D1573345

APULEIUS: *METAMORPHOSES*

Apuleius' famous novel, *The Metamorphoses*, tells the story of a man who was magically changed into an ass, and who had various (humorous, sad, exciting, disturbing, erotic, horrific) adventures before he regained his human form. As well as being genuinely interesting and great fun to read, *The Metamorphoses* is of great value for the study of narrative technique, literary style, religious practices, contemporary culture in a Roman province and much more. This book contains selections from the novel and is aimed at students moving on to genuine, unsimpli-fied Latin prose after completing an introductory Latin course. It contains a useful introduction; detailed notes providing a lot of help with grammar, expression and translation; a full vocabulary; and passages of appreciation to make the selections come alive as literature and to enhance students' perception and enjoyment of the stories.

PAUL MURGATROYD is Professor of Classics at McMaster University. To date he has published nine books and over sixty articles on Greek and especially Latin literature, and is also a published Latin poet himself. He is the co-author, with Garrett Fagan, of another intermediate Latin reader published by Cambridge University Press, *From Augustus to Nero* (2006).

APULEIUS: *METAMORPHOSES*

An Intermediate Latin Reader

~

P. MURGATROYD

CAMBRIDGE
UNIVERSITY PRESS

CAMBRIDGE UNIVERSITY PRESS

Cambridge, New York, Melbourne, Madrid, Cape Town, Singapore, São Paulo, Delhi

Cambridge University Press
The Edinburgh Building, Cambridge CB2 8RU, UK

Published in the United States of America by Cambridge University Press, New York

www.cambridge.org
Information on this title: www.cambridge.org/9780521690553

First published 2009

Printed in the United Kingdom at the University Press, Cambridge

A catalogue record for this publication is available from the British Library

Library of Congress Cataloguing in Publication data
Apuleius.
[Metamorphoses. Selections]
Apuleius' Metamorphoses : an intermediate Latin reader / [edited by] P. Murgatroyd.
p.   cm.
Latin, with introduction and commentary in English.
Includes bibliographical references.
ISBN 978-0-521-87046-7 (hardback)
1. Mythology, Classical – Fiction.   2. Metamorphosis – Fiction.   3. Latin language – Readers.
I. Murgatroyd, Paul.   II. Title.
PA6213.M4M87   2008
873'.01 – dc22   2008048766

ISBN 978-0-521-87046-7 hardback
ISBN 978-0-521-69055-3 paperback

CONTENTS

~

ILLUSTRATIONS

~

All woodcuts from *The Golden Asse of Lucius Apuleius translated out of Latin by William Adlington and illustrated by Jean de Bosschère* (classmark CCC.4.25) are reproduced by kind permission of the Syndics of Cambridge University Library.

PREFACE

~

Apuleius' *Metamorphoses*, as well as being great fun, is a famous and influential work of various levels and layers, and a sustained feat of story-telling from which readers can learn much (about literary style, narrative techniques, religious usage, contemporary culture and society, and so on). The selections are intended to preserve the main outlines of the novel (with the help of summary), and episodes and tales have been chosen which should prove interesting, amusing and affecting, so that students will want to read on and should actually enjoy translating. I have omitted the tale of Cupid and Psyche in books 4, 5 and 6 as that has already been excerpted (and simplified) by Balme and Morwood 1976.

The book is aimed at those who have recently completed an introductory Latin course and are moving on to genuine, unsimplified Latin prose. Difficult language and constructions are omitted rather than emended. Initially, for the sake of brevity and clarity (to reach as wide an audience as possible), cuts are made not only within passages but also within sentences to things like abstruse references, unnecessary details and exuberance and fullness of expression (for example, in the first passage of the selections I drop *lubricas ambages et* from Apuleius' *fortunarum lubricas ambages et instabiles incursiones et reciprocas vicissitudines ignoras* at *Met.* 1.6). As the book progresses there is less and less excerption, and 8.R and 9.A–M are exactly as Apuleius wrote them (although I had to revert to some excerpting after that when covering the lengthy book 11). In view of the target readership lots of help is given in the notes at the start; but later on it is gradually reduced, and readers are encouraged more and more to work things out for themselves. The notes are mainly intended to assist basic comprehension, but do contain remarks on expression and style (to convey some notion of Apuleius' artistry), while the appreciation consists of literary criticism and alerts students to the humour and narrative skills in particular (to increase their perception and plain enjoyment). For students who need to brush up on the basics, at the end of the notes on each passage there are initially suggestions for reviewing declensions and conjugations and also the more important constructions (as encountered in the particular passage). The references are to pages in Morwood 1999 (abbreviated as : M) and Wheelock 2000 (abbreviated as : W) and to sections in the reference grammar at the end of Jones and Sidwell 1986 (abbreviated as : RLRG). Those who used a different introductory Latin course should consult the appropriate parts of that for their reviewing.

I must thank my Latin 2A03 and 2AA3 classes of 2003, 2004 and 2005 for acting as (very useful and willing) guinea pigs with a first draft of this book. The readers for Cambridge University Press also provided stimulating criticisms and suggestions.

PM

INTRODUCTION

~

1 Apuleius' life and works

Not that much is known for sure about the life of Apuleius. He was born in Madaura (a town in North Africa) round about 125 AD, the son of an important and rich man. After learning grammar, rhetoric and some philosophy in Carthage (a city in North Africa), he went to Athens for the equivalent of his university education, and there studied poetry, music, geometry, dialectic and especially philosophy (showing a great interest in the works and thought of the famous Greek philosopher Plato). While based in Athens, he travelled widely in Greece and beyond, and he spent some time in Rome. On his way to Egypt (probably late in 156 AD) he broke his journey at the African town of Oea, and there met Pontianus, who had studied with Apuleius in Athens, and who urged him to marry his wealthy and widowed mother (Pudentilla), to protect her fortune for her sons. Apuleius did marry her, but when Pontianus died not long after, the rest of the family took him to court, accusing him of poisoning Pontianus and bewitching Pudentilla to win her affection. Apuleius successfully defended himself in an elegant and learned speech (the *Apologia*). After that he went to live in Carthage, and in the 160s AD rose to a position of eminence there as an orator and philosophical lecturer. Nothing is known of him after the 160s.

Apuleius was a highly civilized and accomplished man, who travelled widely and had a broad range of interests and talents. He was also a very versatile writer, in both Greek and Latin, in both poetry and prose. Among his poems were love lyrics, satirical epigrams and hymns. In prose he produced novels and speeches and wrote on music, arithmetic, history, medicine, agriculture, astronomy and particularly philosophy. For more on his life see Harrison 2000 1ff.; for more on his writings see the brief summaries in Walsh 1995 xivff., and the much fuller account in Harrison 2000 10ff.

2 *The ancient novel*

Apuleius' *Metamorphoses* belongs to the genre of the novel. Various types of extended narrative fiction written totally or very largely in prose are conveniently grouped together under the heading of novel (or 'romance'). Greek versions flourished especially in the first century AD onwards, and famous Greek authors in this genre include Chariton, Xenophon, Longus (whose *Daphnis and Chloe* is well known), Achilles Tatius and Heliodorus. The best represented type in Greek is the 'ideal' romance (as produced by the five writers just mentioned), an adventure story in which love pre-dominates. There is a standard pattern whereby boy meets girl, the two fall in love, the pair are parted shortly before/after marriage, are exposed to various dangers (such as storms, pirates, attempts on life and chastity), barely escape and are finally reunited in a happy ending. Within this typical format there is variety (plotting may be simple or complex, the tone may be serious or humorous, and so on). There were also Greek novels in which the erotic element was not dominant, such as Lucian's *True Story* (a fanci-ful account of an imaginary voyage) and *The Alexander Romance* (a largely fictional and often fantastical life of Alexander the Great). For more on the Greek novel see Anderson 1982 and Hägg 1983; and for readable, modern translations see Reardon 1989.

Surviving novels in Latin (in addition to the *Metamorphoses*) include Iulius Valerius' Latin version of *The Alexander Romance*, the anonymous *Story of Apollonius King of Tyre* (which looks like a translation or adaptation of a Greek original, and has a plot similar to that of many Greek romances, concerned with a young man who is separated from his wife and daughter, travels far and has various adventures before being reunited with them in the end) and, most importantly, Petronius' *Satyricon* (written in the first century AD). This long picaresque novel survives only in part, but what we have is racy, vivid and realistic, and contains lots of sexual subject matter, irony and (especially bawdy) humour. It concerns the wanderings and disreputable escapades of the narrator and various companions. It is narrated by Encolpius, an impoverished and immoral young man, who is not too bright or sophisticated, and who is a parody of an epic hero, pursued by the wrath of the fertility god Priapus (who inflicts punishment on Encolpius by subjecting him to sexual assaults and an embarrassing bout of impotence). The best preserved episode centres on Trimalchio (an ex-slave who has become a millionaire) and depicts this vulgar upstart's ludicrously unsuccessful attempt to ape high society, as he puts on his idea of a sophisticated dinner party, in which there is a dog-fight in the dining room, he has a noisy and violent quarrel with his wife in front of his guests, he constantly brags and shows off his wealth (picking his teeth with a silver tooth-pick, before eating!) and so on. The novel is often satirical, and here it satirizes the stupidity, cupidity, pretentiousness, superstition etc. of the host and his equally ignorant guests. For further comment on the *Satyricon* see Walsh 1970 and Courtney 2001; and for a lively and reliable translation consult Sullivan 1986 or Walsh 1997.

As well as conforming generally to the genre, Apuleius' work has specific similarities to Petronius and the Greek novel. Like the *Satyricon*, the *Metamorphoses* concerns a rather dim anti-hero, contains extensive humour and irony, and has its satirical aspects too; the close links with the Greek *Onos* are covered in the next section; see also Hijmans and van der Paardt, 1978, 8f., 17ff.; Schmeling 1996, 502f.; Sandy 1997, 242ff.; and Harrison 1999, 229ff.

3 Apuleius' Metamorphoses

The *Metamorphoses*, which has exerted considerable influence on European literature (Haight 1927; Walsh 1970, 224ff.; Harrison 1999, xxxviiif.), was also known in the ancient world as *Asinus Aureus* (= *The Golden Ass*), a title which probably denoted a golden (i.e. splendid, precious) story about an ass. We do not know for sure when in Apuleius' lifetime it was composed, but it was probably later on, after his trial, as (to judge from the *Apologia*) his accusers made no use of this novel of his with its tales of sorcery when charging him with bewitching Pudentilla (see further Harrison 2000, 9f.).

The narrator is a young Greek called Lucius, who in the course of the novel reveals himself as a rather disagreeable rogue (selfish, lecherous, callous, cowardly, foolish, gullible and so on). At the start he makes a business trip to Thessaly (in northern Greece) and stays with a man called Milo, to whom he has a letter of introduction. As he is fascinated with magic and wants to find out all about it, Lucius is delighted to be in an area renowned for witchcraft and stubbornly ignores various warnings about the dangers of sorcery and curiosity such as his own. When he learns that Milo's wife is a witch, he begins an affair with her maid Photis, so that he can through Photis discover the secrets of her magic arts. Reluctantly Photis allows him to watch her mistress rub on an ointment, change herself into an owl and fly off to her young lover. He presses Photis to get the ointment for him, so that he too can become a bird, but in her nervous haste she brings him the wrong ointment, and when he rubs it on, he changes into an ass. She assures the enraged Lucius that eating roses will restore his human form and promises to bring him some at dawn. Meanwhile he goes off to the stables, but later that night the house is robbed and Lucius is driven off, laden with plunder, to the robbers' den. There now follows a series of frustrated attempts to get to roses and escape his fate as a working animal for the robbers and later for other owners too, during which he witnesses and hears about various unpleasant incidents and has various unpleasant experiences himself (being flogged, overworked, nearly castrated, almost killed and disembowelled etc.). Finally when his last master learns that a woman has bribed his keeper so that she can have sex with Lucius, the man decides that he will put the ass in a show, copulating with a condemned murderess. The horrified Lucius bolts, just before being put on show, to a nearby beach, where he falls asleep and dreams that the Egyptian goddess Isis promises that in her sacred festival the next day a priest of hers will have some roses for him. He duly gets the roses from him on the following day and regains his human shape. Subsequently, with quite some trouble and expense, he becomes initiated into the rites of Isis and into those of her husband Osiris, moving to Rome and becoming a priest of Osiris there. (This is of necessity merely a summary, and you are encouraged to read the whole novel, as translated by Kenney 1998 or Walsh 1995.)

Apuleius had a particular Greek model for the *Metamorphoses*, but it is not certain what this model was. Among the works ascribed to the second century AD Greek writer Lucian is a short narrative called the *Onos* (= 'The Ass'), in which a certain Lucius tells how he was transformed magically into an ass and had various adventures before reverting to a human. Apuleius has the same overall plot, and several of his passages are very close to sections in the *Onos* (although there are numerous differences too, over incidents, details and the ending: see Walsh 1970, 145ff.; Sandy 1997, 237ff.). Most critics now think that both the *Metamorphoses* and the *Onos* derive from a common original (of which the *Onos* is an epitome and the *Metamorphoses* is an adaptation). For this original they turn to Photius, a ninth-century AD Byzantine scholar, who mentions a Greek work (now lost) called the *Metamorphoseis* by a Lucius of Patrae, and who claims that the first two books of the *Metamorphoseis* seem to have been abridged in the *Onos*. However, some modern experts have argued that in fact it worked the other way round, that the *Metamorphoseis* was an expansion of the *Onos*, and Photius does allow for this possibility. So Apuleius may have based his novel on the *Metamorphoseis*; but alternatively he may have used the *Onos*, if he did not know of the *Metamorphoseis*, or if (as an expansion of the *Onos*) the *Metamorphoseis* had not been produced by the time that Apuleius was writing. One would certainly expect to find independence in an author as lively and intellectual as Apuleius, but the exact extent of his originality is unclear. Although we can see definite differences from the *Onos*, that work may not have been his model; and, of course, if his source was the *Metamorphoseis*, we have no way at all of telling how much Apuleius added to or subtracted from a composition which we no longer possess. For detailed discussion of this whole complex issue see especially Mason 1994.

Apuleius' version of the ass-tale is consistently entertaining and also highly sophisticated. In the first ten books the racy and engaging narrative contains a piquant mixture of wonder and horror, tenderness and cruelty, tragedy and comedy. Humour predominates, is generally dark and bawdy, and often involves irony and verbal play. Apuleius likes to tease his readers (puzzling, misleading and surprising them), but in so doing he is making a serious philosophical point too, about the deceptiveness of appearances, in line with Platonic thought (compare *Apologia* 53, and see further Penwill 1990). Also serious is his exploration in the course of the novel of various themes, such as sex, magic, curiosity and the influence of fortune (Schlam 1992, 48ff.). He effectively utilizes rhetoric (Schmeling 1996, 504) and a broad range of narrative techniques, like foreshadowing, embedding, aperture and characterization (see the Appreciation below). This is also a very learned work: in addition to a complex blend of literary reminiscences, there is allusion to religion, myth, philosophy, science, law etc. (see above and cf. also Walsh 1970, 52ff.; Finkelpearl 1998; and Harrison 2000, 222ff.). In the light of all this the *Metamorphoses* has reasonably been termed a 'sophist's novel', as Apuleius parades his educational attainments and his alignment with the Second Sophistic, a revival of declamation and general cultural flowering in the contemporary Greek world (see further Harrison 2000, 215ff.; and Sandy 1997).

The eleventh (and final) book at first sight seems to constitute a startling change, as the reprobate Lucius suddenly becomes devout, the Egyptian goddess Isis intervenes to restore his human form, and he becomes initiated into the rites of Isis and her husband Osiris. The interpretation of all this and its effect on the novel as a whole is controversial, and you should realize that this book follows just one possible explanation of this obviously important issue.

Most scholars are swept along by and take at face value all the solemnity, religiosity and cultic detail. Basically they fall into two camps. Some believe that 11 just does not work and is a clumsy and pointless addition. But this seems superficial and makes a whole book extraordinarily inept, spoiling the entire novel (certainly not what one would expect from Apuleius). Other critics feel that the final book represents a deliberate surprise and gives the work a brand new direction, turning it into the edifying tale of a fallen soul who suffered grievously until rescued by the merciful Isis. But Apuleius dwells on and clearly relishes all the low-life material in the first ten books to a degree surprising in someone with a stern moral purpose; and if 11 was a celebration of Isis and Osiris (and we have no evidence that Apuleius was a devotee of theirs), it would be rather long, boring and irritating. In fact, there are numerous elements which militate against the face-value approach (such as Lucius' improbable facility for seeing religious visions, the cost of the cults to him, his own doubts about them, and all the stopping and starting, as the end seems to have been reached, but then the story continues). Winkler (1985, 209ff.) spotted some of these subversive aspects and concluded that 11 suggests both a comic and a serious interpretation of Lucius' religious experience, leaving us unsure whether he is a privileged initiate or a dupe. More recently Harrison 2000 (238ff.) pointed out still more undermining (cf. also Murgatroyd 2004) and argued convincingly that book 11 is ultimately parodic, presenting Lucius as a gullible victim of the venal and exploitative cults of Isis and Osiris, which fits with Apuleius' negative attitude to religion earlier in the *Metamorphoses*, with the characterization of Lucius as lacking sense and proportion, and with the essentially entertaining tone of the work. It seems that in fact a trick is played on readers here: after making it appear initially (in the first 26 chapters of the original) that the *Metamorphoses* has abruptly turned into a serious novel of redemption, Apuleius finally comes clean as all the visions, initiations and expense for Lucius reach ridiculous proportions, amid an amusing succession of false endings (see the Appreciation on 11.A–B and 11.C–E). So (like Lucius) the work regains its original form, as a fundamentally comic tale of an anti-hero who is still asinine even after he escapes from the skin of an ass; and book 11 becomes typically clever, cynical and ironical, acquiring real bite and toying with readers by means of the longest and most elaborate of many teases in the novel.

These selections of necessity have a tight focus with regard to literary criticism and opt to highlight the (attractive, important and often neglected) humour and narrative techniques; but this is a work of many facets and various levels, and there are other approaches which should also be taken into account for full and informed appreciation of this long and complex novel. In addition to the controversy over the thrust of the final book, scholars have emphasized different aspects worthy of consideration. Tatum 1979 shows how the *Metamorphoses* is connected to Apuleius' other compositions, whereas Winkler 1985 investigates it as a piece of hermeneutic playfulness and a philosophical comedy about religious knowledge, much concerned with the interpretation of texts and revision of meaning. James brings out the structural unity, especially thanks to the recurrence of themes with variations. In a set of essays Krabbe 1989 covers the relationship of Apuleius' *Metamorphoses* to Ovid's; females in the novel; verbal and thematic links; and comparisons with modern literature. Krabbe 2003 has more essays, on interweaving of motifs, verbal patterns, allusion and number games. According to Schlam 1992 the work is serio-comic and is given unity by a network of motifs; for Shumate 1996 it is a narrative of the experience of conversion; while Finkelpearl 1998 concentrates on the extensive literary allusion. Harrison 2000 sees this as an essentially erudite and entertaining composition, and relates it to Apuleius' philosophical and literary interests, and to contemporary philosophy and religion in general.

4 Apuleius' Latin

Another important aspect is Apuleius' rhetorical and highly individual manner of writing in the *Metamorphoses* – a virtuoso display that is by turns striking and stylish, eloquent and effective, flamboyant and exuberant. Although his syntax tends to be simple and easy to follow, favouring plain co-ordination (with words and phrases just tacked on one after another, with or without connecting links, rather than in involved subordinate clauses), his diction is elaborate and recherché. His expression is lush and expansive (amply descriptive, and saying the same or virtually the same thing more than once), and also bold and colourful (he has much archaic, poetic and rare language, he invents new words, and gives novel meanings to old ones). Apuleius is also fond of verbal play in various forms (such as the double entendre and the combination of words with similar sounds, like *savia suavia*). His polished prose contains all the major features of style, especially balance, contrast, isocolon, tricolon and pointed word order such as juxtaposition and chiasmus (for explanation of these terms see the next section). He also pays close attention to rhythm and sound, repeating vowels, consonants and whole syllables, often extensively and expressively. For illustration of all of the above see the notes, and for further discussion consult Tatum 1979, 135ff.; and Kenney, 1990, 28ff.

5 *Glossary of technical terms*

The following grammatical and stylistic terms may not be familiar to all students. For more information on them and on other terminology employed in this book see Kennedy 1962 and Woodcock 1959.

ablative of attendant circumstances denotes the circumstances under which an action is performed (*mortuus est ingenti luctu* 'he died to the accompaniment of/amid great grief')

ablative of cause expresses the reason behind a state or action (*pallidus formidine* 'pale because of fear')

ablative of description: a noun and adjective in the ablative are attached to another noun to describe it (*vir nigris capillis* 'a man with black hair')

ablative of instrument/means denotes the thing (instrument) with which or means by which an action is performed (*gladio caedit hostes* 'he kills the enemy with a sword')

ablative of manner expresses the manner in which something happens or is done (*magna cura scribit* 'he writes with great care')

ablative of measure of difference expresses the amount of difference in a comparison (*altior decem pedibus* 'taller by ten feet')

ablative of respect specifies that in respect to which a verb or adjective applies (*corde tremit* 'he trembles in respect to his heart')

ablative of route expresses the route taken (*longa via eo* 'I am going by a long road')

accusative of exclamation: an accusative noun or pronoun generally accompanied by an adjective is used in exclamations (*me miserum* 'o poor me!')

accusative of respect specifies that in respect to which a verb or adjective applies (*nudae lacertos* 'bare in respect to the arms')

alliteration: repetition of the same initial letter(s) in closely successive words (e.g. *sedebat, scissili palliastro semiamictus*)

assonance: repetition of the same or similar vowels (e.g. rabid malice)

asyndeton: the omission of connecting links (like *et* and *sed*)

chiasmus: an ABBA arrangement (e.g. ablative, accusative, accusative, ablative; or noun, verb, verb, noun)

cumulative impact: the powerful effect achieved by piling up point after point in a sentence or passage

dative of agent: the dative is sometimes used on its own in place of *a(b)* and the ablative

dative of disadvantage: the person to whose disadvantage something happens or is done is put into the dative (*nobis stulti sumus* 'we are stupid to the disadvantage of ourselves')

dative of purpose: a gerund, noun or noun plus gerundive can be put into the dative to express purpose (*urbi condendae locum elegerunt* 'they chose a place for founding a city')

deliberative subjunctive is employed when people deliberate about what is/was to be said etc. (*quid faceret* 'what was he to do?')

dicolon denotes a group of two

genitive of cause expresses the reason behind a state or action (*iustitiae miror* 'I marvel at his justice')

genitive of definition expresses that of which a thing consists (*praeda hominum* 'spoil consisting of men')

genitive of quality/description: a noun and adjective in the genitive are attached to another noun to describe it or indicate a distinctive quality (*vir summae virtutis* 'a man of supreme bravery')

genitive of respect denotes that with respect to which an adjective applies (*audax ingenii* 'bold with respect to intellect')

historic infinitive: the infinitive used for variety in place of a past tense of the indicative, and often found alongside imperfects, perfects and historic presents

historic present: a verb in the present tense which refers vividly to a past action as if it is happening at the present time (often found in conjunction with the perfect and imperfect indicative)

homoeoteleuton: similarity of sound in word endings

impersonal expression: the third person singular passive of a verb is used in place of the verb with a personal subject (*curritur* 'it is run' instead of *currunt* 'they run')

inverted cum clause is the name given to the construction whereby X is happening when Y happens

isocolon: the grouping together of individual words or phrases with an equal number of syllables

jussive subjunctive expresses a command (*fiat lux* 'let there be light')

juxtaposition: the placement of words right next to each other for a particular point (for emphasis, to stress contrast etc.)

litotes is affirmation by negation of the contrary (*non tacitus* 'not silent' = 'loud')

local ablative denotes a place where or whence without a preposition (*muris stant* 'they are standing on the walls')

objective genitive denotes the object of the activity implied by a noun or adjective (*vir propositi tenax* 'a man holding to his purpose' = *vir propositum tenet*)

onomatopoeia is a term used when the words sound like what they are describing

partitive genitive names the whole of which part is being considered (*fortissimus Graecorum* 'the bravest one of the Greeks')

polysyndeton: frequency of connecting links (like *et* and *-que*)

possessive dative: the dative of a noun or pronoun is employed to denote the possessor (*est mihi filia parva* 'I have a little daughter')

potential subjunctive expresses a possibility, what would or might happen/be happening/have happened (*hoc velim* 'I would like this')

tricolon denotes a group of three; with a tricolon crescendo the three members become successively longer (like 'friends, Romans and countrymen'); with the tricolon diminuendo the three members become successively shorter (like *occidit brevis lux* 'brief light dies')

TEXT

~

A young man called Lucius is travelling on business in Thessaly (an area in northern Greece renowned for magic) when he meets two men on the road. One of them (Aristomenes) is recounting a tale which the other one disbelieves, but Lucius with his thirst for novelty is quite ready to believe Aristomenes and begs him to tell his story, which he does. Lucius quotes Aristomenes' own words.

1.A *Aristomenes went to Hypata in Thessaly to buy up some cheese cheap, but another trader got in first. While in that town, he came across an old friend (Socrates) who was thought to have died.*

Socraten contubernalem meum conspicio. humi sedebat, scissili palliastro semiamictus, paene alius lurore, ad miseram maciem deformatus. 'Hem,' inquam 'mi Socrates, quid istud? domi iam defletus es; uxor (persolutis feralibus officiis) luctu et maerore diuturno deformata, domus infortunium novarum nuptiarum gaudiis a suis parentibus hilarare   5 compellitur. at tu hic larvale simulacrum viseris.'
'Aristomene,' inquit 'fortunarum instabiles incursiones et reciprocas vicissitudines ignoras.' et sutili centunculo faciem suam iamdudum punicantem prae pudore obtexit ita ut ab umbilico pube tenus cetera corporis renudaret.   10

[Only words within inverted commas represent actual translations of the Latin. The expression 'i.e.' introduces explanation or paraphrase (not translation). For any unfamiliar technical terms, see Introduction section 5.]

1 **Socraten**: accusative singular (Greek form).
1 **conspicio**: this is the historic present (the present tense used vividly in place of a past main verb).
1 **humi**: locative ('on the ground'), like *domi* in line 3.
2 **paene alius lurore**: i.e. not looking like himself (*lurore* is ablative of cause).
3 **inquam**: historic present (like *inquit* in 7). This usage will not be pointed out any more.
3 **mi**: vocative of *meus*.
3 **quid istud**: i.e. *quid est istud*.
3–4 **persolutis feralibus officiis**: ablative absolute.

4 **deformata**: perfect participle passive, agreeing with uxor.

4 **domus** is genitive and goes with *infortunium* (accusative, object of *hilarare*).

5 **gaudiis**: ablative of instrument/means.

6 **hic** is the adverb ('here').

7 **Aristomene**: vocative.

9 **ita ut**: introduces a consecutive (result) clause.

9 **pube tenus**: *tenus* normally follows the noun that it governs (as here).

9–10 **cetera corporis**: 'the other things [i.e. parts] of the body'.

REVIEW 1st and 2nd declension nouns (M p. 16, W p. 446, RLRG sections H1 and H2), ablative absolute (M pp. 79f., W pp. 155f., RLRG section P) and consecutive/result clauses (M pp. 99ff., W pp. 196f., RLRG section S2a).

1.B *Aristomenes cleans him up and takes him to an inn, where Socrates tells how after being robbed he fell into Meroe's clutches.*

Unam e duabus laciniis meis exuo, eumque propere vestio, et ilico lavacro trado. sordium enormem eluviem operose effrico. ad hospitium lassus ipse fatigatum perduco. lectulo refoveo, cibo satio, poculo mitigo, fabulis permulceo. iam allubentia est sermonis et ioci et scitum etiam cavillum, cum ille imo de pectore cruciabilem suspiritum ducens, 'Me miserum,' 5 infit 'qui, dum voluptatem gladiatorii spectaculi consector, in has aerumnas incidi. secundum quaestum Macedoniam profectus, dum mense decimo nummatior revertor spectaculum obiturus, in quadam avia convalli a vastissimis latronibus obsessus atque omnibus privatus tandem evado. 10

'Ad quandam cauponam Meroen (anum sed admodum scitulam) deverto, eique causas peregrinationis et spoliationis refero. quae me cenae gratae atque gratuitae ac mox cubili suo applicat. et statim miser ab unico congressu annosam ac pestilentem coniunctionem contraho; et ipsas etiam lacinias quas latrones contegendo mihi concesserant in eam contuli, 15 operulas etiam quas adhuc vegetus saccariam faciens merebam, quoad me ad istam faciem quam paulo ante vidisti bona uxor et mala fortuna perduxit.'

3 **fatigatum** agrees with the *eum* that is to be understood here.

3–4 **lectulo…permulceo**: *eum* is to be supplied as the object of the verbs; the ablatives are ablatives of instrument/means. The asyndeton (absence of connecting links such as *et*) makes for brevity and so suggests an eager briskness on Aristomenes' part.

4 **allubentia** with the genitive means 'inclination for', while *est* means 'there is'.

5 **cum**: this is an inverted *cum* clause (= X was happening WHEN Y happened). The historic present (*infit*) is normal in this construction.

5 **me miserum**: accusative of exclamation ('poor me!').

6 **consector**: the present tense (with a past force) is normal in *dum* clauses when the main verb is past ('while I was pursuing'), so long as *dum* does not mean 'all the time that'.

7 **secundum** is the preposition.

7 **Macedoniam profectus**: the omission of the preposition (*ad*) with regions is one of the many poeticisms found in Apuleius. *Profectus* is the past participle of the deponent verb *proficiscor*.

8 **obiturus**: future participle of *obeo*.

9 **obsessus**: perfect participle passive of *obsideo*.

9 **omnibus** ('all things') is ablative with *privo* (we would say 'robbed OF everything').

11 **Meroen**: (Greek) accusative of *Meroe*.

12 **quae**: the relative is used to connect sentences (= *et illa*).

12–13 **cenae gratae atque gratuitae**: datives. Apuleius likes to play like this with words that have similar sounds.

15 **contegendo**: dative (of purpose) of the gerund of *contego* ('for covering', i.e. to cover myself).

15 **contuli** is perfect indicative of *confero* and is to be understood as the verb governing *operulas* as well.

17 **bona uxor** refers ironically to Meroe.

REVIEW 3rd declension nouns (M pp. 16f., W p. 446, RLRG section H3), *cum* and *dum* clauses (M pp. 122f., 124f., W pp. 208f., 219, RLRG section T b, c, d, e) and the gerund and gerundive/future periphrastic (M pp. 108ff., W pp. 157, 276ff., RLRG sections N and O).

1.C *When Aristomenes criticizes Socrates for preferring an old whore to his family, his friend warns him to be quiet because she is a witch.*

'Tu dignus,' inquam 'es extrema sustinere, qui voluptatem veneriam et scortum scorteum lari et liberis praetulisti.' at ille, 'Tace, tace,' inquit 'ne quam tibi lingua intemperante noxam contrahas.' 'Ain tandem?' inquam. 'potens illa caupona quid mulieris est?' 'Saga,' inquit 'et potens fontes durare, montes diluere, manes sublimare, deos infimare, sidera exstinguere, Tartarum ipsum illuminare. ut se ament efflictim non modo incolae verum etiam Anticthones folia sunt artis et nugae merae. amatorem suum, quod in aliam temerasset, unico verbo mutavit in castorem, quod ea bestia ab insequentibus se praecisione genitalium liberat, ut illi quoque simile proveniret. cauponem aemulum deformavit in ranam, et nunc ille dolio innatans vini sui adventores officiosis roncis raucus appellat. alium de foro, quod adversus eam locutus esset in arietem deformavit, et nunc aries ille causas agit.

5

10

1 **extrema**: neuter accusative plural.

1–2 **voluptatem . . . liberis**: note the elaborate pattern of alliteration (repetition of initial letters in succeeding words) and the jingle in *scortum scorteum*. Apuleius likes playing with sound for its own sake, but here there seems to be a certain forcefulness.

2 **praetulisti**: perfect active indicative of *praefero*.

2–3 **ne . . . contrahas**: in this negative purpose clause *quam* (indefinite) means 'any' and *lingua intemperante* is ablative of instrument/means.

3 **ain** = *ais* (from *aio*) plus -*ne* (interrogative particle). *Ain tandem* means 'do you really say [so]?'

4 **quid mulieris**: 'what of a woman' (*mulieris* is partitive genitive), i.e. what type of a woman.

4–6 fontes . . . illuminare: her magic feats are presented with brisk asyndeton and striking artistry (object followed by infinitive each time; contrasts within the three grouped pairs; chiasmus (an ABBA order) in the last two pairs – Underworld, heaven, heaven, Underworld; alliteration; rhyme).

6–7 ut . . . merae: i.e. making men of Hypata and people from the opposite side of the world love her (*se*) deeply is merely a trifling part of Meroe's magical skills. Here *ut* means 'that', and this substantive clause is the complement of *folia sunt artis et nugae merae*. Such a use of *se* (rather than *illam*) is a colloquialism.

8 quod . . . temerasset: *temerasset* is the syncopated (shortened) form of *temeravisset* (pluperfect subjunctive because the speaker does not vouch personally for the reason and is just giving Meroe's grounds for the action). With such syncopation -*vi*- or -*ve*- is omitted from pluperfect, perfect and future perfect forms. *Temero* with *in* ('commit an act of violation in respect of', i.e. misbehave with) is not found elsewhere and is an instance of the many rare usages in Apuleius.

9–10 quod . . . liberat: because the speaker does vouch for the reason this time, we find *quod* ('because') with the indicative. The ancients believed that a secretion used in medicine was found in the beaver's scrotum and that the animal when hunted saved itself from capture by biting off that bodily part and leaving it behind for its pursuers. The participle *insequentibus* is used as a noun here.

10 simile is neuter nominative singular in this purpose clause.

11–12 roncis raucus: note the comic onomatopoeia (the words sound like what they describe). The adjective is used as an adverb here.

12 alium de foro: i.e. another man, a lawyer (trials took place in the forum).

12 quod: 'on the grounds that' (see above on lines 8 and 9–10).

REVIEW 4th and 5th declension nouns (M p. 17, W p. 446, RLRG sections H4 and H5), direct commands (M pp. 88f., W pp. 5, 49, 185, RLRG section L-V (a) 3), sequence of tenses (M pp. 86f., W pp. 201ff., RLRG section L-V c) and causal clauses (M pp. 126f., W pp. 211f., RLRG section U).

1.D *Socrates goes on to tell how the indignant citizens of Hypata decided to stone Meroe to death, but she used magic to imprison them all in their houses until they swore not to harm her.*

'Indignatio percrebruit statutumque ut in eam saxorum iaculationibus vindicaretur. quod consilium virtutibus cantionum antevertit. cunctos in suis domibus tacita numinum violentia clausit, ut non claustra perfringi, non fores evelli quiverint, quoad consone clamitarent deierantes sese neque ei manus admolituros et, si quis aliud cogitarit, salutare laturos subsidium. et sic illa propitiata totam civitatem absolvit. at coetus illius auctorem nocte intempesta cum tota domo in aliam civitatem (summo vertice montis exasperati sitam et ob id ad aquas sterilem) transtulit. quoniam densa aedificia locum novo hospiti non dabant, ante portam proiecta domo discessit.' 5

10

1 **statutumque**: understand *est*. This is an impersonal expression ('it was decreed'), and it is followed by an indirect command (*ut . . .*).

1 **iaculationibus**: ablative of instrument/means.

2 **vindicaretur**: another impersonal expression ('punishment should be inflicted on . . . ').

2 **quod**: the relative is used to connect (= *sed illud*).

3 **tacita . . . violentia**: ablative of instrument/means.

3–4 **ut . . . quiverint**: the asyndeton is indicated by the comma inside this result (consecutive) clause. *Perfringi* and *evelli* are present passive infinitives with *quiverint* (perfect subjunctive of *queo*).

4 **deierantes** introduces reported statement in which *sese* (= *se*) refers back to the speakers, and *esse* is to be understood as forming two future infinitives with *admolituros* and *laturos* (from *fero*). The *-que* in *neque* looks forward to *et* ('they would not . . . and they would . . .'). With *si quis aliud cogitarit* the reference is to anyone who thinks otherwise (i.e. does not go along with the oath), and *cogitarit* (syncopated form of *cogitaverit*) represents the future perfect indicative of the original direct speech, which unusually is not changed into a subjunctive when it becomes reported speech.

6–7 **coetus . . . auctorem**: i.e. the person behind the meeting at which the decree to stone Meroe was made.

7 **nocte intempesta**: 'at dead of night' (ablative of time when).

8 **sitam . . . sterilem**: these two words agree with *civitatem*.

8 **ad**: 'with regard to'.

8 **transtulit**: perfect indicative active of *transfero*.

10 **proiecta domo**: ablative absolute.

REVIEW adjectives (M pp. 19ff., W p. 447, RLRG sections J1 and J2), indirect commands (M pp. 89ff., W pp. 253f., RLRG section R2) and indirect statement and subordinate clauses in indirect speech (M pp. 82ff., W pp. 164ff., 444, RLRG sections R1 and R4).

1.E Now afraid of Meroe, Aristomenes wants to get some rest and leave before dawn. But that night the room's doors are burst open.

'Mira,' inquam 'memoras. mihi incussisti formidinem ne numinis ministerio similiter usa sermones nostros anus illa cognoscat. itaque maturius nos reponamus et, somno levata lassitudine, antelucio aufugiamus.' Socrates iam sopitus stertebat altius. ego vero, adducta fore, pessulisque firmatis, grabatulo etiam pone cardines supposito, super eum   5 me recipio. ac primum prae metu aliquantisper vigilo; dein circa tertiam vigiliam paululum coniveo. commodum quieveram et repente ianuae reserantur, immo vero (fractis et evulsis funditus cardinibus) prosternuntur. grabatulus breviculus impetus tanti violentia prosternitur; me excussum recidens in inversum tegit.   10

1 **ne** introduces a fear clause, in which *ministerio* is ablative after *usa* (perfect participle of *utor*).

3 **maturius nos reponamus**: the comparative adverb (compare *altius* in line 4) here has the sense 'rather early'. The subjunctive is jussive ('let us . . .'), like *aufugiamus* in line 4.

3 **somno levata lassitudine**: ablative of instrument/means (*somno*) and ablative absolute.

4–5 **adducta . . . supposito**: ablative absolutes. *Pone* is the preposition, and *pone cardines* denotes a position right against the door (inside the room).

6–7 **circa tertiam vigiliam**: about midnight or in the small hours (the hours of the night were divided into four watches whose length varied according to the length of the whole night).

7 **commodum**: this adverb is just one of the many colloquial touches in Apuleius' diction.

8 **fractis . . . cardinibus**: ablative absolute.

9 **violentia**: ablative of instrument/means.

10 **recidens in inversum**: 'falling back down into an inverted position', i.e. falling upside down.

REVIEW pronouns (M pp. 26ff., W pp. 448f., RLRG section I), fear clauses (M pp. 102f., W p. 285, RLRG section S2e) and expressions of time and place (M pp. 71ff., W pp. 255ff., RLRG sections L c, f and g).

1.F *Aristomenes sees Meroe and Panthia (another witch) enter, intent on taking revenge on Socrates, and on Aristomenes himself.*

De Aristomene testudo factus ac grabatuli sollertia munitus, video mulieres duas altioris aetatis. lucernam lucidam gerebat una, spongiam et nudum gladium altera. Socraten bene quietum circumstetere. infit illa cum gladio, 'Hic est, Panthia, carus Endymion meus, qui non solum me diffamat probris verum etiam fugam instruit. at ego scilicet, Ulixi astu   5
deserta, vice Calypsonis aeternam solitudinem flebo.' et porrecta dextera meque Panthiae demonstrato, 'At hic bonus,' inquit 'consiliator Aristomenes, qui fugae huius auctor fuit et nunc morti proximus iacet. faxo eum sero, immo statim, immo iam nunc, ut et praecedentis dicacitatis et instantis curiositatis paeniteat.'   10

1 **de . . . factus**: i.e. with the bed on his back Aristomenes seems to have turned into (*de* means 'from being') a tortoise.

1 **grabatuli sollertia munitus**: Apuleius is fond of such personification (treating a thing as if it is a person). 'The cleverness of the bed' stands for 'the clever bed' (compare *Ulixi astu* in line 5).

2 **altioris aetatis**: genitive of quality (or description).

2 **lucernam lucidam**: (as often) there is etymological play here, as Apuleius obviously connects both words with *luceo* ('be light').

3 **Socraten**: Greek accusative (this form will not be pointed out any more).

3 **circumstetere** = *circumsteterunt* (alternative form of the third person plural of the perfect indicative active).

3–4 **illa cum gladio**: 'the one with the sword' (i.e. Meroe).

4 **Endymion** was a handsome young hero loved by Selene (the Moon), who gazed on him and kissed him during his sleep (which is frequently depicted as being eternal).

5 **scilicet** is ironical, as often (and so is *bonus* in line 7).

6 **vice Calypsonis**: 'like Calypso'. She was a sea nymph, who fell in love with the Greek hero Odysseus (= Ulysses) and detained him on her island for many years, until the gods finally made her let him go, much to her sorrow.

6–7 **porrecta . . . demonstrato**: ablative absolutes (this construction will no longer be pointed out as a matter of course).

7 **at hic**: supply *est* as the verb (as so often in Latin).

9–10 **faxo . . . paeniteat**: *faxo* is an archaic form of *fecero* (future perfect indicative), and *facio ut* means 'I bring it about that . . .' The words *eum . . . nunc* (where Meroe corrects herself, as her anger mounts) belong syntactically inside the *ut* clause and get emphasis from being placed before it. *Paenitet* is an impersonal verb, meaning it causes someone in the accusative (*eum*) to feel regret for something in the genitive (*praecedentis . . . curiositatis*). *Iam nunc* = 'right now'. *Et . . . et* means 'both . . . and'.

9–10 **praecedentis . . . curiositatis**: such homoeoteleuton (similarity of sound in word endings) is common in Apuleius simply for the sake of melodiousness, but here it seems to have an impressive solemnity. *Instantis* is the adjective.

REVIEW 1st conjugation verbs (M pp. 36f., 46f., W pp. 452ff., RLRG sections A–D) and (no example in this passage) generic relative clauses (M p. 100, W pp. 269f., RLRG section Q2).

1.G *Meroe decides that Aristomenes must survive so that he can bury Socrates, then plunges a sword into Socrates' neck, pulls out his heart and stops up the wound with a sponge.*

Sudore frigido miser perfluo, at Panthia, 'Quin igitur,' inquit 'hunc bacchatim discerpimus vel virilia desecamus?' Meroe, 'Immo,' ait 'supersit, qui miselli huius corpus parvo contumulet humo.' et capite Socratis in alterum dimoto latus, per iugulum sinistrum capulo tenus gladium totum demergit, et sanguinis eruptionem utriculo admoto   5
excipit. immissa dextera per vulnus illud ad viscera, cor miseri contubernalis mei Meroe scrutata protulit, cum ille stridorem incertum per vulnus effunderet et spiritum rebulliret. vulnus spongia offulciens Panthia, 'Heus tu,' inquit 'spongia, cave in mari nata per fluvium transeas.' remoto grabatulo, varicus super faciem meam residentes,   10
vesicam exonerant, quoad me urinae spurcissimae madore perluerent.

   2 **bacchatim**: the female worshippers of Bacchus, when possessed by the god, used to tear animals apart with their bare hands, and occasionally they did this to men as well. The adverb occurs here only in Latin (like *varicus* in line 10). Such rare diction in Apuleius often draws the attention to something significant.

   3 **supersit**: jussive subjunctive ('let him . . . ').

   3 **parvo contumulet humo**: the verb is in the subjunctive because this is a relative clause expressing purpose. It is very unusual for *humus* to be masculine (rather than feminine).

   4 **iugulum sinistrum**: 'the left side of his throat'.

   4 **capulo tenus**: *tenus* normally follows the noun that it governs.

   6 **cor**: the extraction of the heart kills Socrates, but as well as that the heart had magical properties and so was made use of by witches.

   7 **protulit**: perfect indicative active of *profero*.

   9–10 Panthia's address to the sponge is deliberately ambiguous (teasing). There are various possible senses for *cave* ('make sure that you do', 'mind that you don't'), *per* ('along', 'across', 'through', 'by means of') and *transeas* ('cross over', 'pass', 'make your way'). Whatever the precise sense of the words here, as a result of this charm at the end of the story the sponge drops out of the wound when Socrates tries to drink from a river. *Mari* is ablative of *mare*. *Nata* is the perfect participle of the deponent *nascor*.

   11 **quoad . . . perluerent**: the subjunctive expresses purpose ('until such time as . . . '). The main verb (*exonerant*) is an historic present and here makes the sequence secondary (historic). The urine, as well as being offensive and indicating contempt, has magical properties (keeping Aristomenes in the witches' power).

REVIEW 2nd conjugation verbs (M pp. 38f., 48f., W pp. 452ff., RLRG sections A–D) and purpose clauses (M pp. 96ff., W p. 189, RLRG section S2b).

1.H Half-dead with shock and fearing that he will be suspected of murdering his companion, Aristomenes decides to leave the inn.

Commodum limen evaserant, et fores ad pristinum statum integrae resurgunt. at ego, nudus et frigidus et lotio perlutus (quasi recens utero matris editus), immo semimortuus verum ipse mihi supervivens, 'Quid,' inquam 'me fiet, ubi iste iugulatus mane paruerit? cui videbor veri similia dicere perferens vera? "Proclamares saltem suppetiatum, si resistere vir   5 tantus mulieri nequibas. sub oculis tuis homo iugulatur et siles? ergo, quoniam evasisti mortem, nunc illo redi."' haec identidem mecum replicabam, et nox ibat in diem. optimum itaque factu visum est anteluculo furtim evadere et viam trepido vestigio capessere. sumo sarcinulam meam, subdita clavi pessulos reduco.   10

   1 **commodum** is an adverb (like *recens* in line 2).

   3 **editus** is from *edo*.

   3 **verum**: 'but'.

   3–4 **quid . . . me fiet?**: 'what will be done with me?' (*me* is ablative of instrument/means).

   4 **paruerit**: future perfect indicative of *pareo*.

   4–5 **cui . . . dicere**: *videor* here means 'seem' (as it does in line 8) and governs the infinitive *dicere*, while *similia* (neuter accusative plural, object of *dicere*) here takes the genitive (we would say 'similar TO the truth').

   5–6 represent the kind of objections that Aristomenes thinks people will make if he tells them the true story of what happened.

   5–6 **proclamares . . . nequibas**: in this unreal condition the imperfect subjunctive refers to the past ('you would have . . . '), while *nequibas*, which also has reference to the past, is unusually an indicative instead of a subjunctive (in the *si* clause this is mainly archaic). *Suppetiatum* is supine in -*um* expressing purpose (i.e. to get someone to help him).

   7 **illo redi**: *illo* is the adverb ('to that place', i.e. to death), and *redi* is second person singular of the imperative of *redeo*.

   8 **ibat**: imperfect indicative of *eo*.

   8 **factu** is supine in -*u* and goes with *optimum* ('best to do').

   9 **trepido vestigio**: the singular is put in place of the plural (as often).

   10 **clavi**: ablative singular of *clavis*.

REVIEW 3rd conjugation verbs (M pp. 40f., 50f., W pp. 452ff., RLRG sections A–D), temporal clauses (M pp. 118ff., W pp. 211f., RLRG section T) and conditional clauses (M pp. 114ff., W pp. 228ff., RLRG section S2c).

1.I Aristomenes asks the porter to let him out of the inn's front door, but he refuses, so Aristomenes returns to his room, convinced that he will be executed for murder, and tries ineptly to hang himself.

'Heus tu, ubi es?' inquam. 'valvas stabuli absolve.' ianitor pone stabuli ostium cubitans, 'Quid? tu,' inquit 'ignoras latronibus infestari vias? etsi

tu, alicuius facinoris conscius, mori cupis, nos cucurbitae caput non
habemus ut pro te moriamur.' 'Non longe,' inquam 'lux abest. et quid
viatori de summa pauperie latrones auferre possunt, inepte?' ille   5
semisopitus, 'Unde autem,' inquit 'scio an, convectore tuo iugulato, fugae
mandes praesidium?' memini me, terra dehiscente, ima Tartara
prospexisse. ac recordabar Meroen non misericordia iugulo meo
pepercisse sed saevitia cruci me reservasse. in cubiculum itaque reversus,
cum nullum aliud telum mortiferum fortuna quam grabatulum   10
sumministraret, restim qua erat intextus aggredior expedire. ac tigillo
iniecta parte funiculi et altera in nodum coacta, ascenso grabatulo,
laqueum induo. sed repente putris et vetus funis dirumpitur, atque ego
recidens Socraten superruo cumque eo in terram devolvor.

1 **pone** is the preposition ('behind').

2 **latronibus ... vias**: in this indirect statement *latronibus* is either ablative of cause or ablative of instrument/means.

3 **mori**: present infinitive of *morior*.

3–4 **nos ... habemus**: plural for singular (*nos = ego*), as often in Latin. Having the head of a gourd means being empty-headed or an idiot.

4 **ut** introduces a consecutive or result clause ('so as to ... ').

5 **viatori ... possunt**: *viatori* is the dative of disadvantage that is common with verbs of depriving (we say: take away FROM). *De summa pauperie* is rather odd Latin. The phrase modifies *viatori*. The preposition here looks like an extension of *de* (meaning 'of') used to indicate that with which one is connected, from which one originates, to which one belongs etc.

6 **unde ... scio an**: 'whence do I know whether ... ' (i.e. for all I know ...).

7–8 **me ... prospexisse**: in this indirect statement Aristomenes means that he foresaw his own death, with the earth seeming to gape open in front of him and reveal the depths of the Underworld.

8–9 **misericordia ... reservasse**: in this (elegantly balanced) indirect statement *misericordia* and *saevitia* are ablatives of cause; *iugulo* is dative with *pepercisse* (from *parco*); and *reservasse* is the syncopated form of *reservavisse*.

10 **quam** means 'than' and goes with *nullum aliud*.

11 **tigillo** is dative with *iniecta* (from *inicio*, meaning 'throw on').

12 **altera**: understand *parte funiculi* with this word.

12 **coacta** is from *cogo*.

REVIEW 4th conjugation verbs (M pp. 42f., 52f., W pp. 452ff., RLRG sections A–D), concessive clauses (M pp. 127f., W pp. 211f., RLRG section V) and indirect questions (M pp. 94f., W p. 204, RLRG section R3).

1.J When the porter rushes in shouting, Socrates sits up. Delighted, Aristomenes points out to the porter that this is the companion he was accused of murdering and then quickly leaves with Socrates.

Ecce ianitor introrumpit clamitans, 'Ubi es tu, qui alta nocte immodice
festinabas et nunc stertis involutus?' casu nostro an illius absono clamore

experrectus, Socrates exsurgit et, 'Non,' inquit 'immerito stabularios hos
omnes hospites detestantur. nam iste curiosus clamore vasto me
marcidum altissimo somno excussit.' emergo laetus atque insperato   5
gaudio perfusus et: 'Ecce, ianitor fidelissime, comes et frater meus, quem
occisum a me calumniabaris.' et Socraten deosculabar amplexus. at ille,
odore spurcissimi umoris percussus quo me lamiae illae infecerant,
vehementer aspernatur. 'Apage te,' inquit 'foetorem extremae latrinae!' et
causas coepit huius odoris comiter inquirere. at ego miser, afficto absurdo   10
ioco, 'Quin imus,' inquam 'et itineris matutini gratiam capimus?' sumo
sarcinulam et capessimus viam.

> 1 **alta nocte** denotes the dead of night.
> 2 **involutus**: i.e. in bedclothes.
> 2 **casu ... clamore**: ablatives of cause.
> 5 **altissimo somno** is ablative ('from') with *excussit*.
> 7 **occisum**: understand *esse*. This is a perfect infinitive passive in indirect statement after *calumni-abaris*.
> 9 **foetorem extremae latrinae** is in apposition to *te* ('you stench of an absolutely disgusting latrine').
> 11 **itineris ... capimus**: *gratiam* here could mean 'profit' or 'agreeableness', so Aristomenes may be saying let's profit by and/or let's enjoy an early start.

REVIEW 3rd/4th conjugation verbs in -*io* (M pp. 44f., 54f., W pp. 452ff., RLRG sections A–D), irregular verbs (M pp. 57ff., W pp. 457ff., RLRG section E) and supines (M p. 97, W pp. 264f., RLRG section A7).

1.K *Aristomenes can see no wound on Socrates' neck and decides that he must have been dreaming, but then Socrates says that he himself dreamed that his throat was cut and his heart removed.*

Sedulo arbitrabar iugulum comitis et mecum, 'Vesane,' aio 'qui vino
sepultus extrema somniasti. ecce Socrates integer, sanus, incolumis. ubi
vulnus, spongia? ubi cicatrix?' et ad illum, 'Non' inquam 'immerito
medici cibo et crapula distentos saeva somniare autumant. mihi, quod
poculis minus temperavi, nox diras imagines obtulit, ut adhuc me credam   5
cruore humano aspersum.'
    Ille surridens, 'At tu' inquit 'non sanguine sed lotio perfusus es. verum
tamen ipse per somnium iugulari visus sum mihi, et cor ipsum mihi avelli
putavi. et nunc spiritu deficior et gradu titubo et aliquid cibatus refovendo
spiritu desidero.' 'En,' inquam 'paratum tibi adest ientaculum.' et caseum   10
cum pane propere ei porrigo et, 'Iuxta platanum istam residamus' aio.

> 1 **arbitrabar**: the verb with this sense ('observe') occurs only in Plautus before Apuleius (who is fond of such usages and words found in early Roman Comedy). *Cibatus* in 9 is also a Plautine term. *Mecum* (literally 'with myself') = 'to myself'.

1–2 **vino sepultus** (from *sepelio*) is a poetic expression (much of Apuleius' language is taken from poets, from Ovid in particular). There is dark humour in the allusion to burial in such a story.

2 **extrema somniasti**: the syncopated form of *somniavisti* has as its object *extrema* (neuter accusative plural, like *saeva* in 4).

2 **integer, sanus, incolumis**: there is forceful asyndeton and fullness in this tricolon (a group of three, common in Apuleius).

2–3 **ubi . . . cicatrix?**: *est* must be supplied in both sentences.

4 **distentos**: 'those swollen' (referring to people who have eaten and drunk too much).

4 **autumant**: this archaic (and so, as often, solemn) word introduces an indirect statement.

5 **obtulit** is from *offero*.

5–6 **ut . . . aspersum**: the *ut* introduces a result (consecutive) clause, and *esse* must be supplied with *aspersum* (perfect infinitive passive in an indirect statement after *credam*).

8 **per . . . mihi**: i.e. I dreamed that I was killed by having my throat cut (*per* means 'during').

8 **mihi avelli**: *mihi* is dative of disadvantage (= 'from me'), while *avelli* is present infinitive passive in an indirect statement.

9 **spiritu . . . gradu**: ablatives of respect. 'I am lacking in respect of breath' means: I am out of breath.

9 **aliquid cibatus**: 'something of food' (partitive genitive), i.e. some food.

9–10 **refovendo spiritu**: i.e. to restore my wind. The gerundive and noun here are in the dative (of purpose).

11 **residamus**: jussive subjunctive.

1.L Socrates weakens as he eats, and when he tries to drink from a river, the wound opens, the sponge drops out and he falls down dead.

Eumque avide essitantem aspiciens, intentiore macie atque pallore buxeo deficientem video. et brevitas commeantium metum mihi cumulabat. quis enim de duobus comitum alterum sine alterius noxa peremptum crederet? verum ille, ut detruncaverat cibum, sitire impatienter coeperat. haud longe radices platani lenis fluvius ibat. 'En,' inquam 'explere latice   5
fontis lacteo.' assurgit et appronat se avidus affectans poculum. necdum extremis labiis summum rorem attigerat, et iugulo eius vulnus dehiscit, et illa spongia de eo repente devolvitur, eamque parvus comitatur cruor. denique corpus exanimatum in flumen paene cernuat. altero eius pede retento, aegre ad ripam superiorem attraxi, ubi comitem misellum arenosa   10
humo contexi. ipse trepidus per avias solitudines aufugi et, quasi conscius caedis humanae, ultroneum exilium amplexus, nunc Aetoliam colo.

2 **brevitas commeantium**: *brevitas* occurs here only with the sense 'scarcity'. The participle is used as a noun ('travellers').

3 **alterum . . . noxa**: 'the one . . . without wrongdoing on the part of the other'.

3–4 **peremptum crederet**: understand *esse* with *peremptum* (from *perimo*); this is an infinitive in indirect statement. *Crederet* is a potential subjunctive ('would believe').

4 **ut detruncaverat**: *ut* (with the indicative) means 'when'. The verb has real point in connection with the mutilated Socrates.

5 **longe radices**: most unusually *longe* is a preposition, governing the accusative ('far from').

1 Socrates is pulled from the river.

5 **ibat**: imperfect indicative of *eo*.

5–6 **explere latice fontis lacteo**: *explere* is second person singular of the present imperative passive of *expleo*, used reflexively ('fill yourself'). There is alliteration and assonance (repetition of vowels) in *latice . . . lacteo* (the adjective contains the notion of nourishment).

6 **avidus**: here (as often in Latin) the adjective has an adverbial force.

6 **necdum**: i.e. *et nondum*.

7 **iugulo**: 'in his throat'. This is a local ablative (which depicts place where or whence without a preposition).

10 **attraxi**: supply *eum* as the object.

APPRECIATION

1.A–L (Metamorphoses 1.6–19).

Throughout 1.A–L the reader is expertly manipulated. The beginning (1.A) has impact because it is (aptly) gloomy and also contains a 'hook' (we are intrigued over Socrates' situation). In 1.B we learn how he came to be in Hypata, but are soon involved in another engaging puzzle (how can one act of sex with the inn-keeper Meroe involve him in a permanent and demeaning relationship with her?). In 1.C Socrates finally reveals that she is also a sorceress, and we are left to conclude that she bewitched him (but, oddly and unsettlingly, later he seems ready to leave her and does in fact go away – has Aristomenes somehow snapped him out of a trance, or what?). The tale's characteristic eeriness begins, and comes across strongly, at 1.C–D, with the succession of grim examples of Meroe's powers. In 1.E the tension starts to rise, with the fear that Meroe might magically overhear them, and the decision to flee (will this anger her, and will they get away?) but also to stay there for the night first (vulnerable?). After the shock of the doors being smashed in, Meroe's entrance is ominous, and also intriguing (why the sponge?). Aristomenes seems to have escaped notice, but then Meroe turns to him and threatens revenge for just the kind of instigation and cleverness that she punished at 1.C–D. We fear a similar dire magic punishment for him imminently. But in 1.G he escapes this, only for the witches to urinate over him; and now it seems that the worst is over, but in fact there is much more in store for him. The detailed depiction of Socrates' death (with various weird and mystifying touches) and Aristomenes' panicky reaction to it (with the nightmarish inability to escape) mean that Socrates' sudden revival in 1.J comes as a great surprise. We are kept in suspense over what exactly had happened to him (and there is the red herring of Aristomenes' assumption that he had dreamed the murder) until the very end. After the disturbing touch of them both apparently having the same dream, there is foreboding when Socrates begins to feel weak, and especially when he approaches the river. Then the point of the witch's words to the sponge is finally made clear, but in keeping with the mystery of magic we are never told what actually was done to Socrates (we have to infer that he was killed and then reanimated as a living corpse to cause more trouble and upset for his friend).

There is also a typically sophisticated complexity of thought and arrangement here. For example, at 1.Bff. Socrates (in trouble because of the inn-keeper Meroe) is taken by his friend to an inn, and there complains of that inn-keeper (and thereby causes himself still more trouble). At 1.I–J the live Aristomenes (trying to kill himself, but saved from death) crashes on to the dead Socrates, who is thus seemingly rescued from death and brought back to life. And by the end of the story Aristomenes is in exactly the state for which he criticized his friend at the start (absent from his original home without explanation and living in a new place with a new wife). Structurally the all-important visit of the witches at 1.F–G is the pivot. It is framed by Aristomenes lying down behind locked doors, afraid and contemplating escape before dawn in 1.E and 1.H; and before it Socrates is thought to be dead (by his wife) but is really alive, while after it he is thought to be alive (by his friend) but is really dead. There is also ring-composition, whereby elements at the start of the narrative are recalled at the end, to round it off neatly (e.g. Socrates sitting on the ground, suffering from pallor and *macies*, looking like a ghost/actually dead, and receiving funeral rites).

There is a characteristically dark humour as well. Among the verbal play Aristomenes describes himself at 1.H.3 as half-dead but surviving himself (beside the corpse of Socrates soon about to come back to life), at 1.J.5f. as drenched in joy (when he is soaked in urine) and at 1.K.1f. as buried in wine (next to his dead friend whom he will soon be burying). Irony abounds too. For instance, in 1.B Socrates on his way to witness violence (the gladiatorial show) himself becomes a victim of violence, and escapes from the robbers to the still more dangerous and rapacious sorceress; at 1.C–D he glibly recounts her punishment of a lover who offended her and her power over locks and doors, shortly before being punished himself for offending her, and being punished thanks to her power over locks and doors; and at 1.J he jokes about why Aristomenes smells of urine when that was due to the witches, and they did a lot worse than that to Socrates himself.

Then there is Meroe, who has her grimly comic side, thanks especially to her malicious sense of humour, seen in the gruesome revenge with nasty tit for tat at 1.C–D; the sneering references in 1.F to Socrates as (handsome, young) Endymion and (clever, brave and noble) Ulysses; and all the unpleasant tricks played on Aristomenes. With Socrates the humour lies mainly in the play on the revered fifth-century BC Greek philosopher of that name (on significant names in Apuleius cf. Hijmans and van der Paardt 1978, 107ff.). By way of contrast our Socrates is a businessman who exposes his genitalia, and in his case his namesake's indifference to his appearance, trouble with his wife and belief that sex could be dangerous are taken much further. In place of the philosopher's moving end (unjustly condemned and taking poison after talking of the immortality of the soul) there is a lurid murder by witches here, then this Socrates comes back to life, but then (evidently not immortal) dies a grotesque second death.

But the most amusing character is Aristomenes, who from 1.E on makes a series of inept decisions which get him into more and more trouble. When seriously afraid that Meroe may overhear him magically, he actually announces that he will take Socrates away from her but stay at the inn that night (alerting her to his plans and their whereabouts for the next few hours); and right after hearing of her control over doors (in 1.D), he tries to protect himself by locking the room door. She duly turns up and murders Socrates, and he decides on flight (which would look like an admission of guilt), without trying to hide the body or make up a story, even though the locals know all about Meroe and he can show her handiwork on the corpse. Next he makes a mess of his attempts to escape (merely rousing the porter's suspicions) and to kill himself (suicide being the only way that he can see to escape execution). Socrates revives, but as Aristomenes' head is soaked in urine, he should realize that the witches did in fact come and remove the heart, and so get well away from Socrates before he deteriorates and has to be buried (as was predicted). Instead he goes off with him, in front of a witness. When his feeble explanation that he must have dreamed the murder is called into question by Socrates' own dream that he was murdered, and when Socrates reveals that he is feeling very weak, Aristomenes suggests breakfast, offering bread and cheese to a man whose throat has been cut! And then, when his friend becomes much worse, he forgets all about the witch's words to the sponge about the river, and actually suggests that Socrates drink from the river. In addition to that he is gaily parading his own idiocy in all this before his listeners, and foolishly telling the whole story to a complete stranger (Lucius), who might report him. As a final joke, Lucius (who is not too bright himself) nowhere criticizes Aristomenes' stupidity and remains blissfully unaware that this is a cautionary tale for him on the dangers of curiosity, magic and its female practitioners (for such foreshadowing see further Murgatroyd 2001a).

Aristomenes and his companion turn off to a farm, and Lucius goes on to Hypata, where he stays with a rich miser (Milo), to whom he has a letter of introduction from a friend. The next day (in book 2 of the Metamorphoses*) Lucius meets an aunt of his who lives in Hypata and who warns him that his host's wife is a witch with an eye for handsome young men like him. This only makes him keen to find out about her magic arts and he decides to do this by seducing her maid (Photis), who is attractive and seemed taken with him when she tucked him up the night before. When he returns to Milo's house, he finds Photis stirring a pot of stew. He tells what he did next.*

2.A *In a playful exchange full of sexual innuendo, Lucius flatters Photis and she warns him off, before finally giving in to him.*

'Quam pulchre quamque festive,' inquam 'Photis mea, ollulam istam cum natibus intorques! quam mellitum pulmentum apparas! felix et beatus, cui permiseris illuc digitum intingere.' tunc illa, 'Discede,' inquit 'miselle, a meo foculo, discede. nam si te vel modice meus igniculus afflaverit, ureris intime nec ullus exstinguet ardorem tuum nisi ego, quae ollam et lectulum suave quatere novi.' tum ad me conversa limis et morsicantibus oculis, 'Heus tu, scolastice,' ait 'dulce et amarum gustulum carpis. cave ne nimia mellis dulcedine diutinam bilis amaritudinem contrahas.' eam complexus coepi saviari. iamque prona cupidine allibescenti, 'Pereo,' inquam 'immo iamdudum perii, nisi tu propitiaris.' illa, rursum me

5

10

2 Lucius falls in love with Photis.

deosculato, 'Bono animo esto,' inquit. 'prima face cubiculum tuum adero. abi ergo ac te compara: tota enim nocte tecum fortiter proeliabor.'

1 The repetition of words and fullness of expression (saying the same thing twice) are typical of Apuleius' exuberant style but here also make for emphasis and enthusiasm in Lucius' flattery.

1 ollulam on the surface refers to the cooking pot, but receptacles like this often stood for the vagina (compare the play on this sense with *ollam* in 5). Diminutives are common in Apuleius. Here it has an affectionate tinge, as often.

2 quam is exclamatory ('what a!') and goes with *mellitum*.

2–3 With *felix et beatus* understand *erit ille* (which *cui* picks up: 'the man who . . . '). *Permiseris* is future perfect indicative of *permitto*. *Illuc* denotes both the stew and Photis.

3–4 discede . . . discede: the imperative gets stress from the repetition and placement (words are emphasized by being positioned at the very start or end of a sentence). *Foculo* also hints at the vagina.

4 igniculus afflaverit: again there is a double entendre (*igniculus* denotes not just the cooking-fire but also the heat of Photis' genitalia). The verb is future perfect indicative.

5 nec ullus = *nemo*.

6 suave: the neuter accusative singular of the adjective is used as an adverb here, as frequently happens, especially in poetry.

6 morsicantibus is applied neatly to a cook and paradoxically to eyes (it denotes primarily a flickering of the eyes like nibbling, but also suggests Photis tasting Lucius to see what he is like and nipping him (by teasing him), and it conjures up love-bites too). The tasting and digesting imagery in 7–8 is also apt in this culinary context.

7–8 cave . . . contrahas: *cave ne* means 'take care that you don't . . . ' *Nimia . . . dulcedine* is ablative of cause, and *bilis amaritudinem* alludes to indigestion. Love was conventionally bitter-sweet.

9 allibescenti agrees with an understood *illi* ('to her').

11 **bono animo esto**: i.e. be of good cheer, cheer up (ablative of description plus second person singular of the imperative of *sum*).

11 **prima face**: i.e. when the torches are first lit to light the house.

11 **adero**: *adsum* with the accusative (meaning 'be present in') is almost unique to Apuleius.

12 **abi**: second person singular of the present imperative of *abeo*.

12 **compara . . . proeliabor**: the reference is to making oneself ready for sex and indulging in vigorous sexual intercourse.

APPRECIATION

2.A *(Metamorphoses 2.7–10).*

This exchange (typical of the often bawdy *Metamorphoses*: on sex in the novel see Hijmans and van der Paardt 1978, 95ff.) is all very playful and appealing on the surface, but it has a darker undertone, so that its bittersweet theme is particularly apt. Lucius is making advances to Photis primarily as a way of getting access to her mistress' magical arts, and only secondarily because Photis is attractive. He is being calculating, deliberately exploiting a female slave who feels affection for him. There is a comic rebound later on when this access to magic via Photis leads to his metamorphosis into an ass. That means that there is grim irony in Lucius himself taking the initiative here, entering on the road to his downfall amid all this merriment (especially joking about a pot in line 1, when a pot with the wrong magic ointment in it will cause his problems later), and stressing the good fortune of the man who gets involved with Photis. We can also see in retrospect hidden and unwitting point to Photis' words in 3f. (Lucius really should get away from her, and will soon be really wretched) and 7–8 (like a schoolboy, he has things to learn; and he will soon be experiencing bitterness for quite some time).

2.B *That night Lucius retires to his room, where Photis has made arrangements for their assignation and left out wine for them. She arrives, drinks with him and then takes pity on his state of arousal.*

Commodum cubueram et ecce Photis mea laeta proximat, rosa in sinu tuberante. ac me pressim deosculato et corollis vincto, arripit poculum ac, aqua calida iniecta, porrigit. sequens et tertium inter nos alternat poculum, cum ego iam vino madens, 'Miserere' inquam 'et subveni maturius. nam ubi primam sagittam saevi Cupidinis in ima praecordia 5 mea delapsam excepi, arcum meum ipse vigorate tetendi et oppido formido ne nervus rigoris nimietate rumpatur.' laciniis suis cunctis renudata, in speciem Veneris pulchre reformata, paulisper feminal rosea

palmula obumbrans, 'Proeliare' inquit 'et fortiter proeliare! nec enim tibi
cedam nec terga vertam. comminus in aspectum, si vir es, derige, et   10
grassare naviter et occide moriturus.' inscenso grabatulo, super me
sensim residens ac crebra subsiliens, me satiavit. his colluctationibus ad
confinia lucis pervigiles egimus, poculis interdum lassitudinem refoventes
et libidinem incitantes.

    1–2 rosa … tuberante: Latin often uses the singular in place of the plural, as here. Flowers were common at parties, and roses were associated with Venus and love. *Tubero* (like *proximo* in line 1) is not found before Apuleius and so draws the attention.

    3 aqua … iniecta: the Greeks and Romans regularly added water to their wine to temper and dilute it. *Iniecta* is from *inicio*.

    4 miserere: imperative of the deponent *misereor* (compare the deponent imperatives *proeliare* and *grassare* in 9 and 11).

    5 maturius: the sense of the comparative adverb is 'quite quickly'.

    6–7 arcum … rumpatur: Lucius here moves from Cupid's arrows inspiring love in him to the phallic imagery of his own taut bow and bowstring. *Tetendi* in 6 is the perfect indicative of *tendo*, and *ne* in 7 introduces a positive fear clause ('I am absolutely terrified that … ').

    7–8 Venus in literature and art was often represented as holding a hand in front of her private parts coyly or teasingly.

    9–11 These lines contain a series of military images referring to engagement in vigorous sexual intercourse and 'dying' at the climax.

    10 terga vertam: the plural is used in place of the singular, as often. Soldiers turned their backs in flight from the enemy.

    10 comminus … derige: to direct one's force into an opponent's sight at close quarters means to close in and launch a frontal assault.

    11 moriturus is the future participle of *morior*.

    12 crebra: the neuter accusative plural of the adjective is used as an adverb, as frequently happens in Latin (especially in poetry).

    13 egimus: *ago* is intransitive here and mean 'be busy' or 'proceed'.

APPRECIATION

2.B *(Metamorphoses 2.16–17).*

This frankly erotic and entertaining incident also has an underlying bite to it. Lucius here thinks he is in control and so clever, but he isn't really. It is Photis who makes the arrangements for the assignation, hands out the drinks, resembles the goddess Venus (whereas he likens himself to a victim of Cupid), issues orders, initiates sex and is physically above Lucius at the beginning and end (emphasizing her dominance). She also outdoes his flattering wit at 5–6 with more extensive and urgent verbal play at 9–11. All this foreshadows his coming inferiority to Photis as an ass and mirrors the way in which on a larger scale Lucius imagines that he is savvy and in command of events generally, but is in fact the plaything of fortune and his own curiosity and desires, now approaching his comeuppance. Note also that the roses with which Lucius is festooned at 1–2 will later become the means of escape from his asinine form, but will be beyond his reach for a long time; his joking (and swiftly granted) appeal to Photis for help in 4–5 will be replaced by a serious need of her assistance (not forthcoming) after his metamorphosis; there will be poetic justice for his deliberate misleading of her at 5f. (over being in love) when she unwittingly misleads him (by giving him the wrong pot of magic ointment); and in retrospect we can discern an unintentional nasty edge to her *si vir es* in 10 and *moriturus* in 11 addressed to one who will before long end his existence as a man.

After many more such nights of love with Photis Lucius is invited to dinner at his aunt's. In conversation there he remarks that the local witches are said to steal parts of corpses for use in magic, and someone replies that they don't even spare the living and one man's face was in this way completely mutilated by them. All the guests laugh and turn to look at Thelyphron, who is reclining on his own in a corner. He tries to leave, but is persuaded by Lucius' aunt to come out with his story. Lucius now recounts the tale that Thelyphron told.

2.C *When very young, Thelyphron went to see the Olympic Games and then visited Thessaly. Short of funds in the town of Larissa, he became interested when the job of guarding a corpse was advertised. A passer-by explained how difficult and dangerous the job was.*

Dum paupertati meae fomenta conquiro, conspicor medio foro senem. praedicabat, siqui mortuum servare vellet, de pretio liceretur. ad quempiam praetereuntium, 'Quid?' inquam 'hicine mortui solent aufugere?' 'Tace,' respondit ille. 'nam oppido puer et peregrinus es, meritoque ignoras Thessaliae te consistere, ubi sagae mulieres ora   5
mortuorum demorsicant, eaque sunt illis artis magicae supplementa.' 'Et quae,' inquam 'custodela ista feralis?' 'Primum,' respondit ille 'perpetem noctem eximie vigilandum est, inconivis oculis semper in cadaver intentis, quippe cum deterrimae versipelles, in quodvis animal ore converso, latenter arrepant. aves et canes et mures induunt. tunc diris cantaminibus   10
somno custodes obruunt. nec satis quisquam definire poterit quantas latebras nequissimae mulieres pro libidine sua comminiscuntur. et siqui non integrum corpus mane restituerit, quidquid inde decerptum fuerit, id omne de facie sua desecto sarcire compellitur.'

2 **praedicabat . . . liceretur**: *praedicabat* is followed by an indirect command (with *ut* omitted); *siqui* is made up of *si* and *qui* = 'anyone' (in place of the more usual *quis*); and *vellet* is imperfect subjunctive of *volo*. The sense is: 'he proclaimed that if anyone was willing . . . , he should . . .'

3 **praetereuntium**: the participle is used as a noun ('passers-by').

3 **hicine** = *hic* (the adverb) plus the interrogative particle -*ne* (with forms of *hic* ending in -*c* combined with -*ne* the *i* is normally inserted like this).

5 **Thessaliae te consistere**: *Thessaliae* is locative, and *te consistere* is accusative and infinitive in indirect statement.

5 **ora** (from *os*) is neuter accusative plural.

6 **eaque** refers to the pieces bitten off by the witches.

6–7 **et quae . . .**: supply *est* (as so often in Latin).

7–8 **perpetem . . . est**: *perpetem noctem* is accusative of duration of time, and *vigilandum* is the gerundive (expressing obligation) used in an impersonal expression (literally: 'it is to be stayed awake', i.e. one must stay awake).

8 **intentis** is the perfect participle passive of *intendo*.

9 **quippe cum** means essentially 'since'.

9 **in . . . converso**: i.e. the witches' appearance having been changed into that of any animal they please.

12 **comminiscuntur**: the indicative rather than the subjunctive in an indirect question is found mainly in early Latin and in poetry.

12 **siqui** = *si quis*.

13 **corpus . . . inde:** both these words refer to the body guarded.

13 **restituerit** is future perfect indicative (like *fuerit* later in the line). This tense will no longer be pointed out as a matter of course.

13–14 **id omne** picks up *quidquid* and is the object of *sarcire*.

14 **de . . . desecto**: 'with something sliced off from . . .'

2.D *Thelyphron accepts the job and is taken to the mourning widow, who begs him to guard her husband's body as carefully as he can.*

His cognitis, animum meum commasculo et ilico accedens praeconem, 'Clamare' inquam 'iam desine. adest custos paratus.' 'Mille' inquit 'nummum deponentur tibi. sed heus, iuvenis, cave cadaver a malis Harpyis probe custodias.' 'Ineptias' inquam 'mihi narras. vides hominem ferreum et insomnem, certe perspicaciorem ipso vel Lynceo vel Argo.'   5

Ilico me perducit ad domum quampiam. intro vocat me et, conclave umbrosum aperiens, demonstrat matronam flebilem fusca veste contectam. quam propter assistens, 'Hic' inquit 'ad custodiam mariti tui accessit.' at illa, crinibus antependulis dimotis, etiam in maerore luculentam proferens faciem, 'Vide' inquit 'quam expergite munus obeas.'   10
'Sine cura sis' inquam.

3 **nummum** is an archaic form of the genitive plural (this form is common in poetry).

3–4 **cave . . . custodias**: 'make sure that you guard . . .' *Ut* is omitted (it is more normally included with the subjunctive after *caveo*).

4 **Harpyis**: the Harpies were winged female monsters who carried off children and the souls of the dead, and who famously persecuted a blind prophet called Phineus whenever he tried to eat (suddenly seizing his food, devouring it and soiling it with their foul droppings).

5 **Lynceo vel Argo**: ablatives of comparison ('than'). Lynceus was renowned for his keen sight and accompanied Jason on his quest for the Golden Fleece. Argus had eyes all over his head (or body), and

so Juno got him to watch over a cow she suspected (really Io, a mistress of Jupiter, metamorphosed into an animal to escape Juno's notice).

8 quam propter: *quam* (referring to the matron) is the relative used to connect (translate as 'her'), and it is governed by *propter* (such postponement of prepositions was common in verse).

10 vide plus the subjunctive means 'take care that . . .'

10 quam expergite: 'as vigilantly as possible' (this sense of *quam* is much more frequent with superlative adverbs like *celerrime*).

11 sis: jussive subjunctive.

2.E The widow calls in witnesses and formally establishes the body's undamaged state. Later she rounds on Thelyphron for asking in a house of mourning for food and drink to consume during his vigil.

Consurrexit et ad aliud me cubiculum inducit. ibi corpus introductis
septem testibus revelat et, diutine insuper fleto, obtestata fidem
praesentium, singula demonstrat anxie, verba quodam tabulis
praenotante. 'Ecce' inquit 'nasus integer, incolumes oculi, salvae aures,
illibatae labiae, mentum solidum. vos in hanc rem, boni Quirites,   5
testimonium perhibetote.' et consignatis tabulis facessit.

At ego 'Iube,' inquam 'domina, cuncta quae sunt usui necessaria nobis
exhiberi.' 'At quae' inquit 'ista sunt?' 'Lucerna' aio 'praegrandis, et oleum
ad lucem luci sufficiens, et calida cum oenophoris et calice, cenarumque
reliquiis discus ornatus.' 'Abi,' inquit 'fatue, qui in domo funesta cenas et   10
partes requiris. an comissatum te venisse credis? quin sumis potius loco
congruentes luctus et lacrimas?' respexit ancillulam et 'Myrrhine,' inquit
'lucernam et oleum trade confestim et, incluso custode, cubiculo protinus
facesse.'

1–2 introductis . . . testibus: dative (indirect object).

2 insuper fleto: 'with it having been wept [by her] over [the corpse]'. This is an impersonal use of *fleo* in an ablative absolute.

4–5 The forceful asyndeton works like a series of hammer blows.

6 perhibetote: this form of the imperative (second person plural) was common in law. *Perhibere testimonium in* means 'bear witness to'.

7 cuncta . . . necessaria: i.e. all that he would need as a guard.

7 nobis: plural for singular (= *mihi*).

9 ad lucem luci sufficiens: 'sufficient for light [in the lamp] until the light [of day]'. Such verbal play and the alliteration in the following words too make for an inappropriate jauntiness.

11 partes: 'parts [of dinners]', i.e. leftovers.

11 comissatum te venisse: supine in -um to express purpose, followed by an accusative and infinitive in indirect statement.

11–12 The alliteration in these lines seems forceful and solemn.

13 cubiculo: local ablative (a preposition meaning 'from' is omitted).

2.F *He tries to keep his spirits up, but in the depths of the night a weasel slinks in. He drives it out, only to fall into a death-like sleep.*

Sic desolatus ad cadaveris solacium, animum meum permulcebam
cantationibus, cum ecce crepusculum et nox provecta et nox altior et iam
nox intempesta. mihique oppido formido cumulatior quidem, cum
repente introrepens mustela contra me constitit optutumque acerrimum
in me destituit, ut tantillula animalis prae nimia sui fiducia mihi turbarit   5
animum. 'Quin abis,' inquam 'impura bestia, teque ad tuos similes
recondis, antequam nostri vim praesentariam experiaris? quin abis?' terga
vertit et cubiculo protinus exterminatur. nec mora cum me somnus
profundus in imum barathrum repente demergit, ut ne deus quidem
Delphicus ipse facile discerneret, duobus nobis iacentibus, quis esset   10
magis mortuus. sic inanimis et indigens alio custode paene ibi non eram.

> 1 **sic . . . solacium:** *ad* means 'for the purpose of'. Thelyphron is being flippant with the idea of
> himself consoling a corpse and with the play in de*SOLA*tus and *SOLA*cium.
>
> 2 **cum:** this is an inverted *cum* clause (compare those in 3 and 8) in which *fuit* is to be supplied as
> the verb.
>
> 3 **formido cumulatior:** understand *erat*.
>
> 5 **sui fiducia:** *sui* is objective genitive of *se* (we would say 'confidence IN itself').
>
> 5 **mihi** is possessive dative with *animum* ('my mind').
>
> 5 **turbarit** is the syncopated form of *turbaverit* (perfect subjunctive in a result clause).
>
> 6 **ad tuos similes:** if the text is correct here, *similes* must be used as a noun in the sense of 'likenesses',
> i.e. kin (referring to weasels and other vermin).
>
> 7 **nostri** is the gentive of *nos* and is plural for singular (= *mei*).
>
> 7–8 **terga . . . exterminatur:** *terga* is plural for singular; *cubiculo* is a local ablative (supply *de* or *e*
> meaning 'from'); and *exterminatur* is used reflexively ('removed itself').
>
> 8 **nec mora:** understand *erat* ('there was no delay when . . . ' = immediately).
>
> 9–10 **ne . . . Delphicus:** *ne . . . quidem* means 'not even'. The *deus* here is Apollo, who had a famous
> oracular shrine at Delphi in Greece and who was a wise and omniscient god of prophecy.
>
> 10 **duobus nobis iacentibus:** the reference in this ablative absolute is to the corpse and Thelyphron.
>
> 11 **indigens alio custode:** i.e. Thelyphron was himself like a dead man who needed someone to
> guard him.
>
> 11 **paene ibi non eram:** i.e. in his death-like sleep he was almost no longer there on earth but in the
> Underworld.

2.G *He wakes at dawn to find the corpse unharmed. The widow is grateful, but when he thoughtlessly offers to act as such a guard again whenever she needs one, he is beaten up and thrown out.*

Tandem expergitus et nimio pavore perterritus, cadaver accurro. et
admoto lumine revelataque eius facie, rimabar singula, quae cuncta
convenerant. ecce uxor misella flens cum testibus introrumpit anxia, et

statim corpori superruens ac diu deosculata, recognoscit omnia, et
requirit actorem. ei praecipit bono custodi redderet sine mora praemium. 5
'Summas' inquit 'tibi, iuvenis, gratias agimus, et ob sedulum istud
ministerium inter familiares dehinc numerabimus.' ego insperato lucro
diffusus in gaudium, 'Immo,' inquam 'domina, de famulis tuis unum
putato, et quotiens operam nostram desiderabis, fidenter impera.' me
statim familiares, omen nefarium exsecrati, raptis cuiusque modi telis, 10
insequuntur. laceratus atque discerptus domo proturbor.

2–3 **quae cuncta convenerant**: i.e. all the parts of the face were as they should be. The use of the
pluperfect in place of the perfect or imperfect (as here) was common in early Latin and especially in
poetry. The alliteration (of *q* and *c*) seems emphatic and dramatic.

4 **superruens ... deosculata**: the first verb is not found before Apuleius (and so it draws attention
to this action); understand *corpus* as the object of the second verb.

5 **bono ... praemium**: *ut* is omitted (far more common than this simple subjunctive is *ut* with the
subjunctive in the indirect command after *praecipio*). *Bono custodi* is indirect object of *redderet*.

7 **inter familiares ... numerabimus**: supply *te* as the object. *Familiaris* means 'close friend' here
but 'servant' in line 10.

8–9 **de ... putato**: 'consider [me] as one of your ...' *Putato* (= *puta*) is an archaic form of the
imperative, common in legal language.

9 **nostram**: plural for singular (this usage will no longer be pointed out as a matter of course).

10 **omen**: his words suggest that a later husband or husbands will also die and need to be guarded
by Thelyphron.

10 **cuiusque** is genitive singular of *quisque*.

11 **domo**: 'from the house'.

2.H *While Thelyphron recovers nearby, the corpse is carried off in the
funeral procession. Suddenly a distraught old man turns up, begging for
help and accusing the widow of murdering her husband.*

Ac dum in proxima platea refovens animum infausti atque improvidi
sermonis mei reminiscor, ecce iam ultimum defletus processerat mortuus,
rituque patrio pompa funeris publici ductabatur per forum. occurrit
atratus quidam maestus in lacrimis canitiem revellens senex, et manibus
ambabus invadens torum, voce assiduis singultibus impedita, 'Per fidem 5
vestram,' inquit 'Quirites, perempto civi subsistite, et extremum facinus
in nefariam scelestamque istam feminam severiter vindicate. haec enim
miserum adulescentem (sororis meae filium) in adulteri gratiam et ob
praedam hereditariam exstinxit veneno.' Saevire vulgus et ad criminis
credulitatem impelli. conclamant ignem, requirunt saxa, parvulos ad 10
exitium mulieris hortantur. emeditatis illa fletibus, adiurans cuncta
numina, tantum scelus abnuebat.

  2 **ultimum**: the neuter accusative singular of the adjective functions as an adverb ('for the last time').

  3 **rituque patrio**: the ablative *ritu* means in accordance with some practice (here the practice is 'ancestral' – *patrio*).

  4 **atratus . . . senex**: note the flurry of emotive words, building pathos and sympathy for the old man (to counteract the widow).

  5 **assiduis singultibus**: ablative of instrument/means with *impedita* (which agrees with *voce*).

  5–6 **per fidem vestram**: the appeal 'by your honour' means: as you are honourable men, help (i.e. avenge) your fellow-citizen.

  6 **perempto** is perfect participle passive of *perimo*.

  7 **severiter vindicate**: the adverb is rare and emphatic. So too there is no parallel for the construction with *vindico* (which means 'inflict punishment for an' *extremum facinus* 'on' *nefariam* etc.).

  8 **in adulteri gratiam**: i.e. in order to please/oblige her adulterous lover (*in* here has the sense 'for the sake of').

  8–9 **ob . . . hereditariam**: i.e. to secure her inheritance as spoil.

  9–10 **saevire . . . impelli**: these are historic infinitives (used in place of past main verbs).

  10–11 **conclamant . . . hortantur**: the brisk asyndeton suggests swift action. The crowd want to burn the widow alive or stone her to death. *Parvulos* probably refers to street-urchins (although text and interpretation are disputed).

  11 **emeditatis**: this deponent verb's participle has a passive force.

2.1 To establish the truth, the old man gets a prophet to reanimate the corpse, which duly states that it was murdered by the widow. When she denies this, the people are unsure whom to believe.

Ergo senex ille: 'Veritatis arbitrium in divinam providentiam reponamus. Zatchlas adest, Aegyptius propheta primarius, qui mecum pepigit reducere paulisper ab inferis spiritum.' iuvenem quempiam producit in medium. huius diu manus deosculatus, 'Miserere,' ait 'sacerdos, miserere. in aeternum conditis oculis modicam lucem infunde. ad ultionis solacium   5 exiguum vitae spatium deprecamur.' propheta herbulam quampiam ob os corporis et aliam pectori eius imponit. tunc incrementa Solis augusti imprecatus, venerabilis scaenae facie studia praesentium ad miraculum arrexit.

  Immitto me turbae et pone lectulum editiorem lapidem insistens   10 cuncta curiosis oculis arbitrabar. iam tumore pectus attolli, iam spiritu corpus impleri. assurgit cadaver et profatur: 'Malis novae nuptae peremptus artibus et addictus noxio poculo, torum tepentem adultero mancipavi.' tunc uxor egregia coarguenti marito resistens altercat. populus aestuat, diversa tendentes.   15

  1 **reponamus**: jussive subjunctive.
  2 **pepigit** is from *pango*.
  4 **miserere**: second person singular of the imperative of *misereor*.

5 **in aeternum** (meaning 'forever') goes with *conditis*, while *oculis* refers to the corpse's eyes (having light in the eyes = being alive).

5 **ad ... solacium**: *ad* means 'for', and *ultionis* is genitive of definition ('consisting of revenge'). The old man wants the corpse to be reanimated briefly so that he can get revenge.

7 **pectori eius**: i.e. on the chest of the corpse.

7 **incrementa Solis**: i.e. the Sun-god evident in his growing (rising) disk.

8 **facie** means 'sight', and *studia ad* means 'enthusiasm for'.

10 **editiorem**: the comparative means 'rather high'.

11–12 **attolli ... impleri**: historic infinitives.

13 **peremptus** is from *perimo*.

14 **egregia** is ironical.

15 **diversa tendentes**: the participle picks up *populus*, which is singular, but implies plurality. *Diversa* denotes opposite viewpoints.

2.J The young man's corpse proves its truthfulness by revealing a shocking secret about Thelyphron that only it could know.

Sed hanc cunctationem sequens adulescentis sermo distinxit. 'Dabo,' inquit 'dabo vobis intemeratae veritatis documenta perlucida, et quod

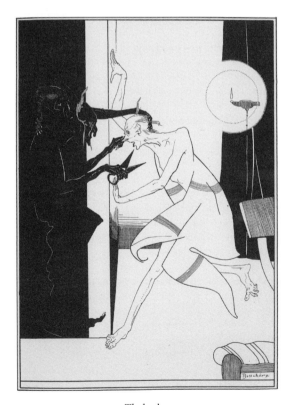

3 Thelyphron.

prorsus alius nemo cognoverit indicabo.' tunc digito me demonstrans:
'Nam cum corporis mei custos hic sagacissimus exsertam mihi teneret
vigiliam, cantatrices anus (iniecta somni nebula) me nomine ciere non   5
prius desierunt quam dum membra frigida ad artis magicae nituntur
obsequia. hic (tantum sopore mortuus), quod eodem mecum nomine
nuncupatur, ad suum nomen ignarus exsurgit. et foribus cubiculi
diligenter occlusis, per quoddam foramen prosectis naso prius ac mox
auribus vicariam pro me lanienam sustinuit. utque fallaciae reliqua   10
convenirent, ceram in modum prosectarum formatam aurium ei
applicant examussim nasoque ipsius similem comparant. et nunc
assistit miser hic, praemium non industriae sed debilitationis
consecutus.'

His dictis perterritus, temptare formam aggredior. nasum prehendo: 15
sequitur; aures pertracto: deruunt. ac dum directis digitis praesentium
denotor, dum risus ebullit, inter pedes circumstantium evado. nec lari me
patrio reddere potui, sed capillis deiectis aurium vulnera celavi; nasi
dedecus linteolo isto pressim agglutinato obtexi.

> **1 cunctationem** refers to the crowd's hesitation over what to do (whether to punish the widow or
> disbelieve the corpse).
> **2–3 quod . . . cognoverit**: with *quod* understand *id* ('a thing which'). *Cognoverit* is the perfect
> subjunctive of *cognosco* with a potential sense ('could find out').
> **5–6 non . . . dum**: 'did not stop . . . sooner than until' (i.e. did not stop . . . until).
> **6–7 ad . . . obsequia**: 'were striving towards obedience to . . . ' (i.e. the corpse's limbs were trying
> hard to obey the witches' magic art).
> **7 tantum**: 'only' (only in a death-like sleep and actually alive, he responded to the witches' summons
> more readily than the corpse).
> **7 eodem . . . nomine**: i.e. by the same name as me (the corpse was also called Thelyphron).
> **8 ad**: 'in response to'.
> **9 prosectis** agrees with both *naso* and *auribus*.
> **10–11 utque . . . convenirent**: 'so that the other things [the rest] might be consistent with their
> trickery' (i.e. to put the finishing touch to their trickery).
> **11 in modum**: 'in the manner of' (i.e. so as to resemble).
> **12 nasoque ipsius similem**: understand *nasum*, with which *similem* agrees (the reference is to a
> fake nose just like his own).
> **15 formam**: supply *meam*.
> **18 potui**: *possum* here means 'bring myself to/have the courage to'.

APPRECIATION

2.c–j (Metamorphoses 2.21–30).

This intricate and sophisticated narrative is certainly effective on a first reading,
thanks to the various puzzles, tricks and surprises in it. One begins it wondering

why Thelyphron is laughed at and upset, and who is the subject of his story (it's about a man with a badly disfigured face, but he himself as far as we are told at this point is not mutilated, so could it be about a relative or friend of his?). Then there is the misleading picture of the widow as a genuinely loving and concerned wife. The ever increasing tension over whether the frivolous and naive Thelyphron will succeed in his dangerous task really mounts when the weasel enters in 2.F, only to be dissipated when it leaves. But then Thelyphron is put to sleep, and it seems certain that the corpse will now be attacked. But again there is relief when the body is found to be whole, reinforced by humour when Thelyphron offers his services as a guard again. In 2.H (as he now largely drops out and seems unimportant) the tale takes a startling new direction, with the pathetic old man's charge of murder, and there is a sudden reversal when we learn that the widow fakes tears and apparently has a lover. In 2.I there is a still more dramatic and surprising turn of events as the corpse is reanimated and corroborates the old man's accusation, with some sensational extra details. The biggest shock of all comes in 2.J, when the focus suddenly shifts back to Thelyphron and we finally learn that he is in fact the maimed subject of the story. Apuleius tricks us infuriatingly by holding back until the very end the tell-tale detail of the bandage, but in doing so he manages to satisfy the logic of his larger narrative of the *Metamorphoses* (one presumes that Lucius, who is not too bright, just did not see the bandage as a give-away, and even after he heard the whole story and came to recount it still did not view Thelyphron as an obvious candidate for mutilation, and so did not mention the bandage until it figured in the man's tale). For more on the teasing here see Winkler 1985, 110ff.

If anything, 2.C–J is even more entertaining on a second reading. One goes back to it with a whole new understanding and sees extra levels of humour and artifice. Among the more general aspects, we can appreciate now what an outrageously good actress the widow is and how (nastily) Thelyphron suffered disfigurement while being used just as a front and in unwitting support of the very person who murdered the corpse he guarded. There are particular aspects in individual sections too. In 2.C there is verbal play in *fomenta* (literally 'bandages') in line 1, irony in Thelyphron of all people being told that witches attack people's faces in lines 5–6, and some tricky foreshadowing at 9ff. (witches changing shape and causing sleep, and guards having to make up lost body parts from their own faces). In 2.D.5 it is comical of Thelyphron (who later didn't even know that he had a false nose and ears) to claim that he is perceptive, and to introduce the comparisons to Lynceus and Argus: after the allusion to witches as Harpies in line 4, one recalls now that Lynceus was with Phineus but did not see the Harpies until they had already attacked him; and Argus, while watching over Io, was put to sleep and maimed (beheaded) by a supernatural power (Mercury). So too the darkness and concealment associated with the widow at 7ff. can now be seen to have additional point. At 2.E.7 Thelyphron calls the widow *domina* (which can also denote a lover's 'mistress'); then at 9f. he asks this poisoner for food and drink; and at 11f. he is told by this woman, who is just pretending to grieve appropriately, that he should adopt an appropriate grief. In 2.F his joke about being left to console a corpse (line 1) unwittingly looks forward to his substitution for disfigurement, which would bring some relief to the dead man; and at 6f. he tells the weasel to be off when he himself should be desperately trying to get away, and threatens it with immediate violence just before being subject to violence himself at the hands of the weasel/witch. In 2.G the mutilated Thelyphron examines the corpse's face for signs of mutilation (1f.), is described in 5 as a good guard by the widow (he is good for her in that he has satisfied her needs, but he has not protected himself), and refers to himself as mangled in 11 with more truth than we initially realize. The volte face in 2.H (about the widow), showing that appearances are deceptive, subtly prefigures that in 2.J (about Thelyphron). The reference to inflicting punishment on a female by stoning her in lines 7 and 10 there recalls the same penalty for the murderous Meroe at 1.D.1f., but later one sees a further neat link in the temporary re-animation of a man killed by the woman. At 2.I.1 there is more to the settling of the truth than we initially realize (it is the truth about Thelyphron too); and at 8ff. there is a sly humour in him being so eager for the ensuing miracle, so keen to find out what the corpse will do, and putting himself in a prominent position for all to see. There are many more instances of this kind of cleverness which you can find yourself through a careful rereading of the narrative.

Also dexterous is the way in which this anecdote is integrated smoothly within the *Metamorphoses* as a whole and is connected with various passages elsewhere in the novel. For example, it echoes Aristomenes' tale (1.A–L) because of its dark humour, supernatural subject matter, Thessalian setting and details in common (murder, one man in a room at night with another and asleep, the room entered by a witch, harm to a body, the temporary revival of it etc.). In addition, like 1.A–L and much else at the start of the novel, it is yet another warning for Lucius (about the dangers of magic), blithely ignored by him, and Lucius of all people passes on what is in fact a story very close to his own (about a rather dim young man who travels to Thessaly, ignores admonition about sorcery, then has an adventure involving magic and metamorphosis, and is as a result disfigured). For more links to the rest of the novel see Hijmans and van der Paardt 1978, 52; Tatum 1979, 39f.; Harrison 1999, 164ff.

4 Photis tells Lucius of her mistress's witchcraft.

In book 3 Lucius presses Photis (who has been inadvertently responsible for his public humiliation) to let him watch her mistress performing magic, and despite the danger she agrees. Thanks to Photis he spies on her mistress rubbing herself with ointment from a jar, turning into a bird and flying off to her lover. He then persuades Photis to fetch the same jar for him, so he too can change into a bird.

3.A *Photis creeps into her mistress's room but by mistake fetches the wrong jar. Lucius eagerly rubs on the ointment and turns into an ass.*

Summa cum trepidatione irrepit cubiculum et pyxidem depromit arcula.
quam ego amplexus ac deosculatus, abiectis propere laciniis totis, avide
manus immersi et, haurito plusculo, cuncta corporis mei membra
perfricui. iamque libratis bracchiis in avem similem gestiebam. nec ullae
plumulae nec usquam pinnulae; sed plane pili mei crassantur in setas, et   5
cutis tenella duratur in corium; et in extimis palmulis, perdito numero,
toti digiti coguntur in singulas ungulas; et de spinae meae termino grandis
cauda procedit. iam facies enormis et os prolixum et nares hiantes et
labiae pendulae; sic et aures immodicis horripilant auctibus. nec ullum
miserae reformationis video solacium, nisi quod mihi iam nequeunti   10

5 Lucius is turned into an ass.

tenere Photidem natura crescebat. ac querens de facto Photidis (sed iam
humano gestu et voce privatus), postrema deiecta labia, umidis tamen
oculis obliquum respiciens ad illam, tacitus expostulabam.

2 **quam** refers to *pyxidem* (the relative used to connect sentences).

4 **in . . . gestiebam**: 'I had a strong desire for a similar bird' (i.e. I longed to become a bird like
Photis' mistress). The expression is odd, and *in* with the verb in this sense occurs first here and is rare.

4–5 **nec . . . pinnulae**: supply *sunt mihi*. The (rare) diminutives have point: there is not the slightest
sign of Lucius turning into a bird. Note the alliteration, assonance and parallel arrangement of words
here (and at 5–6 the repetition of the order of noun, adjective, verb and prepositional phrase in *pili . . .
corium*).

5–7 **et . . . ungulas**: *perdito* is from *perdo*, and *numero* means 'plurality'. There are four balanced
pairs here (epithet preceding noun each time), together with alliteration and extensive homoeoteleuton.

8–9 **facies . . . pendulae**: understand *est mihi*. In this group of four pairs the nouns are followed by
epithets each time, the first two pairs are singular and the second two are plural, and the even-numbered
pairs refer to Lucius' mouth.

10 **nisi quod**: 'except for the fact that'.

11 **tenere** means both 'embrace' and 'have intercourse with'.

13 **obliquum**: the neuter accusative singular of the adjective is used as an adverb. The sidelong look
denotes disapproval and distrust.

APPRECIATION

3.A *(Metamorphoses 3.24–5).*

In addition to its importance for the plot, the metamorphosis is caught at
length and in detail to point up the comedy. There is irony at 2–4, where

almost every word brings out how eager Lucius is and how he makes sure that
he applies the ointment thoroughly. At 4–9, piquantly, controlled and elegant
expression is used to describe the uncontrolled change into an ugly ass. There is
also visual humour throughout (just picture the scene, especially at 4 and 12f.).
Then there is the appropriateness of the transformation. In the ancient world
asses were famous for curiosity, stubbornness and stupidity, and they were
sometimes viewed as being worthless as well, so becoming one is a wickedly
apt punishment for a character such as Lucius. The ass (with its large penis)
was also a byword for lust, which fits with the lecherous Lucius, who has been
having lots of sex with Photis. Amusingly and pointedly, when he turns into
an ass he immediately demonstrates several of these traits in his new form as
well: he takes solace from the fact that his penis is bigger, as if that mattered,
especially when he thinks that he cannot copulate with a woman anyway (and
he is wrong there, because he does just that later on, in book 10); and he puts
the blame on Photis, refusing to see that he is, if anything, more at fault, as he
cajoled her into letting him dabble in magic. (Quite possibly also relevant is
the ass' connection with Seth, the enemy of Isis, who releases Lucius from his
asinine state and accepts him as a priest in book 11: see Tatum 1979, 43ff.)

*Photis is distraught but says that eating roses will restore Lucius' human form
and she will rush some to him at dawn. He considers biting and kicking her
to death, and only desists because he needs her help. As an ass he goes off to
the stable to spend the night there, but before dawn the house is robbed and
Lucius and the other animals in the stable are loaded with loot and driven off.
In book 4 the robbers stop off in a village on their way back to their den.*

4.A *Welcomed by friends, they put Lucius out to pasture. He eats
vegetables in a nearby garden and then thinks he sees some roses.*

Diem circa medium in pago quodam apud familiares latronibus senes
devertimus. sic enim sermo prolixus et oscula mutua sentire praestabant.
iamque nos omni sarcina levatos in pratum proximum tradidere. pone
stabulum prospectum hortulum iam fame perditus fidenter invado, et
crudis oleribus ventrem sagino. video frondosi nemoris convallem   5
umbrosam, cuius inter virecta rosarum mineus color renidebat. Veneris et
Gratiarum lucum illum arbitrabar. tunc cursu me concito proripio, ut
sentirem non asinum me, verum equum currulem nimio velocitatis
effectum. sed loco proximus tantum ripae fluvialis marginem densis
arboribus saeptam video. hae arbores pariunt in odori modum floris   10

caliculos punicantes, quos vulgus indoctum rosas laureas appellant.
cuncto pecori cibus letalis est.

2 **sic ... praestabant**: *sic* goes with *sentire*, and *mihi* is to be understood with *praestabant* ('... gave me to believe so').

3 **nos** refers to Lucius the ass and the other animals carrying loot.

3 **tradidere**: alternative form for *tradiderunt* (perfect indicative). The robbers are the subject.

4 **prospectum** agrees with *hortulum*, and *perditus* is from *perdo*.

6–7 **Veneris ... arbitrabar**: Lucius considers it their grove because it is so charming and loveable and because roses were sacred to the goddess of love Venus (often accompanied by the Graces, minor goddesses who were the personification of grace or charm).

7 **ut** introduces a result (consecutive) clause.

8–9 **sentirem ... effectum**: in the indirect statement here *esse* is to be supplied with *non asinum me* and also with *effectum* (making it into a perfect passive infinitive). *Verum* means 'but'.

9 **loco** is dative, with *proximus*, while *tantum* means 'only'.

10 **in ... floris**: i.e. like the rose (*in modum* means 'in the manner of'). These 'laurel roses' (i.e. oleanders) have no scent, unlike real roses.

11 **appellant**: *vulgus* is the subject (the noun is singular but implies plurality – hence the plural verb).

4.B In despair Lucius decides to commit suicide, but is suddenly assaulted by the owner of the garden. He escapes from him, only to be attacked by the villagers and is very nearly killed by them.

Talibus fatis implicitus, sponte illud venenum rosarium sumere gestiebam. sed hortulanus cuius olera vastaveram cum grandi baculo furens decurrit, adreptumque me plagis obtundit adusque vitae periculum, nisi tandem ipse mihi tulissem auxilium. nam pedum posteriorum calcibus iactatis in eum crebriter, fuga me liberavi. sed ilico 5
uxor eius, simul eum prostratum et semianimem ex edito despexit, ululabili cum plangore ad eum prosilit. cuncti pagani, fletibus eius exciti, statim conclamant canes. tunc morti proximus, cum viderem canes magnos et multos in me exasperari, fugam desino ac me celeri gradu rursum in stabulum recipio. at illi, canibus iam aegre cohibitis, me loro 10
valido ad ansulam destinatum caedendo confecissent profecto, nisi dolore plagarum alvus artata, crudisque illis oleribus abundans, et lubrico fluxu saucia, fimo fistulatim excusso, quosdam extremi liquoris aspergine, alios putore nidoris faetidi a meis scapulis abegisset.

Nec mora cum nos ac praecipue me longe gravius onustum producunt 15
illi latrones stabulo.

3 **decurrit**: the gardener and his wife live up a hill.

4 **nisi ... auxilium**: the pluperfect subjunctive (of *fero*) is used in a past unreal condition ('if I had not brought ...'). The protasis ('and he would have killed me') has to be understood, on the basis of the preceding words (*obtundit adusque vitae periculum*).

5 **calcibus** is from *calx*.

6 **simul** is the conjunction ('as soon as').

11 **caedendo** is the gerund (ablative of instrument/means).

11–14 **confecissent…abegisset**: again the pluperfect subjunctives are used in a past unreal condition ('they would have killed … if my bowels had not driven away …'). They tied him to a hook with a strap, and beat him, and would have killed him, if he had not driven them off with an attack of diarrhoea. In the involved *nisi* clause *alvus* is the subject, and it is modified by *artata* and *abundans* and *saucia* (*lubrico fluxu saucia* = troubled by diarrhoea); *fimo … excusso* is an ablative absolute; *quosdam … alios* means 'some … others'; and *abegisset* is from *abigo*. Note the ornate sound and style here (including assonance, alliteration, homoeoteleuton, and patterning of adjectives and nouns in *extremi … faetidi*) to describe an attack of diarrhoea!

15 **nec mora cum**: understand *erat* ('there was no delay when …', i.e. immediately).

15 **gravius** is the comparative adverb.

16 **stabulo**: local ablative (undertand *e* or *de*).

APPRECIATION

4.A–B *(Metamorphoses 4.1–4)*.

This lively episode, with its various surprises (as it goes on and on) and its flurry of close calls, is effectively structured. It begins with Lucius halting in his journey, having his load removed and stuffing his belly with raw vegetables; it ends with Lucius emptying his belly of raw vegetables, being loaded up again and resuming his journey. After the deceptively quiet, relaxed and friendly start (which increases the impact of what follows), there is a series of ups and downs, with the significant themes of rescue and frustration prominent and intertwined. Lucius' rescue from his ass form is frustrated, but he is frustratingly rescued from death four times, on the first and third occasions by others, and on the second and fourth by his own (posterior) efforts. So too for nearly killing Lucius, the gardener is nearly killed by Lucius, and for nearly killing the gardener, Lucius is nearly killed by the villagers. For the broader picture of structure in the *Metamorphoses* see Hijmans and van der Paardt 1978, 43ff.; Krabbe 1989, 123ff.; and Schlam 1992, 29ff.

Farce, crudity and schadenfreude all add to the entertainment, and so do several witty turns. For instance, in 4.A Lucius, who objected to carrying the robbers' plunder, becomes a plunderer himself; and the allusion to roses and Venus recalls 2.B (where Photis turned up for the night rendezvous with roses and was likened to Venus), so that one sees poetic justice in Lucius, who misled Photis with a false appearance there, being himself misled by a false appearance here. In 4.B the gardener who tries to punish Lucius' theft by beating him to death actually stops him from committing suicide; after trying to kill himself Lucius goes on to evade death at the hands of others; and finally the vegetables which he stole (as well as being returned in a way) save him from punishment.

Lucius finally reaches the robbers' den (a mountain cave). The brigands with him (just one part of a large gang) are about to eat when another group from the gang of robbers return from their plundering. When one of Lucius' abductors taunts the others with losing men (including their leader Lamachus) in their raids, a member of the other group tells the story of their recent losses.

4.C *They arrive in Thebes and decide to rob a rich man called Chryseros. Lamachus rashly slips his hand through the large keyhole of Chryseros' front door and tries to dislodge the bolt inside.*

Vix Thebas heptapylos accessimus; sedum sedulo fortunas inquirebamus popularium. nec nos latuit Chryseros quidam, nummularius qui magnis artibus magnam dissimulabat opulentiam. solus ac solitarius, parva sed satis munita domuncula contentus, pannosus ac sordidus, aureos folles incubabat. ergo placuit ad hunc primum ferremus aditum, ut cunctis   5
opibus otiose potiremur.

  Noctis initio foribus eius praestolamur, quas neque sublevare neque dimovere nobis videbatur, ne valvarum sonus cunctam viciniam suscitaret. tunc sublimis vexillarius noster Lamachus spectatae virtutis suae fiducia (sensim immissa manu) claustrum evellere gestiebat. sed   10
nequissimus Chryseros paulatim arrepit, grandique clavo manum ducis nostri repente ad ostii tabulam offigit. et gurgustioli sui tectum ascendit, atque inde clamitans rogansque vicinos diffamat incendio repentino domum suam possideri. sic suppetiatum decurrunt anxii.

---

  1 **heptapylos**: this is feminine accusative plural (of a two-termination Greek adjective).

  1 **accessimus; sedum**: note the parataxis (avoidance of subordinate clause). Translate: 'We had scarcely ... when we made inquiries about ... '

  3–4 **solus . . . sordidus**: the repeated use of the dicolon (group of two) brings out Chryseros' shrewdness (as opposed to the robbers).

  5 **placuit . . . aditum**: 'it was pleasing [i.e. we decided] that we should make our attack'. *Ut* has been omitted. the simple subjunctive (without *ut*) after *placeo* is unusual. *Ferremus* is imperfect subjunctive of *fero*.

  7 **foribus eius**: local ablative ('at his door').

  7 **quas** (referring to the *fores*) is the object of the two infinitives, which depend on *nobis videbatur* ('it seemed good to us to ... ').

10 **fiducia** + gen means 'with confidence in' (ablative of manner).

14 **possideri**: present infinitive passive in indirect statement. The neighbours (concerned for their own homes in the vicinity) react to shouts of 'fire' more than they would to shouts of 'thieves'.

14 **suppetiatum**: supine in -*um* to express purpose.

4.D *The robbers hack off Lamachus' arm at the elbow and take him away. He cannot follow them fleeing or stay behind safely, so he commits suicide. They carry his body off to the sea for burial.*

Tunc nos, in ancipiti periculo constituti vel opprimendi nostri vel deserendi socii, remedium validum (eo volente) comminiscimus. antesignani nostri partem (qua manus umerum subit) abscidimus, atque ibi bracchio relicto, multis laciniis offulto vulnere, ceterum Lamachum raptim reportamus. instantis periculi metu terremur ad fugam, nec vel   5
sequi propere vel remanere tuto potest vir sublimis animi. adhortatur per dexteram Martis bonum commilitonem cruciatu simul et captivitate liberaremus; cur enim manui, quae rapere et iugulare sola posset, fortem latronem supervivere? cumque nulli nostrum persuadere posset, manu reliqua sumptum gladium suum diuque deosculatum per medium pectus   10
ictu fortissimo transadigit. tunc nos, magnanimi ducis vigore venerato, corpus reliquum (veste lintea diligenter convolutum) mari commisimus. et nunc iacet noster Lamachus elemento toto sepultus.

1–2 **vel ... socii** explains the dilemma – the danger 'either of us being caught or of our companion being abandoned' (the genitive of *nos*, though plural, always has a gerundive ending in -i agreeing with it).

3 **qua manus**: 'where the lower arm'.

4 **ceterum Lamachum** ('the rest of Lamachus') is an unintentionally comic way of referring to the leader minus his forearm (compare *corpus reliquum* in 12 below).

5 **instantis** is from *insto*.

6–7 **per dexteram Martis**: it is amusing for a man who is himself lacking a hand to appeal *per* ('by') the right hand of Mars like this.

8 **liberaremus**: we find both *ut* plus subjunctive and also the subjunctive on its own in the indirect command after *adhortor*.

8–9 **cur ... supervivere**: the indirect statement continues here. A rhetorical question (asked for effect rather than in a genuine desire for information) like this was regarded as a disguised statement and so when reported went into the accusative and infinitive ('why was a brave brigand surviving the hand which ... ').

9 **nostrum** is (partitive) genitive of *nos*.

10 **deosculatum**: the perfect participle of the deponent has a passive force here (as does *venerato* in 11).

13 **elemento toto sepultus**: i.e. buried (*sepultus* is from *sepelio*) in the sea. This element is whole (unlike Lamachus!).

6 Portrait of Apuleius.

4.E *Next the unlucky Alcimus, while throwing an old woman's belongings*
out of her bedroom window to the other robbers below, is tricked by her
and pushed out of the window to his death.

Alcimus sollertibus coeptis consonum Fortunae nutum non potuit
adducere. cum dormientis anus perfracto tuguriolo conscendisset
cubiculum iamque protinus interstinguere eam debuisset, prius maluit
rerum singula per fenestram forinsecus (nobis scilicet rapienda)
dispergere. Cumque cuncta naviter emolitus nec toro aniculae quiescentis   5
parcere vellet, eaque lectulo suo devoluta vestem stragulam iactare
similiter destinaret, sic nequissima illa deprecatur: 'Quid, fili, paupertinas
pannosasque resculas miserrimae anus donas vicinis divitibus, quorum
haec fenestra domum prospicit?' quo sermone callido deceptus, Alcimus
(verens ne ea quae prius miserat quaeque postea missurus foret non sociis   10
suis sed in alienos lares abiceret) suspendit se fenestra sagaciter
perspecturus omnia, praesertim domus attiguae fortunas arbitraturus.
quod eum satis improvide conantem senile illud facinus inopinato pulsu
praeceps inegit. qui super vastissimum lapidem decidens, rivos sanguinis
vomens, narratisque nobis quae gesta sunt, vitam evasit. quem (prioris   15
exemplo sepulturae traditum) bonum secutorem Lamacho dedimus.

1–2 **Alcimus . . . adducere**: i.e. he could not get Fortune to smile favourably on his enterprise (of
robbing the old woman).

2 **tugurIolo** by its novelty highlights the victim's poverty.

4 **rerum singula**: 'individual things [i.e. items] of her possessions'.

4 **nobis . . . rapienda**: the gerundive expresses purpose, and *nobis* is dative of the agent ('to be seized
by us').

5 **emolitus** = *emolitus esset*.

5–6 **nec . . . vellet**: i.e. he wanted to steal the old woman's bedclothes too (*vellet* is imperfect
subjunctive of *volo*).

6 **eaque . . . devoluta**: ablative absolute with local ablative ('from').

7–8 **quid . . . resculas**: *quid* means 'why', and *fili* is vocative. Poverty is stressed by alliteration, assonance, juxtaposition (placement of words right next to each other for effect – e.g. for emphasis) and the diminutive.

8 **donas vicinis**: by throwing them on to the neighbours' property.

9 **domum** goes with *quorum* ('whose house').

10 **ea quae . . . quaeque** (= *et quae*) are objects of *abiceret* in 11. The robber is afraid of throwing stuff out on to the rich neighbours' property rather than to his comrades.

10 **missurus foret**: *missurus* is future participle of *mitto* (*miserat* earlier is from the same verb), and *foret = esset*.

11 **fenestra** is local ablative ('from').

12 **perspecturus**: the future participle (as later in this line) denotes purpose. This usage is confined in Latin to poets and poeticizing prose authors.

13 **quod** ('which thing', i.e. this) is the object of *conantem*.

13 **senile illud facinus** = 'the old criminal'.

14 **praeceps inegit**: 'pushed headlong' (*praeceps* is the adverb, and *inegit* is from *inigo*).

15 **narratisque . . . sunt**: i.e. after telling us what had happened. In this ablative absolute *illis* ('those things') has to be supplied as the antecedent of *quae gesta sunt* (from *gero*), and *nobis* is dative.

15–16 **prioris . . . traditum**: i.e. also buried at sea like Lamachus.

16 **bonum secutorem** is in apposition to *quem* (= 'as a good . . . ').

The robber tells how they then left Thebes for the next city (Plataea). There a rich man called Demochares was about to put on a lavish gladiatorial show, but the bears to be used in it sickened and died. The robbers carried off the largest corpse, cleaned it out and put one of their gang (Thrasyleon) inside it, carefully disguised as a bear, as part of a plan to burgle Demochares' house.

4.F *They take Thrasyleon in a cage to Demochares' home, pretend that the bear was sent for the show by a friend of his and persuade him to keep the cage in the grounds by his house.*

Sciscitati nomen cuiusdam Nicanoris (qui ius amicitiae summum cum Demochare colebat), litteras affingimus, ut venationis suae primitias bonus amicus videretur ornando muneri dedicasse. iamque provecta vespera, Thrasyleonis caveam Demochari cum litteris illis adulterinis offerimus. qui miratus bestiae magnitudinem, suique contubernalis   5 opportuna liberalitate laetatus, iubet nobis decem aureos annumerari. tunc multi mirabundi bestiam confluebant; quorum satis callenter curiosos aspectus Thrasyleon impetu minaci frequenter inhibebat. Demochares iubet novalibus suis confestim bestiam summa cum diligentia reportari. sed ego 'Caveas,' inquam 'domine, fatigatam coetui   10 multarum et non valentium committere ferarum. quin potius domus tuae patulum ac perflabilem locum prospicis?' talibus monitis Demochares perterritus, ut ex arbitrio nostro caveam locaremus facile permisit. 'Nos'

inquam 'ipsi parati sumus hic pro cavea ista excubare, ut bestiae cibum
tempestivum et potum solitum accuratius offeramus.' 'Nihil indigemus   15
labore vestro' respondit ille. 'iam familia nutriendis ursis exercitata est.'

1–2 **qui . . . colebat**: i.e. who was a very close friend of Demochares (*ius* means 'bonds' and *colo*
means 'cultivate').

2 **primitias**: i.e. to make it seem that Nicanor was sending the first animal caught in a hunt of his
to adorn Demochares' show (*ornando muneri*, in the next line, is dative of purpose).

6 **opportuna liberalitate**: ablative of cause.

7 **mirabundi** has an object here only and so takes the attention (if the truth was known, there was
even more reason for astonishment).

7 **callenter**: the unique word stresses the irony (in fact what Thrasyleon does now makes people
think that he is ferocious and so contributes substantially to his eventual death).

9 **novalibus** is dative and denotes a park separate from the house.

10 **caveas . . . fatigatam**: *caveas* (which looks like an unwitting pun on *cavea* 'cage') is the jussive
subjunctive of *caveo*, and with *fatigatam* you must supply *feram* ('beware of entrusting a tired wild
animal to . . . ').

11 **domus** ('property') includes the grounds of the house.

13 **ut** introduces an indirect command (after *permisit*).

15 **accuratius**: i.e. more meticulously than your servants.

15 **nihil** is used adverbially here ('not at all').

16 **nutriendis ursis** is dative with *exercitata* ('practised in').

4.G *The robbers leave, wait at a tomb outside town and return when all in the house are asleep. Thrasyleon opens the door for them.*

Discessimus et, portam civitatis egressi, monumentum conspicamur
procul a via. ibi capulos (quis inhabitabant pulverei mortui) ad futurae
praedae receptacula reseramus. noctis illunio tempore (quo somnus
impetu primo corda mortalium validius invadit) cohortem nostram
gladiis armatam ante ipsas fores Democharis sistimus. Thrasyleon   5
prorepit cavea, statimque custodes (qui propter sopiti quiescebant), mox
ianitorem ipsum gladio conficit. clavique fores repandit, nobisque
prompte convolantibus demonstrat horreum ubi vespera sagaciter
argentum copiosum recondi viderat. quo protinus perfracto confertae
manus violentia, iubeo singulos commilitonum asportare quantum   10
quisque poterat auri vel argenti et in illis aedibus mortuorum occultare
propere, rursumque recurrentes sarcinas iterare; me solum resistentem
pro domus limine cuncta rerum exploraturum sollicite, dum redirent. et
facies ursae mediis aedibus discurrentis ad proterrendos, si qui de familia
forte vigilassent, videbatur opportuna. quis enim (quamvis fortis),   15
immani forma bestiae visitata, non se ad fugam statim concitaret, non
obdito cellae pessulo trepidus sese cohiberet?

2 **quis** is dative plural with *inhabitabant*.

2 **ad**: 'to serve as'.

3 **quo**: ablative of time when.

6 **cavea**: local ablative ('from').

7 **clavi** is ablative of instrument/means.

9 **recondi**: present infinitive passive.

9–10 **quo . . . violentia**: i.e. the gang (*manus*) working all together forced an entrance into the storeroom (*quo* picks up *horreum* in 8, and *violentia* is ablative of means).

11 **auri vel argenti**: these are partitive genitives with *quantum* ('as much gold or silver as each could [carry off]').

11 **occultare** has 'it' (i.e. the gold and silver) as its object.

12–13 **me . . . redirent**: picking up from *iubeo* in 10 this is indirect statement (translate as 'I said that I would . . . ').

13 **cuncta rerum**: i.e. everything (*rerum* is partitive genitive).

13 **exploraturum**: supply *esse* (this is a future infinitive active).

14–15 **ad . . . opportuna**: 'seemed useful for frightening off any out of the household slaves who by chance . . . '). *Si qui* 'if any' = 'any who'. *Vigilassent* is subjunctive in virtual indirect statement.

16 **concitaret** is potential subjunctive, like *cohiberet* in 17.

17 **obdito** is from *obdo*.

4.H *Unfortunately a slave (woken by the noise) sees the bear and rouses the rest of the household, who come with lights and weapons.*

His omnibus salubri consilio recte dispositis, occurrit scaevus eventus. namque dum reduces socios nostros suspensus opperior, quidam servulus strepitu (scilicet divinitus) inquietus proserpit leniter, visaque bestia (quae libere discurrens totis aedibus commeabat), premens obnixum silentium, vestigium suum replicat, et utcumque cunctis in domo visa   5
pronuntiat. nec mora cum numerosae familiae frequentia domus tota completur. taedis, lucernis, cereis, sebaciis et ceteris nocturni luminis instrumentis clarescunt tenebrae. nec inermis quisquam de tanta copia processit, sed singuli fustibus, lanceis, destrictis denique gladiis armati muniunt aditus. canes etiam venaticos ad comprimendam bestiam   10
cohortantur.

1 **salubri consilio**: ablative of instrument/means.

3 **strepitu** is ablative of cause (with *inquietus*).

4–5 **premens . . . silentium**: this poetic expression (literally 'suppressing silence') is an emphatic way of saying 'keeping silence'.

5 **visa**: i.e. what he had seen (this is neuter accusative plural).

6 **nec mora cum**: understand *erat* before *cum*. This is an inverted *cum* clause ('and there was no delay when . . . ', i.e. and immediately).

7–8 **taedis . . . instrumentis**: the ablatives are all causal. Apuleius' expression is often full, but here all the nouns, highlighted by sound effects, rare language (*sebaciis*) and asyndeton, bring out how competently the house was illuminated (compare the various weapons mentioned in line 9 below).

10 **ad . . . bestiam**: *ad* with the gerundive expresses purpose.

*4.1 Thrasyleon fights with the dogs bravely and escapes into the street,
only to be pursued by them and attacked by local dogs too.*

Tunc ego sensim (gliscente adhuc illo tumultu) domo facesso, sed
Thrasyleonem mire canibus repugnantem latens pone ianuam prospicio.
quamquam enim vitae metas ultimas obiret, non tamen sui nostrique vel
pristinae virtutis oblitus, iam faucibus ipsis hiantis Cerberi reluctabat.
nunc fugiens, nunc resistens variis corporis sui schemis ac motibus,   5
tandem domo prolapsus est. nec tamen, quamvis publica potitus libertate,
salutem fuga quaerere potuit. quippe cuncti canes de proximo angiportu,
satis feri satisque copiosi, venaticis illis (qui domo insequentes
processerant) se ommiscent agminatim. miserum funestumque
spectamen aspexi – Thrasyleonem nostrum catervis canum saevientium   10
cinctum atque obsessum multisque morsibus laniatum.

    Denique, tanti doloris impatiens, populi circumfluentis turbelis
immisceor et sic indaginis principes dehortabar. 'O grande,' inquam 'et
extremum flagitium! magnam et vere pretiosam perdimus bestiam.'

    3 obiret is imperfect subjunctive of *obeo*.
    3 sui nostrique: genitives (of *se* and *nos*) with *oblitus*. By 'himself' he means Thrasyleon's reputation,
and by 'us' he means the robbers' code (of honour, bravery etc.).
    4 Cerberi: this was the huge, three-headed and ferocious monster of a dog that guarded the entrance
to the Underworld.
    6 publica . . . libertate: i.e. having escaped from the confines of the house into the public street,
where he could move more freely.
    8 venaticis illis: understand *canibus* (dative with *ommiscent*).
    9 funestumque: the adjective economically combines the senses 'lamentable' and 'deadly'.
    10–11 catervis . . . laniatum: there is vivid onomatopoeia in the clattering consonants and repeated
-um sound here.
    13 immisceor is reflexive ('I merged myself in').
    13 indaginis brings out the poetic justice and grim rebound (the pretend hunt in which Thrasyleon
the bear was supposedly captured is here succeeded by a real hunt).

*4.1 Servants with weapons join in the attack on Thrasyleon. He dies a
glorious death, keeping his real identity secret to the end.*

Nec tamen nostri sermonis artes infelicissimo profuerunt iuveni. quippe
quidam procurrens e domo procerus et validus incunctanter lanceam
mediis iniecit ursae praecordiis, nec secus alius; et plurimi, iam timore
discusso, gladios de proximo congerunt. Thrasyleon (egregium decus
nostrae factionis) neque clamore ac ne ululatu quidem fidem sacramenti   5

prodidit. sed iam morsibus laceratus ferroque laniatus, obnixo mugitu et
ferino fremitu praesentem casum tolerans, gloriam sibi reservavit, vitam
fato reddidit. tanto tamen terrore tantaque formidine coetum illum
turbaverat ut nemo fuerit ausus iacentem bestiam vel digito contingere.
tandem pigre ac timide quidam lanius paulo fidentior, utero bestiae   10
resecto, ursa magnificum despoliavit latronem. sic etiam Thrasyleon
nobis perivit, sed a gloria non perivit.

    Confestim itaque (constrictis sarcinis illis quas nobis servaverant
fideles mortui) Plataeae terminos concito gradu deserentes, istud
identidem reputabamus: merito nullam fidem in vita nostra reperiri,   15
quod ad manes iam odio perfidiae nostrae demigrarit.

    1 **nostri**: plural for singular ('my').

    3 **nec secus alius**: supply *fecit* ('acted'). Another man did the same.

    5 **neque** looks forward to *ac* ('neither . . . and not even'). The idea here is that he did not betray
his oath of allegiance to the rest of the gang by revealing his identity (but just how would this be a
betrayal?).

    6–8 **sed . . . reddidit**: style and sound are forceful and dramatic here.

    7–8 **vitam fato reddidit**: note the asyndeton (a word such as *sed* has been omitted before this
expression for dying).

    8 **tanto . . . formidine**: alliteration and repetition stress the terror.

    9 **fuerit ausus** = *ausus sit* (from the semi-deponent *audeo*), an unusual form of the perfect
subjunctive (a sort of double perfect).

    11 **ursa . . . latronem**: i.e. he stripped the robber of his bearskin (a comic twist to the stripping of
armour from a dead warrior).

    11–12 **sic . . . perivit**: i.e. we lost Thrasyleon too, but he was not lost to glory (*nobis* is dative of
disadvantage, and *a* means 'in respect of').

    14 **mortui** refers to the coffins used as a hiding-place for the loot.

    15–16 **merito . . . demigrarit**: in this indirect statement after *istud reputabamus* the idea is that
loyalty (here personified, i.e. treated as a person) is only to be found among the dead, who faithfully
guarded the plunder hidden with them. *Odio* is ablative of cause; *demigrarit* = *demigraverit* (perfect
subjunctive, with *fides* as its subject).

APPRECIATION

4.C–J *(Metamorphoses 4.9–21).*

The robber who tells these three tales is what is called an 'unreliable narrator'.
Typically such narrators have a problematic value-scheme, see qualities that
others do not, are mentally deficient and produce suspicious accounts. So this
speaker inverts morality by describing the gang's victims as evil. He actually
likens the thieves to soldiers by applying military terms to them and actually
praises these inept losers (himself included) and their absurd posturing. An
inefficient leader himself, he simply cannot see the mistakes that he and the
other brigands make. To save face, he claims in 4.H to know of things going

on inside the (dark) house which he could not have seen from his position in front of the door (4.G.13). Then he contradicts himself at 4.I.1f. (where he intimates that he was in fact inside the house), and again at 4.J.8 (where he talks of terror despite 4.J.3f.). We also find here something known as a 'seed' (an inserted piece of information whose real relevance only becomes clear subsequently, as it makes a later event more plausible). The thieves' (often fatal) stupidity is evident in all three stories, and by way of reinforcement neither the narrator nor his audience has the wit to perceive it. As a result we are not at all surprised when they are all easily duped and killed in book 7 by Tlepolemus (for more on the links with Tlepolemus' tale at 7.A–B see Frangoulidis 1994).

In the first story (4.C–D) Thebes, where a celebrated mythical exploit took place (when an invading army with seven great heroes as champions attacked the city's seven gates), is the setting for this decidedly unheroic incident. So too the robbers' melodramatic and foolish chief Lamachus bears the same name as a famous Athenian general, a genuinely brave man and energetic leader, who was killed while fighting the enemy on Sicily in 414 BC. Their victim Chryseros (= Lovegold) outwits them at every turn, and his shrewdness makes them seem even more retarded by contrast. When faced with the quandary of Lamachus nailed to the door, they panic and don't think straight (they should have smashed the door down, pretending to help with the fire, and removed the nail). Their equally slow-witted chief acquiesces in the amputation, and then decides that he can't follow them or stay behind (but obviously this large group of men could have carried him with them, as they later do his corpse), and opts instead for the showy and totally unnecessary gesture of suicide, under the misapprehension that he cannot rob and kill one-handed (though he does manage to kill himself one-handed!).

There is another pointless death in the second anecdote (4.E), as Alcimus (= Strongman) is ignominiously beaten by a weak old lady (who seems hardly worth looting at all and hardly worth waking just for her bedclothes). The narrator himself (while commending Alcimus!) highlights his silliness in not killing the old woman and in leaning out of the window. Her speech craftily plays on the robber's greed, and succeeds, despite being an obvious ploy (why on earth would she care if he was throwing her stuff on to her neighbour's property, where the gang could not pick it up?). There is also a mock-solemn touch at 14–15 with *rivos sanguinis vomens*, which is taken from Virgil *Aeneid* 11.668 (of the fallen Trojan Euneus, killed by the young warrior queen Camilla as he faced her in battle).

In the third tale (4.F–J) the speaker proudly recounts how Thrasyleon (= Boldlion) was successfully disguised as a bear, and he does this in front of Lucius, not realizing that he is a human in an ass's skin. Here the brigands are initially rather more clever, but before long the bungling begins again, and is even more extensive this time. There are the bad ideas of using the tomb as a hiding-place (this amounts to desecration, which could well be punished) and letting the bear loose in the house (as is only natural, this results in the alarm being raised and the bear being attacked). A much better plan would have been to be more quiet during the raid (and the noise they make duly wakes up a slave), and to get away quickly with just one load of loot (so Thrasyleon is spotted while waiting for the gang to return). In 4.H we learn that, dangerously, Demochares' house had a large number of slaves, and hunting dogs, which would be capable of tracking (the gang either didn't bother to find all this out in advance or didn't think that it was important), and the efficiency with which the slaves cope with the bear points up the robbers' ineptitude. Next the speaker leaves it far too late to come out with the argument about the loss of an expensive bear; and Thrasyleon himself could have saved his life (by playing a frightened animal, by going back into his cage, and by shouting out that he was a man).

His ostentatious and unnecessary death is depicted as glorious, but what glory is there in being killed during a botched burglary by slaves and dogs, while in a grotesque disguise, and then being skinned by a butcher? The praise of his courage is rich in the mouth of the speaker, who timidly abandoned him to his fate in 4.I (despite being largely responsible for it), as is the philosophizing about loyalty at the end. A few other points add to the fun. This sordid raid in which the 'hero' dies and the rest of the gang flees takes place at Plataea, the scene of a genuinely glorious battle (479 BC), in which the Greek spearmen defeated decisively the invading army of the Persian king Xerxes, and his brave general Mardonius was killed, while the survivors fled. At the same time the attack by the hunting dogs on Thrasyleon in bear form conjures up the renowned and grim myth of Actaeon (a noble hunter who in all innocence saw the goddess Diana naked and was punished by being turned into a stag and killed by his own dogs). On top of that there is a bizarre and low variant on the Trojan Horse in the whole ruse of getting a man inside an animal into the house by means of a lying story, so that others can be admitted to plunder. Read Virgil's account at *Aeneid* 2.13ff., looking out for various parallels and twists, and see also Finkelpearl 1998, 92ff.

After hearing these stories the robbers make an offering to the memory of their dead comrades and then go to sleep. Much later that night they go off on another raid and bring back a beautiful, well-born local girl called Charite (abducted on the day that she was to be married to her handsome young cousin), whom they intend to ransom. To cheer her up, the old woman who looks after the robbers' den tells her the famous story of Cupid and Psyche (in books 4–6). Then the robbers return from another raid and use Lucius to fetch some of the loot they couldn't carry. After he lames himself and gets back to the den with difficulty, they decide to kill him. Before doing that they go off to get the rest of the loot, and Lucius resolves to escape, as there is now only a feeble, half-dead old woman there.

6.A *Lucius breaks his tether and runs off, but the old woman grabs the strap. She holds on to it, despite being kicked, and calls for help.*

Lorum, quo fueram destinatus, abrumpo meque quadripedi cursu proripio. nec tamen astutulae anus milvinos oculos effugere potui. nam lorum prehendit ac me revocare contendit. ego, incussis in eam posteriorum pedum calcibus, protinus applaudo terrae. at illa, quamvis humi prostrata, tenaciter inhaerebat, ut me procurrentem aliquantisper   5
sequeretur. et occipit statim clamosis ululatibus auxilium implorare. sed frustra fletibus tumultum commovebat, cum nullus adforet, nisi sola illa virgo captiva. quae procurrens facinus audet pulcherrimum. extorto etenim loro manibus eius, me (placidis gannitibus ab impetu revocatum) naviter inscendit et ad cursum rursum incitat.   10

> 1 **fueram destinatus** = *destinatus eram* (a sort of double pluperfect, common in later Latin).
> 2 **milvinos**: the kite is a watchful, rapacious and repellent bird of prey.
> 4 **posteriorum … applaudo**: *calcibus* is from *calx*; understand *eam* as the object of *applaudo*. There seems to be onomatopoeia here (repeated p = the hooves' blows), and in 10 (*cursum rursum* of the galloping ass).
> 5 **prostrata** is perfect participle passive of *prosterno*.
> 5 **ut** introduces a result (consecutive) clause.
> 7 **adforet**: imperfect subjunctive of *adsum*.

6.B *As they gallop off, the amorous ass kisses Charite's feet, and she prays for help and promises to reward him richly for rescuing her.*

Equestri celeritate solum replaudens, virgini delicatas voculas adhinnire temptabam. scabendi dorsi mei simulatione nonnumquam obliquata cervice, pedes decoros puellae basiabam. tunc illa 'Vos,' inquit 'superi, tandem meis supremis periculis opem facite. tuque, praesidium meae libertatis meaeque salutis, si me domum pervexeris incolumem,   5 parentibusque et formoso proco reddideris, quas tibi gratias perhibebo, quos honores habebo, quos cibos exhibebo! iubam tuam meis monilibus adornabo, bullisque te multis aureis inoculatum cotidie saginabo. nec inter cibos delicatos et otium profundum deerit tibi dignitas gloriosa. nam depictam in tabula fugae praesentis imaginem meae domus atrio   10 dedicabo. visetur doctorumque stilis rudis perpetuabitur historia. et iam credemus et Phrixum arieti supernatasse et Europam tauro supercubasse. quodsi vere Iuppiter mugivit in bove, potest in asino meo latere vel vultus hominis vel facies deorum.'

1 **SOLUM** is the noun, and *delicatas* means 'amorous'.

2–3 **scabendi . . . cervice**: i.e. Lucius turned his head, pretending to scratch his back. *Scabendi* is gerundive (and goes with *dorsi mei*), while *obliquata cervice* is an ablative absolute.

4–5 **praesidium . . . salutis** refers to Lucius the ass. Note the (excited, exuberant and rather flowery) fullness of expression here.

5 **domum**: 'to home' (no preposition is needed with *domus*).

5 **pervexeris**: future perfect indicative of *perveho* in an open (indicative) condition referring to the future.

6 **reddideris** (also future perfect) has *me* as its object.

6–7 **quas . . . exhibebo**: again there is ebullience and lushness here, in the emphatically full expression, repetition of words, echoing verbs and parallel ordering (compare the balance and juxtaposition in *et . . . supercubasse* at 12). *Honores habeo* means 'display honours' (i.e. 'how much will I honour you!').

9 **deerit**: future indicative of *desum*.

10 **atrio**: local ablative ('in').

11–12 The idea is that because an ass conveyed Charite to safety humans will believe the mythical accounts of a ram carrying Phrixus and a bull bearing Europa. Phrixus and his sister Helle escaped death at the hands of an evil stepmother on a marvellous ram sent by the gods which took them across the sea to Colchis (on the way Helle fell off into the sea and was drowned; and on landing in Colchis Phrixus sacrificed the ram). Jupiter fell in love with the beautiful princess Europa, disguised himself as a bull, coaxed her on to his back, then rushed with her into the sea and swam off to the island of Crete, where he raped her.

12 **supernatasse** is the syncopated form of the perfect infinitive active (= *supernatavisse*), as is *supercubasse* later in this line. Both are in indirect statement.

13 **in bove**: 'in the guise of a bull'.

6.C *While Lucius and Charite disagree over which road to take, the robbers (returning with the rest of their loot) catch them.*

Ad quoddam pervenimus trivium, unde me dirigere dextrorsum gestiebat, quod ad parentes eius ea scilicet iretur via. sed ego, gnarus latrones illac ad reliquas commeasse praedas, renitebar firmiter, atque sic in animo meo tacitus expostulabam: 'Quid facis, infelix puella? quid agis? cur festinas ad Orcum? quid meis pedibus facere contendis? non enim te   5 tantum verum etiam me perditum ibis.' sic nos rapinis suis onusti

deprehendunt latrones. unus e numero, prehenso loro, retrorsum me
circumtorquet. iam domus eorum extremam loricam perveneramus; et
ecce de ramo cupressus, induta laqueum, anus illa pendebat. quam dedere
praecipitem; puellaque distenta vinculis, cenam (quam postuma   10
diligentia praeparaverat infelix anicula) ferinis invadunt animis.

Ac dum avida voracitate cuncta contruncant, iam incipiunt de nostra
poena secum considerare. variae fuere sententiae, ut primus vivam
cremari censeret puellam, secundus bestiis obici suaderet, tertius patibulo
suffigi iuberet, quartus tormentis excarnificari praeciperet.   15

2 **quod . . . via**: *ea . . . via* is ablative of route; *iretur* (from *eo*) is an impersonal expression ('it was gone by that road'). It is subjunctive because the reason is assigned and represents Charite's thoughts.

3 **commeasse** is the syncopated form of the perfect infinitive (in indirect statement). This form will not be explained any more.

5 **meis pedibus**: ablative of instrument/means (the idea is that Charite is making use of Lucius' feet by riding him).

5–6 **non . . . ibis**: the supine in -*um* expressing purpose is employed with *ibis* (future of *eo*) as an old-fashioned periphrasis for *perdes* and has as its objects not only (*non tantum*) *te* but also (*verum etiam*) *me*.

8 **loricam**: the robbers' den was fortified like a military camp.

9 **cupressus**: the tree had funereal associations (used in pyres etc.).

9 **induta laqueum**: i.e. having put on a noose (around her neck) and hanged herself. The perfect participle passive has an active force and governs a direct object here, in imitation of the Greek 'middle' voice (which shares almost all of its forms with the passive but denotes actively doing something for oneself).

9–10 **quam . . . praecipitem**: i.e. the robbers threw the old woman off the mountain where their den was. *Dedere* is third person plural of the perfect indicative of *do* (meaning 'cause to go').

10 **distenta vinculis**: if the text is correct, the expression is unusual and seems to mean that the girl was chained up with her arms (and possibly her legs) spread out.

10–11 **postuma diligentia**: i.e. the results of her diligence extended beyond her death (there is sardonic humour here, and in the ironical *infelix* in 11). This is an ablative of manner.

12–13 The clattering consonants suggest the sound of noisy eating.

13 **secum**: 'among themselves'.

13 **fuere** = *fuerunt* (this form will not be pointed out any more).

13 **ut primus**: in this result clause *primus* is used as a noun ('the first man'), as are *secundus*, *tertius* and *quartus*.

14 **puellam** is to be taken with the following infinitives as well.

6.D One of the robbers proposes a neat solution – to kill Lucius and disembowel him, and to sew Charite up inside his belly, so that she suffers all the proposed punishments in the course of a slow death.

Tunc unus placido sermone sic orsus est: 'Meis consiliis auscultantes
vitam puellae (sed quam meretur) largimini. nec vos memoria deseruit
quid iamdudum decreveritis de isto asino, manducone summo, nunc

7 Plaque from Ur Iyre.

etiam virginalis fugae ministro. hunc igitur iugulare crastino placeat,
totisque vacuefacto praecordiis per alvum nudam virginem insuere (ut,   5
sola facie praeminente, ceterum corpus puellae nexu ferino coerceat),
tunc insiciatum asinum exponere et solis ardentis vaporibus tradere. sic
enim cuncta quae recte statuistis ambo sustinebunt – et mortem asinus, et
illa morsus ferarum (cum vermes membra laniabunt) et ignis flagrantiam
(cum sol nimiis caloribus inflammarit uterum) et patibuli cruciatum   10
(cum canes et vultures intima protrahent viscera).'

 Latrones in eius vadunt sententiam. quam meis tam magnis auribus
accipiens, quid aliud quam meum crastinum deflebam cadaver?

 1 **orsus est**: from *ordior*.

 2 **sed ... meretur** = *vitam quam meretur* (i.e. a brief and very unpleasant life).

 2 **largimini** is imperative (second person plural).

 3 **quid** introduces an indirect question dependent on *memoria* ('the memory [of] what
you ...') – hence the perfect subjunctive *decreveritis* (from *decerno*).

4 **placeat** is jussive subjunctive ('let it be pleasing [to you] to . . . ', i.e. make up your minds to . . .) and governs all four infinitives in this sentence.

5 **totisque . . . insuere**: with *vacuefacto* (dative, with *insuere*) understand *huic*, referring to the ass (he wants them to sew the girl in the totally disembowelled ass). *Per* brings out the extent (she will fill the whole length of the animal's belly).

6 **coerceat**: the subject is the ass.

8 **sustinebunt**: from this one understands later *sustinebit* as the verb governing both *mortem* and *morsus* (and the following accusatives). Note the malicious play on words (*mortem, morsus*).

10 **inflammarit** is the syncopated form of the future perfect.

11 **viscera**: there seems to be a grim pun here. Primarily the word refers to the girl's entrails, but she also now forms the ass's entrails.

12 **in . . . sententiam**: i.e. they supported his opinion. The image is taken from senators (!) separating into groups to show support or opposition to a proposal under consideration.

12 **quam** picks up *sententiam*.

13 **quid . . . cadaver**: i.e. what [could I do] other than mourn myself about to be a corpse tomorrow?

APPRECIATION

6.A–D *(Metamorphoses 6.27–32).*

Verbally and thematically 6.A recalls the incident of the garden and the laurel roses (4.A–B). As well as acting as a binding device, these links between the two episodes tantalize and trick readers. When Lucius hurled himself forward at speed (for the roses) at 4.A.7, he was soon frustrated; when he does so here at 1f., it seems at first that he will be so again (by the old woman), but then he gets free of her, only for his escape to be finally frustrated by the robbers. When he kicked the gardener to the ground with his rear hooves at 4.B.4f., that led at once to greater problems for Lucius from others; after the similar kicking at 3f. here we may expect worse trouble again, but initially it does not materialize, although it does in the end. At 4.B.7f. the woman's howls and tears won her immediate help and allies, ending Lucius' flight and resulting in danger of death for him from that group; here at 6f. the old woman's howls and tears produce no assistance for her, and in fact bring an ally (Charite) for Lucius, and his escape actually seems to be succeeding this time, until finally the group of robbers end it and threaten him with death.

In 6.B the two escapers are shown to be equally silly. Lustful as ever, Lucius actually tries it on with Charite while attempting to get away (distracting and slowing himself down), as if an ass really could sweet-talk a girl, and as if she would be interested in an ass anyway, especially when she is engaged. Her speech is touchingly hopeful, but it also contains a flowery address to a creature, made while galloping along on it. In the midst of her attempt to motivate (the enamoured) Lucius, she mentions her handsome fiancé (and does not include love among the rewards proposed for Lucius). She promises a beast finery suitable for a human, not realizing that the beast is in fact a human; and her offer conjures up a double perversion (Lucius the animal done up in a girl's jewellery). Her allusion to Phrixus and Europa ineptly puts the antihero Lucius on a par with the marvellous golden ram and the king of the gods himself. It also contains unsuspected relevance: she will soon bear responsibility for Lucius' imminent death (like Phrixus, who killed the creature that conveyed him); and like Europa she is seated on a lover in the guise of an animal.

There is even more ineptitude in 6.C. Charite at least does not know that she is taking the wrong road; but Lucius wastes time in completely futile recrimination (instead of promptly bolting), and criticizes her for ruining them, when he is also doing just that himself. His callousness about the old woman's death at 8ff. soon rebounds on him (when his own end is touted in 6.D), and as an animal and glutton (compare 6.D.3) himself he is hardly in a position to criticize the robbers for falling on their meal like beasts at 10ff. The apparently irreconcilable suggestions at 6.C.13ff. for Charite's punishment are succeeded by the ingenious solution in 6.D, economically combining all four proposals for her, and working in the bonus of Lucius' death, and building up a comically gruesome picture (for such over the top horror elsewhere in ancient novels see Walsh 1970, 159; and Tatum 1979, 63). Here with the girl imprisoned inside the ass Apuleius is playing on the idea of the man Lucius inside the animal. There is a tit for tat element too: to punish the beast's greed, its guts will be removed, and it will be crammed (with Charite); for helping her escape, it will help her die agonizingly. There are twists and reversals as well. After fancying the girl, Lucius will get her, naked, to embrace (but sewn up inside his carcase). She will stuff him, as she promised at 6.B.8, but with her own body; and her promise of a happy and glorious life for him is replaced by the prospect of a miserable and inglorious end. So too later on we will see that all this plotting by the robbers to kill Charite and Lucius on the next day will be followed by the killing on the next day of the robbers, themselves confined and left as prey for dogs and vultures. But at this stage in the story it looks as if all Lucius has achieved by his flight from the death decreed for him earlier is to bring on himself an even worse end, one involving his beloved Charite too, and book 6 closes here with a cliff-hanger (leaving us wondering what will happen, so that we read on), and with the picture of an ass weeping, and paradoxically mourning its own demise.

At the start of book 7 another robber turns up, and when he learns that the gang have recently lost their leader and others (in the inept raids described earlier) he tells them that they need new recruits and promptly produces a

*huge, powerful young man in rags, whom he has just met and persuaded
to join them. (The young man is in fact Charite's fiancé, Tlepolemus, who
has come to rescue her, posing as a former chief of a gang of brigands called
Haemus.)*

7.A *Tlepolemus claims that he is the great Haemus and that the
destruction of his gang began with an imperial official driven into exile
and accompanied by his brave and faithful wife Plotina.*

'Praefui validissimae manui totamque prorsus devastavi Macedoniam.
ego sum praedo famosus Haemus, cuius totae provinciae nomen
horrescunt, latrone incluto prognatus, humano sanguine nutritus, heres
et aemulus virtutis paternae. sed omnem pristinam sociorum fortium
multitudinem magnasque illas opes exiguo temporis amisi spatio.   5
    Fuit quidam multis officiis in aula Caesaris clarus atque conspicuus.
hunc insimulatum quorundam astu proiecit extorrem saeviens Invidia.
sed uxor eius Plotina (rarae fidei atque singularis pudicitiae femina),
fugientis comes et infortunii socia, tonso capillo, in masculinam faciem
reformato habitu, auro zonis refertis incincta, inter custodientium   10
militum manus et gladios nudos intrepida, cunctorum periculorum
particeps, et pro mariti salute pervigilem curam suscipiens, aerumnas
assiduas ingenio masculo sustinebat.

2 **cuius**: *nomen* (accusative) goes with this word ('whose name').
5 **magnasque . . . opes**: i.e. the loot they had amassed.
6 **quidam . . . conspicuus**: the clattering consonants have an angry and contemptuous air to them. *Multis officiis* is ablative of cause.
7 **quorundam astu**: i.e. by certain cunning people.
7 **saeviens Invidia**: the reference is to envious enemies (the personification makes the story more dramatic and impressive).
8–13 There is cumulative impact in this long sentence, as various merits and meritorious actions of Plotina are tacked on one after another via a whole series of nouns, adjectives and participles.
8 **rarae . . . pudicitiae**: genitives of quality/description.
9 **fugientis comes**: 'companion of [him] going into exile'.
10 **auro . . . incincta**: i.e. she was wearing a belt filled with gold coins.

7.B *The official lands at Actium and stays at an inn which Haemus robs.
Plotina then appeals to the emperor, and he destroys all the robbers except
Haemus, who just escapes from his troops in disguise.*

Sed cum primum litus Actiacum (quo tunc Macedonia delapsi
grassabamur) appulisset, nocte promota tabernulam quam incubabant

invadimus, et diripimus omnia. sed protinus sanctissima et unicae fidei
femina, precibus ad Caesaris numen porrectis, marito reditum celerem et
aggressurae plenam vindictam impetravit. noluit esse Caesar Haemi 5
latronis collegium, et confestim interivit.

Tota factione militarium vexillationum indagatu confecta atque
concisa, aegre solus mediis Orci faucibus evasi. sumpta veste muliebri,
mitellaque contecto capite, calceis femininis indutus, et asello spicas
hordeacias gerenti residens, per medias acies infesti militis transabivi. nec 10
ab illa tamen paterna gloria vel mea virtute descivi, quamquam
semitrepidus iuxta mucrones constitutus, sed habitus alieni fallacia tectus,
villas seu castella solus aggrediens, viaticulum mihi corrasi.'

Et diloricatis statim pannulis, duo milia profudit aureorum.

1 **cum . . . Actiacum**: *cum primum* means 'as soon as'. Actium is on the west coast of Greece, south
of Macedon.

1 **quo . . . delapsi**: *quo* is the adverb, and *Macedonia* is ablative ('having slipped down to which
place from Macedon, we were . . .').

2 **nocte promota**: i.e. late at night.

3 **unicae fidei**: genitive of quality/description.

4 **Caesaris numen**: the emperor was regarded as a god.

5 **esse**: 'to exist'.

6 **confestim interivit**: the brevity (only two words) brings out the speed with which the band of
robbers was wiped out by squadrons of soldiers.

7 **indagatu**: causal ablative.

8 **mediis . . . evasi**: escaping from the midst of the jaws of Orcus is a poetic (and vivid and dramatic)
expression for just escaping death.

10 **gerenti** agrees with *asello*.

10 **militis**: singular for plural.

11 **illa**: 'that famous'.

12 **semitrepidus**: this unique word draws the attention. A hero like Haemus would only be *half-
afraid* even with detachments of troops so close to him in the area where he now establishes himself.

12 **habitus . . . tectus**: i.e. disguised as a woman (*tectus* is from *tego*).

APPRECIATION

7.A–B (Metamorphoses 7.5–8).

Tlepolemus will shortly be accepted as their new chief by the gang on the
basis of this story, and then will get them drunk, escape with Charite on
Lucius, return with a group of men from his home town, kill the robbers
and carry off their booty. Here he comes across as a real character, a devil-
may-care hero who is much more bright than his opponents and likes taking
risks. This tale is well aimed: it is short and easy to follow; its subject matter
would appeal in itself; it contains action and twists of fortune, and ends on an
upbeat for the thieving fraternity. It also highlights Haemus as a great leader

and brigand, especially at significant points (the start and end). He knows as well that he need not bother too much with logic and fine points of detail, and with amusing ease smuggles past the slow-witted robbers various oddities and improbabilities – why did Plotina disguise herself as a man; why is she (an enemy) here praised so much; why did the emperor recall her husband; and how could the tall, well-muscled Haemus pass himself off as a woman? (You can find more anomalies for yourselves.) More than that, Tlepolemus actually mocks the robbers' dulness and daringly rubs their noses in it – he tells how he once disguised himself and fooled hostile armed men; how a gang made an ill-judged attack on a female of standing, which misfired thanks to a devoted spouse; and how he was responsible for a band of thieves being killed and losing their loot. (Again you can find more of this cleverness for yourselves.)

There is also some typically sophisticated narrative technique. What we have here (as often in the *Metamorphoses*: cf. e.g. Murgatroyd 2001b) is embedding (i.e. one story is told inside another one). The tale of Haemus is embedded within the whole Charite episode (and that is just part of the account of Lucius' experiences as an ass, which is itself inset within the outer story of Lucius' adventures in human form at the beginning and close of the novel). As is frequently the case, the embedded narrative plays an important part in the overall plot (it leads to the rescue), keeps up the suspense (holding back the fates of Lucius and Charite) and has an effective setting (this anecdote about brigands is told to brigands in the brigands' den). The inner story of Haemus also mirrors closely the outer story of the saving of Charite (this is known as *mise en abyme*): in both there is a misguided raid by robbers which leads to their eventual downfall, a loving couple share danger, a brave male (Haemus/Tlepolemus) triumphs thanks to a disguise despite armed men all around, and there is a happy ending and restoration for the couple. There is similar intricacy in connection with the parallels to Tlepolemus in his anecdote. Initially he is like Haemus (leading and destroying a robber gang etc.). Then he puts the spotlight on Plotina and resembles her (braving hazards and trouble with his beloved, having gold hidden on his person, securing the return of his beloved, and so on). Finally, after Plotina drops out, he reverts to being like Haemus (tricking armed enemies, attacking a group on his own etc.). We can also now see point in connection with some of the above puzzles – Plotina is disguised as a man because that brings out the connection with Tlepolemus; and he praises her so much because he is thus actually praising himself! For more on links with the surrounding narrative (and with epic poetry too) see Frangoulidis 1992 and 1994; Harrison 1990, 199ff.

Tlepolemus is accepted as leader, gets the gang drunk, escapes with Charite on Lucius' back and then returns with men from his home town to kill the robbers. As a reward Lucius is sent to Charite's farm to father mules on the mares. But once there he is in fact maltreated by the servants, until (in book 8) a slave from Charite's house arrives with the shocking news that Charite is dead. This is the story told by the slave to the farm-hands.

8.A *Charite is dead. The immoral Thrasyllus was refused her hand in marriage and subsequently resorted to crime, posing as the friend of Charite and Tlepolemus and worming his way into their confidence.*

Charite misella casu gravissimo nec incomitata manes adivit.

Erat in proxima civitate iuvenis praenobilis; pecuniae fuit satis locuples, sed scortis et diurnis potationibus exercitatus, atque ob id factionibus latronum male sociatus, nec non etiam manus infectus humano cruore, Thrasyllus nomine.   5

Hic, cum Charite maturuisset, inter praecipuos procos summo studio petitionis munus obierat; morum tamen improbatus, repulsae contumelia fuerat aspersus. ac dum puella in boni Tlepolemi manum venerat, nutriens amorem et permiscens indignationem, cruento facinori quaerebat accessum. nanctus denique occasionem, sceleri quod diu   10
cogitarat accingitur. ac die quo praedonum infestis mucronibus puella fuerat astu virtutibusque sponsi sui liberata, turbae gratulantium (exsultans insigniter) permiscuit sese; occultato consilio sceleris, amici fidelissimi personam mentiebatur. iamque sermonibus assiduis et conversatione frequenti carior cariorque factus, in profundam ruinam   15
cupidinis sese paulatim praecipitaverat.

Spectate quorsum furiosae libidinis proruperint impetus.

---

1 **misella**: note the affectionate and pathetic diminutive.

1 **casu gravissimo**: ablative of cause

1 **adivit** is from *adeo* (compare *obierat*, from *obeo*, in 7).

2 **pecuniae**: the genitive with *locuples* ('well supplied with') is found here only in surviving Latin.

3 **diurnis potationibus**: drinking in the daytime was considered especially scandalous in antiquity.

4 **nec non**: 'and not not' = 'and'.

4 **manus**: accusative of respect ('as to his hands').

7 **morum**: 'due to his morals'. This is probably a genitive of cause (an originally Greek construction, confined mainly to poetry in Latin).

8 **fuerat aspersus** = *aspersus erat.*

8 **manum** here denotes the power of the husband over his wife, so the reference is to Charite marrying Tlepolemus.

11 **mucronibus** is ablative ('from') with *fuerat . . . liberata* (= *liberata erat*).

12 **turbae gratulantium**: *turbae* is dative, with *permiscuit*; the participle is used as a noun ('well-wishers').

15 **carior cariorque**: the repetition catches well Thrasyllus' constantly growing popularity and suggests repeated activity.

15 **factus**: 'having become' (*facio* provides the perfect tenses of *fio*).

17 **spectate**: i.e. let me show you (said to the farm-hands).

17 **quorsum . . . impetus**: i.e. what he was led to do by his mad lust.

8.B *One day Tlepolemus goes hunting with Thrasyllus, looking for harmless prey, but instead his dogs disturb a huge, ferocious boar.*

Die quadam venatum Tlepolemus (assumpto Thrasyllo) petebat, indagaturus feras. quid tamen in capreis feritatis est? nec enim Charite maritum suum quaerere patiebatur bestias armatas dente vel cornu. iamque apud frondosum tumulum obsaeptis capreis, canes immittuntur, statimque partitae totos praecingunt aditus. signo repentino reddito, latratibus fervidis dissonisque miscent omnia. nec ulla caprea nec pavens dammula nec prae ceteris feris mitior cerva, sed aper immanis atque invisitatus exsurgit, toris callosae cutis obesus, pilis inhorrentibus corio squalidus, setis insurgentibus spinae hispidus, dentibus attritu sonaci spumeus, oculis aspectu minaci flammeus, impetu saevo frementis oris totus fulmineus. et primum canum procaciores (quae comminus contulerant vestigium) interficit; dein calcata retiola (qua primos impetus reduxerat) transabiit.

5

10

2 **indagaturus**: the future participle expresses purpose.

2 **quid . . . feritatis**: 'what of wildness' (partitive genitive). The speaker in an aside is remarking on the fact that Tlepolemus was not allowed to go after really wild (dangerous) game like boars and stags.

7–8 **immanis atque invisitatus**: the first adjective is pregnant (it combines 'huge' and 'savage' and 'frightful'), while the second means both that the animal had not been seen by the hunters and that nothing like it had been seen ever before.

8 **toris . . . obesus**: 'bulky with the muscles of [i.e. under] his tough skin'. This is the first in a series of phrases (marked off by commas) describing the boar. Take them slowly, one by one, as they come.

8 **pilis inhorrentibus**: ablative of respect ('as to the hair bristling on its hide'). *Setis insurgentibus* in the next phrase is also ablative of respect.

9 **dentibus** is ablative of respect (with *spumeus*), while *attritu sonaci* is ablative of cause.

10 **oculis** is ablative of respect (with *flammeus*), while *aspectu minaci* is ablative of cause.

11 **totus** has an adverbial force here ('totally').

11–12 **comminus . . . vestigium**: i.e. had engaged the boar at close quarters (*contulerant* is from *confero*).

12 **qua . . . impetus**: *qua* means 'where', and *impetus* refers to the boar's first attack, checked at the hunters' nets set up round the hill.

*8.c As the servants hide, Thrasyllus persuades Tlepolemus to pursue the
boar, but then brings down his horse, leaving him helpless.*

Nos, pavore deterriti, arboribus abscondimus. Thrasyllus vero, nactus
opportunum decipulum, sic Tlepolemum captiose compellat: 'Quid,
stupore confusi vel etiam cassa formidine similes humilitati servorum
istorum, tam opimam praedam amittimus? quin equos inscendimus?
quin ocius indipiscimur?'   5

   Protinus insiliunt equos, summo studio bestiam insequentes. illa
retorquet impetum et, dente compulso, quem primum insiliat rimatur.
sed prior Tlepolemus iaculum quod gerebat insuper dorsum bestiae
contorsit. at Thrasyllus ferae pepercit, sed equi quo vehebatur Tlepolemus
postremos poplites lancea feriens amputat. quadrupes, recidens qua   10
sanguis effluxerat, toto tergo supinatus, invitus dominum suum devolvit
ad terram. eum furens aper invadit iacentem, ac primo lacinias eius, mox
ipsum resurgentem multo dente laniavit. nec coepti nefarii bonum piguit
amicum vel suae saevitiae litatum saltem tanto periculo cernens potuit
expleri. sed percito atque plagosa crura contegenti suumque auxilium   15
miseriter roganti per femus dexterum dimisit lanceam, tanto fidentius
quanto crederet ferri vulnera similia futura prosectu dentium. ipsam
quoque bestiam facili manu transadigit.

  1 **nactus** is from *nanciscor.*

  2 **quid**: 'why?'

  3 **cassa formidine**: ablative of respect.

  3–4 **similes . . . istorum** = 'like those lowborn slaves' (Apuleius is fond of using abstract nouns in
place of adjectives in this way).

  5 **indipiscimur**: understand *praedam* as the object.

  7 **dente compulso**: 'its tusks having been whetted' (as with *compello*, Apuleius often gives well-
known words a new sense).

  7 **insiliat** is deliberative subjunctive ('it should attack').

  9 **pepercit**: from *parco.*

  9–10 **equi . . . amputat**: i.e. he hamstrung the hind legs of Tlepolemus' horse.

  10 **qua** is the adverb ('where').

  11 **toto . . . supinatus**: i.e. sprawling full length on its back.

  13 **multo dente**: i.e. making much use of its tusks (goring).

  13–14 **nec . . . amicum**: Thrasyllus felt no horror at his crime. The impersonal verb *piget* means 'it
makes someone (acc) feel horror at something (gen)'. *Bonum* is ironical, and *coeptum* is a noun here.

  14–15 **vel . . . expleri**: 'nor could he be satisfied seeing that at least a propitiatory offering had been
made to his savagery by such a great danger' (i.e. his savagery could not be appeased by seeing his
victim's terrible danger).

  15–16 **percito . . . roganti**: the three dative participles refer to Tlepolemus and are possessive datives
('the right thigh of him panicked and . . . '). There is a tricolon crescendo (a group of three in which
the three members become successively longer) in pathos here.

16–17 tanto ... quanto: these are ablatives of measure of difference ('by that much more boldly by how much he believed that ... ', i.e. all the more boldly because he believed that ...).

17 futura: supply *esse* (this is a future infinitive in indirect statement, after *crederet*).

17 prosectu is dative (with *similia*).

8.D *The servants at the hunt are saddened by the death, and Thrasyllus pretends to be upset also. When the news reaches Charite she is devastated, rushes to the corpse and nearly dies of grief.*

Definito iuvene, exciti latibulo familia maesta concurrimus. at ille, quamquam prostrato inimico lactus, vultu tamen gaudium tegit et frontem asseverat et dolorem simulat et cadaver (quod ipse fecerat) avide circumplexus omnia lugentium officia sollerter affinxit; sed solae lacrimae procedere noluerunt. sic ad nostri similitudinem (qui vere lamentabamur) conformatus, manus suae culpam bestiae dabat.

Necdum satis scelere transacto, Fama dilabitur et cursus primos ad domum Tlepolemi detorquet et aures infelicis nuptae percutit. quae, amens et vecordia percita cursuque bacchata furibundo, per plateas populosas et arva rurestria fertur, insana voce casum mariti quiritans. confluunt civium maestae catervae, sequuntur obvii (dolore sociato), civitas cuncta vacuatur. et ecce mariti cadaver accurrit, labantique spiritu se super corpus effudit, ac paenissime ibidem quam devoverat ei reddidit animam. sed, aegre manibus erepta suorum, invita remansit in vita. funus vero (toto feralem pompam prosequente populo) deducitur ad sepulturam.

5

10

15

1 familia maesta: these words are in apposition to the 'we' that is the subject of the verb.

3 asseverat: 'make serious' is a new meaning for a familiar word.

4 lugentium is here used as a noun ('mourners').

4 lacrimae: with this striking personification the tears have a mind of their own and will not take part in such a disgraceful deception.

5–6 sic ... dabat: i.e. acting like us genuine mourners, he blamed the boar for what he had done with his own hand. The *qui* picks up *nostri* (genitive of *nos*), and *bestiae* is dative singular.

7 necdum = *et nondum.*

7 Fama: rumour is here personified (as a goddess).

9 amens ... furibundo: this emphatic tricolon (crescendo) of frenzied grief is framed by words for madness. *Percita* is from *percieo.*

10 fertur: *feror* = 'am borne, go' is common in epic poetry.

11 obvii is used as a noun here ('people who she met').

12 labantique is ablative.

13–14 paenissime ... animam: i.e. she very nearly died of grief (she had sworn that her life was his and she would die without him). *Quam devoverat* picks up *animam.*

14 **suorum** is used as a noun here (denoting relatives and friends).

14 **invita . . . in vita**: the paranomasia (play on words) draws attention to her unwillingness to live on.

14 **funus**: the sense 'corpse' for the word is largely poetical.

8.E *While pretending to mourn, Thrasyllus restrains Charite's grief and stops her from killing herself for his own selfish purposes.*

Thrasyllus clamare, plangere et quas in primo maerore lacrimas non habebat iam (scilicet crescente gaudio) reddere. interdum manus Charites a pulsandis uberibus amovere, luctum sedare, eiulatum coercere; cunctis tamen mentitae pietatis officiis studium contrectandae mulieris adhibere odiosumque amorem suum nutrire. sed, officiis inferialibus exactis, 5 puella protinus festinat ad maritum suum demeare inedia. sed Thrasyllus instantia pervicaci (partim per se, partim per puellae parentes) extorquet tandem paene collapsa membra cibo confoveret. at illa, invita religiosae necessitati succumbens, vultu non quidem hilaro verum paulo sereniore obiens (ut iubebatur) viventium munia, penitus luctu ac maerore 10 carpebat animum; diesque totos totasque noctes insumebat luctuoso desiderio. et imagines defuncti (quas ad habitum dei Liberi formaverat) divinis percolens honoribus, ipso se solacio cruciabat.

1 **clamare**: this infinitive and the others at 1–5 are historic infinitives.

2 **Charites** is a (Greek) genitive.

3 **pulsandis uberibus**: the beating of one's breasts (*pulsandis* is gerundive, like *contrectandae* in 4) was an act of mourning.

4 **officiis** is ablative of instrument/means. By restraining and soothing Charite Thrasyllus indulges his eagerness to touch her.

5 **odiosumque amorem**: a pointed juxtaposition.

5 **exactis** is from *exigo*.

6 **demeare inedia**: i.e. starve herself to death, so that she goes to meet her husband in the Underworld.

8 **confoveret**: *ut* is omitted after *extorqueo* ('he compelled her to sustain . . .').

8–9 **religiosae necessitati**: i.e. the need to be dutiful to her parents and give in to their requests that she live on.

10 **obiens**: present participle of *obeo*.

10 **viventium**: the participle is used as a noun here.

11 **dies . . . noctes**: this chiasmus stresses *totus* by juxtaposition and *dies* and *noctes* by emphatic placement (at the start and end).

12 **quas . . . formaverat**: i.e. she had ordered the statues (and/or other artistic representations) to be made to resemble Bacchus (*ad* means 'so as to agree with' and *formo* here means 'have fashioned' by another, rather than 'fashion' personally).

13 **ipso . . . cruciabat**: a pathetic paradox (she gets some solace from her act of devotion but it is also a painful reminder to her of reality).

8.f When Thrasyllus proposes to Charite while she is still in deep mourning, she suspects that he may have been behind the death of Tlepolemus. His ghost appears to her in a dream and confirms this.

Thrasyllus (praeceps et de ipso nomine temerarius) adhuc flentem, adhuc vestes lacerantem, adhuc capillos distrahentem non dubitavit de nuptiis convenire et imprudentiae labe tacita pectoris sui secreta fraudesque ineffabiles detegere. sed Charite vocem nefandam et horruit et detestata est; et velut tonitru percussa corruit. sed, revalescente paulatim spiritu,   5
iam scaenam pessimi Thrasylli perspiciens, ad limam consilii desiderium petitoris distulit. tunc umbra misere trucidati Tlepolemi (sanie cruentam et pallore deformem attollens faciem) quietem pudicam interpellat uxoris:

‘Mi coniunx, quovis alio maritare, modo ne in Thrasylli manum   10
sacrilegam convenias, neve sermonem conferas, nec mensam accumbas, nec toro acquiescas. fuge mei percussoris cruentam dexteram. noli parricidio nuptias auspicari. vulnera illa, quorum sanguinem tuae lacrimae proluerunt, non sunt tota dentium vulnera: lancea mali Thrasylli me tibi fecit alienum.’ et addidit cetera omnemque scaenam sceleris   15
illuminavit.

---

1 **de ipso nomine**: lurking in the name Thrasyllus is the Greek word *thrasys* (which means ‘bold’ and ‘rash’).

1 **adhuc flentem**: this participle and the next two agree with the *eam* that is to be supplied as the object of *convenire* in 3. The repetition of *adhuc* brings out Thrasyllus’ terrible timing.

3 **imprudentiae labe**: i.e. with an imprudent slip (he gives the game away inadvertently by proposing so soon after the death). *Imprudentiae* is genitive of definition.

6 **ad limam consilii**: i.e. to sharpen up her plan.

7 **distulit** is the perfect indicative of *differo*.

7–8 **sanie cruentam et pallore deformem**: the balanced order and isocolon (equal number of syllables) in these two phrases draw attention to the ghastly nature of the ghost’s face.

10 **mi**: vocative of *meus*.

10 **maritare**: second person singular of the passive imperative of *marito* (*maritor* + abl = ‘get married to’).

10 **modo ne**: ‘only provided that you do not’ (the negatives continue inside this clause with *neve*, *nec* and *nec* in 11–12).

10–11 **in . . . convenias**: ‘to come into the hand [i.e. the power] of someone’ was a common way in Latin of saying ‘to marry someone’. To accommodate *sacrilegam*, translate the phrase as ‘accept the hand’.

11 **sermonem conferas**: understand ‘with him’ with this verb and with the next two verbs.

13 **parricidio** is ablative of cause (‘as a result of’).

15 **me tibi fecit alienum**: i.e. separated me from you. In *me tibi* there is tragic juxtaposition of the two lovers who are now parted.

8.G Intent on revenge and suicide, Charite pretends to give in finally to Thrasyllus' repeated proposals and sets up a secret rendezvous.

Illa, luctu redintegrato sed indicio facinoris prorsus dissimulato, et nequissimum percussorem punire et aerumnabili vitae sese subtrahere tacita decernit. rursus detestabilis petitor, aures de nuptiis obtundens, aderat. sed illa, clementer aspernata sermonem Thrasylli, astuque miro personata, 'Adhuc' inquit 'Tlepolemus in meo vivit pectore. boni ergo 5 consules, si luctui legitimo necessarium concesseris tempus, quoad spatium reliquum compleatur anni. quae res etiam tuum commodum respicit, ne immaturitate nuptiarum manes mariti ad exitium salutis tuae suscitemus.'

Thrasyllus identidem pergit susurros improbos inurguere, quoad 10 (simulanter revicta) Charite suscipit: 'Magnopere deprecanti concedas mihi, Thrasylle, ut interdum clandestinos coitus obeamus.' succubuit Thrasyllus et prolixe consentit de furtivo concubitu, noctemque et opertas exoptat tenebras. 'Sed heus' inquit Charite 'veste contectus omnique comite viduatus, prima vigilia tacitus fores meas accedas, unoque sibilo 15 contentus nutricem meam opperiare. te ad meum perducet cubiculum.'

> 2 **percussorem . . . subtrahere**: animated and forceful alliteration.
>
> 5–6 **boni . . . consules**: *boni consulere* means 'to do well' (the genitive is adverbial).
>
> 6 **si . . . tempus**: i.e. if you allow me to keep on mourning for several more months until it is a year since Tlepolemus' death (the legally required period for mourning). *Concesseris* is future perfect indicative of *concedo* in an open (indicative) condition.
>
> 7 **commodum:** this is a noun.
>
> 8 **immaturitate nuptiarum:** i.e. by marrying before the year is up.
>
> 11 **concedas:** jussive subjunctive ('grant to me . . . that we . . . ').
>
> 12 **interdum:** 'meanwhile' (until the year of mourning is up).
>
> 14 **veste** here denotes a cloak.
>
> 15 **viduatus** has subtle point (the verb often means 'to widow').
>
> 15 **prima vigilia:** ablative of time when.
>
> 15 **accedas:** jussive subjunctive, like *opperiare* (= *opperiaris*) in 16.
>
> 15 **sibilo:** to alert the nurse, who will be waiting at the door.

8.H When the eager Thrasyllus arrives at the rendezvous, the nurse gives him drugged wine, and then Charite stands over his sleeping form, bitterly abusing him and threatening terrible vengeance.

Placuit Thrasyllo scaena ferialium nuptiarum. de diei spatio et vesperae mora querebatur. sed ubi sol tandem nocti decessit, ex imperio Charites adornatus et nutricis captiosa vigilia deceptus irrepit cubiculum, pronus spei. tunc anus (depromptis calicibus et oenophoro quod immixtum vino

soporiferum gerebat venenum) crebris potionibus secure haurientem   5
facile sepelivit ad somnum. iamque eo ad iniurias exposito, Charite
masculis animis invadit.

'En' inquit 'fidus coniugis mei comes, en venator egregius, en carus
maritus. haec est illa dextera quae meum sanguinem fudit, oculi isti
quibus male placui. quiesce securus, beate somniare. non ego ferro petam;   10
absit ut simili mortis genere cum marito meo coaequeris. vivo tibi
morientur oculi, nec quicquam videbis nisi dormiens. Chariten non
tenebis; nuptias non frueris. et diu quaeres dexteram quae tuas
expugnavit pupulas, quodque est in aerumna miserrimum, nescies de quo
quereris. at ego sepulcrum mei Tlepolemi tuo luminum cruore libabo.   15
relictis somnolentis tenebris, ad aliam (poenalem) evigila caliginem.
attolle vacuam faciem, vindictam recognosce, infortunium intellege,
aerumnas computa.'

1 **scaena . . . nuptiarum** denotes the rendezvous that is supposed to bring about his marriage to Charite but will in fact bring about death.

2–3 **ex . . . adornatus**: i.e. covered with a cloak, as Charite ordered. *Charites* is genitive singular.

5 **haurientem** agrees with *eum* (to be supplied as the object here).

6 **sepelivit ad somnum**: i.e. plunged into sleep (*sepelio* is chosen especially because of its ominous connotations of death).

8–9 **en . . . maritus**: Charite's speech has great rhetorical power. Note here the repetition and tricolon diminuendo (group of three phrases which get successively shorter), as well as the extensive irony.

9 **meum sanguinem**: she is so close to Tlepolemus that she views his blood as her own.

9–10 **oculi . . . placui**: supply *sunt* ('these are the eyes to which I . . . ').

10 **somniare** is second person singular of the imperative of *somnior* and closes a sardonic chiasmus.

10 **petam**: supply *te* as the object of the verb (meaning 'attack').

11 **absit ut**: jussive subjunctive ('let it be removed that you are . . . ' = 'god forbid that you should be . . . ').

11–12 **vivo . . . dormiens**: i.e. she will not kill him but will blind him, and he will see only in his dreams. *Vivo* is dative of *vivus*.

12–13 **Chariten . . . frueris**: emphatic alliteration, repetition and isocolon.

14–15 **quodque . . . quereris**: 'and, something which is . . . , you will not know who to complain about.' *Quod* (= *id quod*) . . . *miserrimum* is in apposition to *nescies* etc., and *quereris* is deliberative subjunctive.

17 **vacuam**: this is a grimly graphic way of describing a face that lacks the animation and character provided by the eyes. The sound effects and asyndeton in this sentence are forceful too.

8.1 *Charite blinds Thrasyllus, seizes Tlepolemus' sword, rushes to his tomb and announces to all those who follow that she will kill herself.*

Mulier, acu crinali deprompta, Thrasylli convulnerat lumina. eumque
prorsus exoculatum relinquens, dum dolore nescio crapulam cum somno

8 Charite takes her revenge.

discutit, arrepto gladio quo se Tlepolemus solebat incingere, per mediam
civitatem cursu furioso proripit se. scelus gestiens, recta monimentum
mariti contendit. at nos et omnis populus (nudatis totis aedibus) studiose   5
consequimur, hortati mutuo ferrum vesanis extorquere manibus. sed
Charite, capulum Tlepolemi propter assistens gladioque fulgenti singulos
abigens, ubi fletus uberes et lamentationes varias cunctorum intuetur,
'Abicite' inquit 'importunas lacrimas, abicite luctum meis virtutibus
alienum. vindicavi in mei mariti cruentum peremptorem, punita sum   10
funestum mearum nuptiarum praedonem. iam tempus est ut isto gladio
deorsus ad meum Tlepolemum viam quaeram.'

2 **dolore nescio**: ablative of cause. The sense 'unknown, inexplicable' for *nescius* (as here) was
unusual.

4 **scelus**: 'something terrible' (a very rare meaning for the noun).

5 **nos** denotes the speaker and the other slaves belonging to Charite.

7 **propter** is the preposition (postponed) and governs *capulum*.

9–10 **meis virtutibus alienum**: 'not in keeping with my bravery'.

10 **punita sum** is from the deponent *punior*.

11–12 **tempus . . . quaeram**: 'it is time that I seek . . .', i.e. 'it is time for me to seek . . .' (normally
tempus est takes the infinitive). *Isto gladio* is ablative of instrument/means.

8.J After explaining what she learned from Tlepolemus' ghost and how she tricked Thrasyllus, Charite kills herself. She is buried with her husband. Then in remorse Thrasyllus also commits suicide.

Et enarratis singulis quae sibi per somnium nuntiaverat maritus, quoque astu Thrasyllum petisset, ferro sub papillam dexteram transadacto, corruit; et in suo pervolutata sanguine, balbuttiens incerto sermone, efflavit animam virilem. tunc familiares miserae Charites accuratissime corpus ablutum unita sepultura marito perpetuam coniugem reddidere.   5

Thrasyllus vero, cognitis omnibus, certus tanto facinori nec gladium sufficere, sponte delatus ad sepulcrum, 'Ultronea vobis, infesti manes, en adest victima' saepe clamitans, valvis super sese diligenter obseratis, inedia statuit elidere (sua sententia damnatum) spiritum.

> 1–2 **quoque . . . petisset** is an indirect question (*quoque* = *quo* plus -*que*), also (like *singulis*) to be taken with *enarratis* (this is something else that she related fully).
>
> 5 **ablutum**: washing the corpse was part of the funeral rites. The great care with which this is done is indicative of love and respect.
>
> 5 **unita sepultura**: local ablative ('in').
>
> 5 **perpetuam coniugem** is in apposition to *corpus* (i.e. as his wife for all time).
>
> 6–9 This is quite a long sentence with cumulative impact as grim detail after detail is added. Take it slowly, keeping a close eye on punctuation, and sorting out the various participial phrases.
>
> 6 **omnibus** is neuter ('all things').
>
> 6–7 **certus . . . sufficere**: there is an accusative and infinitive construction after *certus* ('convinced that . . . '), and *nec* here means 'not even'. The idea is that to kill himself with a sword would mean a quick death, too easy for one who has committed such a terrible crime (and so he decides below to starve himself to death slowly).
>
> 7 **delatus** is from *defero* (remember that he is blind).
>
> 8 **valvis . . . obseratis**: i.e. he enters the (large) tomb and locks himself in there. The letter *s* is much in evidence from here until the end of the sentence. What do you think is its effect?

APPRECIATION

8.A–J (Metamorphoses 8.1–14).

This is a deeply tragic and grim tale. The dark subject matter (betrayal, death, grief, madness, revenge and so on) is not relieved by anything lighter at any point. In addition to the constant pathos, foreboding and sense of inevitability, there are dispiriting reversals (e.g. Tlepolemus the deceiver (of the robbers) is himself deceived; Thrasyllus goes from suitor to enemy; Charite from happy wife to distraught widow) and a bleak tit for tat (Thrasyllus is himself tricked, rendered defenceless, pierced etc.). Then comes the dismal conclusion, where unexpectedly Thrasyllus also dies, right after Charite, and dies a horrible death at that; and his suicide also thwarts Charite's planned revenge of a long life of suffering for him (8.H), and ensures that he ruins the wedded couple's reunion by joining them in their tomb. The overall impact is heightened by description, narrative pace, characterization and literary associations, as we will see.

The vivid description of the appearance of the boar at 8.B.6ff. really brings out the menace and horror. After emphasizing (three times) that this is not a harmless animal, Apuleius finally reveals that it is a boar, and immediately qualifies *aper* with the economical *immanis* and *invisitatus*. He then gives more specific information, packing in detail after detail (to provide a full and clear picture), appealing to all five senses (so that we can see the boar, and smell it, and hear it etc.) and stressing via repetition ominous elements (the mouth, the noise and fire). This information is conveyed (with powerful asyndeton and sound effects) in six phrases, of which the first five consist of four words each, while the climactic sixth contains six words and ends with the striking and suggestive *fulmineus*. This whole descriptive 'pause' freezes the awful moment as the boar rises up and keeps us in suspense by holding back what the beast actually does now. It also puts us in the position of the hunters (so that we identify with them and experience the terrifying moment with them): first we see that it is a boar; next we get a general impression of it as *immanis* and *invisitatus*; then we perceive more particular aspects, taking in its muscles, skin, bristles etc., and progressing at last to the fearsome head (as it whets its tusks, glares and charges).

That 'pause' demonstrates the way in which the slowness or quickness with which a story is related can influence its effect on readers, and there are other points here where the narrative pace is important. For example, after lingering on the (highly significant) hunt throughout 8.B and 8.C (increasing the tension, and enabling us to visualize the murder clearly) and on the mourning at 8.D.1–6 (to foster gloom and outrage), Apuleius at 8.D.7ff. presents a sudden flurry of activity (with rapid asyndeton, punchy alliteration, and skimming of details), which fits with Charite's animation and conveys the actual speed of events. Again, after the pace is slowed by her long speech (even longer in the original) at 8.H.8–18 (ensuring that her strong emotions come across with full force, and holding back the actual blinding to produce a build-up to it), in 8.I and 8.J Apuleius recounts in swift succession a whole series of (often dreadful) actions, which makes for a dramatic, gripping and sombre climax.

The characterization does much to get us involved, making us feel deeply for Charite (so that the tragedy comes across properly), and eager to see Thrasyllus punished. Tlepolemus hardly figures here and is much diminished from his earlier appearance in the novel (in keeping with his minor role as the victim who is soon eliminated); but Thrasyllus and Charite, as the protagonists, are well developed.

Thrasyllus is built up into a real villain and arouses in us strong emotions (like hatred), seeming all the worse by contrast with others (especially Tlepolemus and Charite). The character sketch at 8.A.2–5 marks him out as a significant figure, and he dominates that opening section, aptly and disquietingly. First impressions are important, and there his passion and generally criminal nature (responsible for the whole catastrophe) receive stress. In 8.C we see the device of accumulation, as Thrasyllus begins to grow as a character (at this vital point) and acquires extra specific traits (he is exploitative, treacherous, rash, callous, sadistic etc.). Then there is the technique of iteration (to reinforce), as several of those traits appear again in 8.D–E. There is also effective manipulation of the *dramatis personae* in those two sections, as we are taken from the criminal to the woman so affected by his crime, and lines on Charite's genuine grief encompass and highlight Thrasyllus' fake grief. At 8.E.3f. Apuleius also employs the telling detail (the caressing of the widow while pretending to restrain her grief is really despicable). In 8.F (as is standard) our attitude is coloured by other people's reactions (on top of the narrator's consistent disapproval, now both Charite and Tlepolemus show revulsion towards Thrasyllus). Satisfyingly, at 8.F–G Thrasyllus' passion undermines his cunning (as he gives the game away), and his own headstrong nature leads to his downfall. Then in 8.J there is a surprising twist at the end, as he suddenly feels remorse and kills himself, although this (precipitate and murderous) act is not really out of character, and it is credible (in view of what he has actually achieved and his own prospects now in the city).

Charite first comes to the fore as a loving and grieving widow at 8.D, and those aspects appear subsequently too, arousing great sympathy for her. At 8.E.12f. there is the memorable detail of the worship of representations of her husband. In 8.F she starts to evolve (into someone quick on the uptake, determined and clever). In 8.G, with a smooth progression in cunning, it begins to seem that this figure who is already diametrically opposed to Thrasyllus (in attitude to Tlepolemus, grief etc.) may also surpass him in cleverness (and this foreshadows and prepares us for her victory over him), as she shows self-control and shrewdness in contrast to Thrasyllus, while using his own trickery on him. From now on, as she establishes her ascendancy over him, she has greater textual prominence and (unlike him) her words are actually quoted in direct speech (and, as is usually the case, reveal much about her personality). She now inspires admiration, awe and even fear as well, and there are lively contrasts in her character (we now see her as active, calculating, hard, hate-filled etc.), making her far from stereotypical. Such substantial change from the rather passive and naive Charite that we met in the robbers' cave and the tender and loving person that she is at the start of this story means that she is what is known as a 'dynamic' character. However, the change seems well motivated, given the circumstances and her great love for her husband and mad grief at his death. Apuleius is also careful to ensure that she does not lose our sympathy by blinding Thrasyllus (he does deserve to suffer, and the actual act of blinding is passed over quickly, with little in the way of detail or vividness, and with only brief mention of his pain).

This tale also contains much literary allusion. In particular it is reminiscent of the supremely sad Dido episode in Virgil's epic *Aeneid*. Apuleius thereby attaches those tragic associations to his story and raises the tone. More than that, and increasing the impact still further, his narrative is more bleak and bloody than Virgil's, and his heroine is more faithful, violent and vengeful than Dido herself. If you examine *Aeneid* 1.338–68 and 4.1–705, you will see the various ways in which Apuleius echoes, varies and tops Virgil. On that model (and the other ones) see Walsh 1970, 53f., 163f.; Schlam 1992, 26; Hijmans and van der Paardt 1978, 70, 151f.; and Finkelpearl 1998, 115ff.

After hearing this story, the farmhands are nervous about how they will be treated by the owner who will succeed Charite, so they load Lucius and the pack-animals with valuables and flee the farm.

8.K That evening they arrive at a village, and are warned not to leave before daylight because of ferocious wolves infesting the area.

Vespera semitam tenebrante, pervenimus ad quoddam castellum frequens et opulens, unde nos incolae nocturna, immo vero matutina etiam prohibebant egressione. lupos enim numerosos, grandes et vastis corporibus sarcinosos ac nimia ferocitate saevientes infestare cunctam illam regionem; iamque ipsas vias obsidere et in modum latronum   5 praetereuntes aggredi; immo etiam, vesana fame rabidos, finitimas expugnare villas. denique ob iter illud, qua nobis erat commeandum, iacere semesa hominum corpora, suisque visceribus nudatis ossibus cuncta candere. ac per hoc nos quoque summa cautione ingredi debere, idque in primis observitare, ut luce clara et die iam provecto, cum lumine   10 dirarum bestiarum repigratur impetus, stipato commeatu difficultates illas transabiremus.

2 nocturna (like *matutina*) is ablative, agreeing with *egressione*. The villagers did not want the farm-hands to leave the village at night or even early in the day, before broad daylight.

3 enim, as often, introduces indirect statement (representing what the villagers said, and continuing for all the rest of this section). There is cumulative impact in this long sentence (as point after point about the wolves is tacked on) and also a careful gradation in horror (a technique continued in the following sentence).

  5 **obsidere**: *lupos* is the subject of this infinitive (and the next two).

  7 **ob**: i.e. the bodies are blocking their route.

  7 **qua . . . commeandum**: *qua* is the adverb, and *nobis* is dative of agent with the gerundive (used impersonally to express necessity).

  8–9 **suisque . . . candere**: *ossibus* goes with *candere* ('white with'), and *nudatis* agrees with *ossibus* (*nudo* + abl means 'strip of'). The assonance and alliteration here are arresting.

  9 **per**: 'on account of'.

  10 **idque**: the *id* is prospective to the *ut* clause ('to have a regard to this, that we . . . ' = 'to ensure that we . . . ').

  10 **luce . . . provecto**: i.e. in broad daylight (these are ablatives of attendant circumstances).

  10 **lumine**: ablative of instrument/means.

8.*L* *Despite the warning they leave before dawn, arming themselves against the wolves. Lucius is terrified, but no wolves attack them.*

Sed nequissimi ductores nostri caecae festinationis temeritate ac metu incertae insecutionis (spreta salubri monitione nec exspectata luce proxima) circa tertiam ferme vigiliam noctis onustos nos ad viam propellunt. ego, metu praedicti periculi inter conferta iumenta latenter absconditus, clunibus meis ab aggressionibus ferinis consulebam; iamque   5 me cursu celeri equos antecellentem mirabantur omnes. sed illa pernicitas non erat alacritatis meae sed formidinis indicium. illi qui nos agebant manus obarmaverant: hic lanceam, ille venabulum, alius gerebat spicula, fustem alius; sed et saxa, quae salebrosa semita sumministrabat; plerique ardentibus facibus proterrebant feras. sed frustra timorem illum satis   10 inanem perfuncti, longe peiores inhaesimus laqueos. nam lupi (forsitan confertae iuventutis strepitu vel certe nimia luce flammarum deterriti, vel etiam aliorsum grassantes) nulli contra nos aditum tulerunt, ac ne procul saltem ulli comparuerant.

  1 **temeritate**: ablative of cause (like *metu* in line 1).

  2 **incertae insecutionis** refers to the *possibility* that they might be pursued (for running away from Charite's farm with valuables).

  2 **spreta** is the perfect participle passive of *sperno*.

  3 **circa . . . vigiliam**: see the notes above on lines 6–7 of passage 1.E.

  4 **metu** is ablative of cause.

  5–6 **iamque . . . antecellentem** is onomatopoeic (sound of hooves).

  8 **hic . . . alius**: different individuals carry different weapons (the verb *gerebat* governs all four accusatives here).

  9 **sed et saxa**: supply *gerebant* (*et* here means 'also').

  10 **facibus** is from *fax*.

  10 **proterrebant**: quite often, as here, the imperfect tense has a conative force (i.e. it is used to express something tried).

12 **strepitu . . . luce**: these are both ablatives of instrument/means with *deterriti*.
13 **tulerunt** is from *fero*.
13–14 **ne procul saltem**: 'not even in the distance'.

8.M Instead of being attacked by wolves, they are attacked by the farmhands of a country estate that they pass, who think that they are brigands, set savage dogs on them and then hurl rocks at them.

Villae vero quam tunc forte praeteribamus coloni (multitudinem nostram latrones rati, eximieque trepidi) canes rabidos et immanes et quibusvis lupis et ursis saeviores nobis inhortantur. qui, praeter genuinam ferocitatem tumultu suorum exasperati, contra nos ruunt, et undique laterum circumfusi passim insiliunt; ac sine ullo dilectu iumenta simul et   5
homines lacerant, diuque grassati plerosque prosternunt. cerneres non tam (hercules!) memorandum quam miserandum spectaculum – canes copiosos ardentibus animis alios fugientes arripere, alios stantibus inhaerere, quosdam iacentes inscendere, et per omnem nostrum commeatum morsibus ambulare. Ecce tanto periculo malum maius   10
insequitur. de summis enim tectis ac de proximo colle rusticani illi saxa super nos raptim devolvunt, ut discernere prorsus nequiremus qua potissimum caveremus clade – comminus canum an eminus lapidum.

9 Ass turning away from its folder.

1 **nostram**: understand *esse* after this word, as the infinitive in an accusative and infinitive construction with *rati* (from *reor*).

3 **lupis et ursis**: ablatives of comparison ('than') with *saeviores*.

3 **nobis** is dative with *inhortantur*. *Inhortari* = to incite something (in the accusative) to attack someone (in the dative).

3 **qui** refers to the dogs in the previous sentence.

4 **suorum** is a noun here ('their masters').

4–5 **undique laterum**: in this unique combination *laterum* is partitive genitive with *undique* ('on all sides of our flanks').

6–7 **cerneres . . . spectaculum**: *cerneres* is a potential subjunctive referring to the past ('you would have seen'). Alliteration, rhyme and balance are used to get the point across strongly (Kenney 1998 catches the gerundives well with 'not so much memorable as miserable').

8–9 **alios . . . alios . . . quosdam**: these all modify *canes* (different dogs do different things to the travellers, who flee, stand or lie down).

10 **morsibus ambulare** is an odd expression (*morsibus* is ablative of manner) and so draws attention to the terrible biting.

10 **tanto periculo**: ablative of comparison.

12 **ut** introduces a result clause.

13 **caveremus** is a deliberative subjunctive in an indirect question ('which disaster we should be on our guard against'). The ablative with *caveo* is rare after early Latin. The disasters to be guarded against are subsequently defined by *canum* and *lapidum*.

8.N When the husband of one of the casualties complains to the farmhands that they are just poor travellers, the attack stops at once.

Quorum quidem unus caput mulieris quae meum dorsum residebat repente percussit. quo dolore commota, statim fletu cum clamore sublato, maritum suum suppetiatum ciet. at ille, deum fidem clamitans et cruorem uxoris abstergens, altius quiritabat: 'Quid miseros homines et laboriosos viatores tam crudelibus animis invaditis atque obteritis? quas praedas vultis? quae damna vindicatis? at non speluncas ferarum vel cautes incolitis barbarorum, ut humano sanguine profuso gaudeatis.' vix haec dicta, et statim lapidum congestus cessavit imber et infestorum canum revocata conquievit procella.

Unus illinc denique de summo cupressus cacumine, 'At nos' inquit 'non vestrorum spoliorum cupidine latrocinamur, sed hanc ipsam cladem de vestris protelamus manibus. iam denique pace tranquilla securi potestis incedere.'

Sic ille; sed nos plurifariam vulnerati reliquam viam capessimus, alius lapidis, alius morsus vulnera referentes, universi tamen saucii.

1 **quorum** picks up *lapidum* at the end of the previous section.
2 **sublato** is from *tollo*.

3 **suppetiatum**: supine in *-um* to express purpose.

3 **deum fidem**: 'the protection of the gods' (*deum = deorum*).

4 **altius**: 'more loudly' (than his wife) or 'rather loudly'.

4 **quid**: 'why'.

7 **ut** introduces a result (consecutive) clause.

7–8 **vix haec dicta**: supply *sunt.*

9 **procella** is unusually applied to animals and is here most expressive (suggesting sudden and terrifying violence, noise etc.)

11 **vestrorum . . . cupidine**: the ablative is one of cause, and *vestrorum* means 'taken from you'.

11–12 **cladem de vestris . . . manibus**: 'this very disaster [i.e. being robbed] by your hands' (*de* denotes cause here).

14 **sic ille**: understand *dixit.*

APPRECIATION

8.K–N *(Metamorphoses 8.15–18)*.

The start of a story gives readers their first impressions and produces the initial impact. By seizing the attention, drawing us in, making things clear (or doing none of that) the opening can affect radically our perception and reception of the whole narrative. Here, in 8.K, we are engaged by means of an early 'hook' (the prohibition of a departure by night or even in the early morning, immediately reinforced by the dramatic and disturbing 3–12). As well as creating atmosphere (menace), this is the 'problem' type of beginning (can they escape such numerous, ubiquitous and fierce wolves?). As such it generates tension, by the very length of the reported speech at 3ff. (the longer it goes on, the more it holds back the solution, while also building up the problem). That tension is later increased when they set out at night, and in fear. There is also reader-deception here, thanks to various red herrings, which ensure that we are led astray as the narrator was. So we are induced to believe that the journey will continue in broad daylight (as the need for that is stressed), that some of the group may be killed (because the wolves' deadliness is highlighted), and that it is the wolves which constitute the danger (they dominate 3ff., where there is a concentration of many, often horrific, details together with much juxtaposition and repetition). As a result a series of surprises ensue when none of this comes true.

Wit and comedy also ensue. In 8.L, after the group aptly sets off in darkness (which in the ancient world connoted gloom, terror, ill omen, chaos and error), Lucius craftily conceals himself in the middle to protect his rear end, and rushes off, in fact into trouble. So too the men carefully arm to protect themselves against attack, but in this way make themselves seem like robbers and so actually attract attack by the farmhands (and the travellers pick up rocks only to be pelted by rocks themselves later on; and to ward off animal assailants they carry torches, which mark them out as a target for human assailants). In 8.M the escape from the wolves is merely the prelude to even greater danger from two unanticipated sources, as the farmhands are afraid of the travellers (who are themselves afraid) and put up a defence against these armed men (who are simply trying to defend themselves). Also diverting is Lucius' selfish viewpoint: as an ass he complains about the dogs (undiscriminating dogs!) attacking animals as well as men; and he sees the shower of rocks as being worse than that because in the middle of the convoy he is sheltered from the encircling dogs but not from the stones raining down from above. In 8.N we see the final spin to the *latrones* theme: from wolves falling on passers-by like *latrones* we moved to the farmhands thinking that the travellers were *latrones*, and at 8.N.5f. one of the latter complains that the farmhands are after booty from them (just like *latrones*) and implies that they have no booty (but, of course, they had stolen valuables from Charite's farm, and so there is poetic justice in an assault on them as *latrones*).

This story which had such a dramatic start has a diminuendo close. We have also progressed from the convoy arriving at the village unhurt (in 8.K) to it leaving the country estate wounded (in 8.N), and from the inhabitants of the village detaining Lucius' company out of concern that they may be harmed to the inhabitants of the estate sending the company on their way unconcerned (unapologetic) at the harm that they have inflicted on them. On the pervasiveness in the *Metamorphoses* of metamorphosis like this in various forms see Tatum 1972; James 1987, 27ff., 199, 306ff.; and Krabbe 1989, 40ff. and 143f. Can you find any more examples of such metamorphosis in this tale?

8.0 *They stop at an attractive grove to recover but an old herdsman appears and implies that this is a place of terror, before rushing off.*

Aliquanto denique viae permenso spatio, pervenimus ad nemus quoddam proceris arboribus consitum et pratentibus virectis amoenum, ubi placuit illis ductoribus nostris refectui paululum conquiescere corporaque sua diverse laniata sedulo recurare. ergo passim prostrati solo, primum fatigatos animos recuperare ac dehinc vulneribus medelas varias adhibere   5 festinant – hic cruorem praeterfluentis aquae rore deluere, ille spongeis inacidatis tumores comprimere, alius fasciolis hiantes vincire plagas. ad istum modum saluti suae quisque consulebat.

Interea quidam senex de summo colle prospectat, quem circum capellae pascentes opilionem esse profecto clamabant. eum rogavit unus e   10 nostris haberetne venui lactem. At ille, diu capite quassanti, 'Vos autem' inquit 'de poculo vel omnino ulla refectione nunc cogitatis? an nulli scitis quo loco consederitis?' et conductis oviculis conversus longe recessit. quae vox eius et fuga pastoribus nostris non mediocrem pavorem incussit.

1 **aliquanto** is the adjective, not the adverb.

2 **proceris . . . amoenum**: the beauty of the place is matched and accentuated by the beauty of the sound and style, which includes homoeoteleuton, parallel ordering (of adjectives, nouns, cases), and isocolon. *Consitum* is from *consero*.

3 **refectui**: dative of purpose.

4 **prostrati** is from *prosterno*. The passive is here used reflexively, of stretching oneself out.

6–7 **hic . . . ille . . . alius**: understand *festinat* as the verb (governing the infinitives) with these subjects (= various travellers).

7 **ad** here means 'in' (of the manner in which something is done).

9–10 **quem . . . clamabant**: *quem* is the object of this verb (*circum* is the adverb). The idea is that the goats make it clear that he is a herdsman, but this (onomatopoeic) verb comically conjures up the idea of talking (shouting) goats.

11 **nostris** is used as a noun, meaning 'our men/our company'.

11 **haberetne venui**: the particle -*ne* ('whether') introduces an indirect question, in which *venui* is dative of purpose.

11 **lactem**: *lac* was normally neuter, and *lactem* as the accusative was very rare.

11 **quassanti** is an alternative form for *quassante*.

12 **nulli** is here a strong form of *non*.

13 **oviculis** after *capellae* in 10 presumably means that he had a mixed flock, but the change from goats to sheep here in connection with this old man may subtly foreshadow the change (from human to snake) in connection with the second old man in 8.Q below.

14 **pastoribus nostris** refers to the servants from Charite's farm who are leading the convoy of travellers.

14 **non mediocrem**: i.e. considerable (such affirmation by means of negation of the contrary is called litotes).

14 **incussit**: the verb agrees in number with its nearest subject but has two subjects (*vox* and *fuga*).

8.P *Another old man appears, weeping and begging them to save his little grandson, who has fallen into a pit and is in danger of dying.*

Ac dum perterriti de loci qualitate sciscitari gestiunt, nec est qui doceat, senex alius (magnus, gravatus annis, totus in baculum pronus et lassum trahens vestigium) ubertim lacrimans per viam proximat; visisque nobis, cum fletu maximo singulorum iuvenum genua contingens, sic adorabat: 'Decrepito seni subsistite meumque parvulum, ab inferis ereptum, canis meis reddite. nepos namque meus et itineris huius suavis comes, dum forte passerem incantantem saepiculae consectatur arripere, delapsus in proximam foveam, in extremo iam vitae consistit periculo, quippe cum de fletu ac voce ipsius avum sibi saepicule clamitantis vivere illum quidem sentiam, sed per corporis mei defectam valetudinem opitulari nequeam.
5

10

at vobis (aetatis et roboris beneficio) facile est suppetiari miserrimo seni
puerumque illum sospitem mihi facere.' sic deprecantis suamque
canitiem distrahentis totos quidem miseruit.

1 **qui doceat**: the subjunctive in the relative clause expresses purpose ('someone to inform').

2 **totus . . . pronus**: i.e. bent over his stick and putting all his weight on it (*totus* is used adverbially here, meaning 'entirely').

3 **vestigium**: singular for plural.

4 **genua contingens**: this was done by the ancients in entreaty.

5–6 **ab . . . reddite**: i.e. save my grandson from death and return him to me, his old grandfather (*cani* means 'grey hairs').

8 **quippe cum** = 'since' (the old man explains that he says that the boy is in danger of dying because he can tell from his tears and frequent cries for his grandfather that he is alive but also in need of help, which the frail old man cannot give him).

9 **clamitantis** modifies *ipsius* and has *avum* as its object.

12–13 **deprecantis . . . miseruit**: the verb is here impersonal ('it makes feel sorry'), and, for example, *miseret me* (acc) *illius* (gen) means 'I am sorry for him'. Here the accusative (*totos*) refers to all the travellers, while the genitive (*senis* = 'old man') has to be understood, and the two participles (*deprecantis* and *distrahentis*) agree with it. The old man is tearing his hair in grief over the boy.

8.Q *The bravest and strongest one of the travellers goes off with the old
man to help. But when they are ready to move on, they send someone to
get him, and he finds him being eaten by a huge snake.*

Sed unus et animo fortior et aetate iuvenior et corpore validior, quique
solus incolumis proelium superius evaserat, exsurgit alacer. et percontatus
quonam loci puer ille decidisset, monstrantem digito non longe frutices
horridos senem illum impigre comitatur.

Ac dum refecti, sarcinulis sumptis, viam capessunt, clamore primum   5
nominatim cientes illum iuvenem frequenter inclamant, mox mora
diutina commoti, mittunt e suis arcessitorem unum, qui comitem
reduceret. at ille modicum commoratus, refert sese, buxanti pallore
trepidus. mira super conservo suo renuntiat: conspicatum se quippe
supinato illi et iam ex maxima parte consumpto immanem draconem   10
mandentem insistere; nec usquam miserinum senem comparere illum.
qua re cognita et cum pastoris sermone collata (qui saevum prorsus hunc
locorum inquilinum praeminabatur), pestilenti deserta regione, velociori
se fuga proripiunt, nosque pellunt crebris tundentes fustibus.

1 **et animo . . . validior**: the three nouns are ablatives of respect. The fullness, sound and style (including polysyndeton = emphatic frequency of connecting links) draw attention to the man's toughness here, so that it is a real surprise when harm befalls him later.

3 **quonam loci**: 'in just what of a place' (partitive genitive), i.e. just where.

4 **horridos** in retrospect has more than one possible sense here.

7 **suis** is used as a noun, meaning 'their people/ their company'.

8 **reduceret**: the subjunctive expresses purpose.

8 **modicum**: the neuter accusative singular of the adjective is here used as an adverb (meaning 'briefly').

9 **conspicatum se**: understand *esse*. This is indirect statement after *renuntiat* (as is *nec usquam . . . illum* at 11).

10 **supinato illi . . . consumpto**: these are datives with *insistere* (11).

10 **ex maxima parte**: *ex* here has the sense 'to the extent of', so that the phrase means essentially 'to a very great extent'.

10 **immanem** economically combines various senses.

12 **cum . . . collata**: 'having been compared with' (the verb is *confero*).

12 **pastoris** denotes the old man with the goats and sheep in 8.O.

13 **velociori** is ablative (for the much more usual *velociore*).

APPRECIATION

8.O–Q *(Metamorphoses 8.18–21)*.

Again aperture is important, but the beginning here (8.O.1–8) is in many ways different from that of the previous tale. This time the (shorter) opening presents a silent tableau, with the focus on the travellers, and contains an act (the pause in the grove) which plays a substantial role in the plot. It raises no 'problem' but just builds atmosphere instead, here an atmosphere of calm and beauty, so that everything is much more relaxed, and one is not so much 'hooked' as charmed and lulled. Suspense is not generated this time, only surprises (two, more neatly structured surprises), as we are misled again, but in a different fashion – by concealing the real nature of the story, by suppressing a vital protagonist (the snake) and by creating a bogus atmosphere (the grove seems delightful and unthreatening; and peaceful rest and recuperation receive a lengthy treatment that is itself leisurely). For more on reader-deception in the *Metamorphoses* see Smith 1994 and Winkler 1985, 1ff., 57ff., 135ff., 204ff.

The first surprise comes when the first *senex* suddenly appears and spoils the tranquil mood by means of a brief, ominous speech (implying great danger) and a brisk, disturbing action (immediate flight). This old man (a real human) frightens at first but is well-meaning and truthful. In 8.P a second old man (really a snake) appears, and he arouses sympathy at first, but is malevolent and lying. Again there is a lulling which is subsequently shattered. As you will see for yourself if you analyse 8.P.2–13, initially this *senex* by his appearance, actions and words does much to arouse pity and calm any suspicions (but, as we realize later, all of this is in fact an extensive and chilling psychological attack and suggests a sinister intelligence at work). The second (still greater) surprise comes in 8.Q, when the sturdy young traveller is found dead. This is carefully ushered in by growing tension at 5–9, and there is an effective build up of horror at 9–11 (with considered placement and selection of words). There are grim inversions here: for example, the ordinary, weak, mild old man becomes an extraordinary, powerful, savage snake; and after begging for help to save someone from death, he inflicts death on a helpless victim. These go hand in hand with the sardonic humour elsewhere in this tale (e.g. the company rest and tend their wounds in a place of terror and death; and after being warned and frightened by the first *senex*, stupidly they do not flee at once but remain, and allow one of their number to be isolated, and to go off to what is quite possibly the source of peril).

Once again the end contains changes from the start that contrast notice-ably with it. At 8.Q.13f. the beautiful, non-menacing grove of the opening is described as *pestilenti . . . regione*, and the travellers depart from it instead of arriving at it; also in place of calm, stationary rest and recovery from wounds there is now hurried flight and the dealing out of many blows.

8.R *They arrive at a village, where they hear how a local slave's infidelity made his wife take revenge and kill herself and their son.*

Celerrime denique longo itinere confecto, pagum quendam accedimus, ibique totam perquiescimus noctem. inibi coeptum facinus oppido memorabile narrare cupio.

Servus quidam, cui cunctam familiae tutelam dominus permiserat suus, quique possessionem maximam illam in quam deverteramus   5
villicabat, habens ex eodem famulitio conservam coniugam, liberae cuiusdam extrariaeque mulieris flagrabat cupidine. quo dolore paelicatus uxor eius instricta cunctas mariti rationes et quicquid horreo reconditum continebatur admoto combussit igne. nec tali damno tori sui contumeliam vindicasse contenta, iam contra sua saeviens viscera,   10
laqueum sibi nectit; infantulumque quem de eodem marito iamdudum susceperat eodem funiculo nectit, seque per altissimum puteum (appendicem parvulum trahens) praecipitat.

Quam mortem dominus eorum aegerrime sustinens arreptum servulum (qui causam tanti sceleris uxori suae praestiterat) nudum ac   15
totum melle perlitum firmiter alligavit arbori ficulneae, cuius in ipso carioso stipite inhabitantium formicarum nidificia borriebant, et ultro citro commeabant multiiuga scaturrigine. quae, simul dulcem ac mellitum corporis nidorem persentiscunt, parvis quidem sed numerosis et continuis morsiunculis penitus inhaerentes, per longi temporis   20
cruciatum ita (carnibus atque ipsis visceribus adesis) homine consumpto

membra nudarunt ut ossa tantum, viduata pulpis, nitore nimio
candentia, funestae cohaererent arbori.

Hac quoque detestabili deserta mansione, paganos in summo luctu
relinquentes, rursum pergimus.   25

2 **totam . . . noctem** is accusative of duration of time ('through/for').

2 **coeptum** is the participle of *coepi*.

7 **cuiusdam** is genitive singular of *quidam*.

7 **paelicatus** is genitive with *dolore* ('grief at . . . ').

9–13 **nec . . . praecipitat**: Apuleius is fond of long sentences like this, tacking on item after item
by means of participles or additional main verbs (linked by *et*, *-que* etc.), rather than employing
subordinate clauses. These sentences are not too hard to decipher, if you stay calm and take them bit
by bit, keeping a close eye on punctuation, and pausing for breath at strong stops (like the semicolon
in 11).

9–10 **tori . . . contenta**: *tori sui* goes with *contumeliam* ('insult to . . . '), which is the object of
vindicasse (syncopated form of *vindicavisse*), a perfect infinitive after *contenta* ('content to have . . . ').

10 **viscera** here means 'flesh and blood' (i.e. child).

11 **de** means literally 'originating with' (indicating paternity). We would say in English 'had borne
TO the same husband' (*susceperat* is the pluperfect indicative of *suscipio*).

12 **eodem funiculo**: ablative of instrument/means.

12 **per**: i.e. through the opening of, into.

13 **appendicem** denotes the child attached to her.

14 **arreptum**: perfect participle passive of *arripio*.

16 **totum** is adjective for adverb ('totally').

16 **cuius in ipso**: 'in whose very' = 'and in its very'.

17–18 **ultro citro**: 'back [and] forth' (the asyndeton is brisk).

18–23 **quae . . . arbori**: *quae* refers to the *formicae*, and *simul* means 'as soon as'. The length of this
sentence reinforces the notion of prolonged biting and (with so many details added one after another)
makes for cumulative impact.

20 **per**: 'during' or 'by means of'.

21 **ita** goes with *membra nudarunt ut* in 22 ('stripped his limbs in such a way that only [*tantum*]
the bones . . . ').

APPRECIATION

8.R *(Metamorphoses 8.22–3).*

Once more the opening (at 1–3) is significant, and once more versatility in
connection with aperture is evident. This much shorter beginning gets us into
the main narrative with unexpected suddenness, before any atmosphere is
created or any 'problem' is raised. Here for the first time in these three prefaces
the narrator intrudes with comment (*coeptum facinus oppido memorabile*) and
curiosity is aroused (by the ambiguity of the comment). In fact there is a
(challenging and mocking) virtuoso performance here, as Apuleius is teasing
and misleading us and setting up surprises yet again, but in a different way.
So we cannot tell if *facinus* has the sense 'deed' or 'crime', and *coeptum* could
mean that it was only started; the whole phrase is an understatement and does
not do full justice to the truly awful tale that follows; and the singular *facinus*
does not prepare us for the ensuing plurality of crimes.

As a result of all this at 4ff. we read on eagerly, dismissing first the slave's infidelity and then the arson as the really remarkable *facinus*. Most will conclude that the *facinus* is the murder-suicide at 10ff., which involves both hanging and leaping down a well, and which is unusual, bizarre and engaging (how exactly does it work?). For these readers the wicked punishment at 14ff. will come as an unexpected addition and as such pack a real punch (reinforced by the deliberate build up in horror, the vividness, the telling details and the stress on devouring). The grim aptness of the punishments increases the overall impact. For example, the wife avenges her husband's burning passion (7) by using fire, and his insult to her marriage bed (9f.) by killing the product of that bed; and the tree to which the amorous slave is tied is fitting, since the fig symbolized the female private parts (can you see any other elements of the penalty at 15ff. that are appropriate and make for poetic justice?).

Yet again the ending inverts the beginning (with its journey completed, arrival at the village and static rest). But the neatness extends beyond that. This is the last in a trio of tales (at 8.K–R) which are carefully linked together: these are successive episodes on the journey with Charite's slaves; various words and details (like death, trees and biting creatures) are common to them; and there is ring structure (do the white bones and devoured body at 8.R.21ff. remind you of anything in 8.K?). In addition, these narratives form a tricolon diminuendo (a group of three in which the second is shorter than the first, and the third is shorter than the second). And the openings parallel the diminution in length of their respective stories. For more on this triad and especially aperture in it see Murgatroyd 1997.

The travellers reach a city, where they sell Lucius to a priest of an oriental goddess. Lucius relates with disgust how he and the other priests with him debauch young men and even have sexual designs on Lucius himself, and how to get alms they fabricate a prophecy and one of them pretends to rave with divine inspiration and flogs himself for an invented act of sacrilege. In book 9 they move on to a village, where they hear an amusing story about a poor man.

9.A *A poor man has an unfaithful wife, who is entertaining her lover one morning when he suddenly returns from work. She hides her lover in a large storage-jar and attacks her husband for being idle.*

Cognoscimus lepidam de adulterio cuiusdam pauperis fabulam, quam vos etiam cognoscatis volo. is, gracili pauperie laborans, fabriles operas

praebendo parvis illis mercedibus vitam tenebat. erat ei tamen uxorcula,
etiam satis quidem tenuis et ipsa, verum tamen postrema lascivia
famigerabilis. sed die quadam, dum matutino ille ad opus susceptum 5
proficiscitur, statim latenter irrepit eius hospitium temerarius adulter. ac
dum veneris colluctationibus securius operantur, maritus (ignarus rerum
ac nihil etiam tum tale suspicans) improvisus hospitium repetit. iamque
clausis et obseratis foribus, uxoris laudata continentia, ianuam pulsat,
sibilo etiam praesentiam suam denuntiante. tunc mulier callida et ad 10
huius modi flagitia perastutula tenacissimis amplexibus expeditum
hominem dolio (quod erat in angulo semiobrutum, sed alias vacuum)
dissimulanter abscondit; et, patefactis aedibus, adhuc introeuntem
maritum aspero sermone accipit: 'Sicine vacuus et otiosus, insinuatis
manibus, ambulabis mihi, nec, obito consueto labore, vitae nostrae 15
prospicies et aliquid cibatui parabis? at ego misera pernox et perdia
lanificio nervos meos contorqueo, ut intra cellulam nostram saltem
lucerna luceat. quanto me felicior Daphne vicina, quae mero et prandio
matutino saucia cum suis adulteris volutatur!'

1 **adulterio . . . pauperis** is an odd and deliberately misleading expression. The genitive denotes not
the adulterer (as would be normal) but the injured party. Translate *adulterium* as 'cuckolding'.

2 **volo** may take *ut* and the subjunctive or the subjunctive on its own to indicate what one wants to
happen ('I want you too to . . . ').

3 **praebendo** is a gerund ('by offering his services . . . ').

3 **parvis . . . mercedibus**: ablative of instrument/means, referring to the scant wages he earned as a
workman.

3 **uxorcula**: the diminutive (of *uxor*) has a contemptuous force.

4 **etiam . . . et ipsa**: both *etiam* and *et* mean 'also'. This is typical Apuleian fullness (like the two
words for 'but' in this line, and *dissimulanter abscondit* in 13).

4 **postrema lascivia**: ablative of cause.

5 **sed** is just transitional here ('now').

7 **veneris colluctationibus**: i.e. in sexual intercourse.

7 **securius**: the force of the comparative may be 'rather' or 'too'.

8 **etiam tum**: 'even then' implies that the affair has been going on for a while, but the slow husband
has not realized.

9 **uxoris . . . continentia**: because the door is locked he thinks that his wife is respectably employed
at home and not wanting visitors.

10 **ad**: 'with regard to'.

11 **tenacissimis amplexibus** goes with *expeditum* ('disentangled from').

12 **dolio** is a local ablative and goes with *abscondit* in 13.

12 **alias** is the adverb ('at other times').

14 **sicine** = *sic* and the interrogative particle *-ne*.

14–15 **insinuatis manibus**: 'with your hands in your pockets'.

15 **obito** is the perfect participle passive of *obeo* in an ablative absolute construction.

16 **cibatui**: dative of purpose ('for food').

18 **quanto me felicior**: *quanto* is ablative of measure of difference; *me* is ablative of comparison; and *est* has to be supplied ('how much more fortunate than me is . . . ').

18 **mero**: it was customary to dilute wine with water. To drink neat wine in the morning was disgraceful, especially for a woman.

9.B *When the husband replies that he has been given the day off but has sold the storage-jar, she claims that she has sold it for a higher sum to a man who is inside it at that very moment, inspecting it.*

Sic confutatus maritus, 'Et quid istic est?' ait. 'nam licet forensi negotio officinator noster attentus ferias nobis fecerit, tamen hodiernae cenulae nostrae prospexi. vide, sis, ut dolium (quod semper vacuum) frustra locum detinet tantum et re vera praeter impedimentum conversationis nostrae nihil praestat amplius. istud ego quinque denariis cuidam   5 venditavi, et adest ut, dato pretio, secum rem suam ferat. quin itaque praecingeris mihique manum tantisper accomodas, ut exobrutum protinus tradatur emptori?'

E re nata fallacia, mulier temerarium tollens cachinnum, 'Magnum' inquit 'istum virum ac strenuum negotiatorem nacta sum, qui rem (quam   10 ego, mulier et intra hospitium contenta, iamdudum septem denariis vendidi) minoris distraxit.'

Additamento pretii laetus, maritus 'Et quis est ille' ait 'qui tanto praestinavit?' at illa 'Olim, inepte,' inquit 'descendit in dolium, sedulo soliditatem eius probaturus.'   15

1 **quid istic est**: 'what is in that matter of yours?' = 'what are you saying?'
1 **licet** with the subjunctive means 'although'.
3 **sis**: a contracted form of *si vis* ('if you wish' = 'please').
3 **ut**: 'how'. The indicative in an indirect question (see *detinet* and *praestat* at 4–5) was colloquial and common in early Comic writers.
3 **quod . . . vacuum**: understand *est*.
4 **praeter** virtually means 'than' (with *amplius* in 5).
5 **quinque denariis**: ablative of price ('for').
6 **adest**: the present tense is used vividly of someone who will be present in the immediate future.
6 **dato** is from *do*.
7 **exobrutum**: agrees with *dolium* (which has to be supplied).
9 **nata fallacia**: ablative absolute (*nata* is from *nascor*). The circumstances (*res*) suggest a trick to the quick-thinking wife.
10 **istum** here virtually means 'here', 'in you'.
10 **nacta sum**: from *nanciscor*.
11 **contenta** is from *contineo*.
12 **minoris**: although the ablative of price is standard (as with *septem denariis* in 11 and *tanto* in 13), the genitive *minoris* is often used to express price ('for less').
13 **additamento**: ablative of cause.
15 **probaturus**: future participle to denote purpose.

9.c The lover emerges from the storage-jar, claiming it is in a bad state and he wants to clean the inside to check it properly. While the husband does this himself, the lover takes advantage of the situation.

Nec ille sermoni mulieris defuit, sed exsurgens alacriter 'Vis' inquit 'verum scire, mater familias? hoc tibi dolium nimis vetustum est et multifariam rimis hiantibus quassum.' ad maritumque eius dissimulanter conversus, 'Quin tu (quicumque es), homuncio, lucernam' ait 'actutum mihi expedis, ut, erasis intrinsecus sordibus, diligenter aptumne usui   5 possim dinoscere – nisi nos putas aes de malo habere?' nec quicquam moratus ac suspicatus, acer et egregius ille maritus, accensa lucerna, 'Discede' inquit 'frater, et otiosus assiste, donec probe percuratum istud tibi repraesentem.' et cum dicto nudatus ipse, delato lumine, scabiem vetustam cariosae testae occipit exsculpere.   10

At vero adulter (bellissimus ille pusio) inclinatam dolio pronam uxorem fabri superincurvatus secure dedolabat. ast illa, capite in dolium demisso, maritum suum astu meretricio tractabat ludicre. hoc et illud et aliud et rursus aliud purgandum demonstrat digito suo, donec, utroque opere perfecto, acceptis septem denariis, calamitosus faber collo suo   15 gerens dolium coactus est ad hospitium adulteri perferre.

1 **nec ... defuit**: an instance of litotes. The meaning is that he supported her words (*defuit* is from *desum*).

1 **vis**: second person singular of the present indicative of *volo*.

2 **mater familias**: 'mistress of the household', 'lady' (*familias* is an alternative form of the genitive singular of *familia*).

2 **tibi**: possessive dative ('of yours').

3 **dissimulanter**: i.e. pretending not to know who the husband was. The adverb occurs in 9.A.13 and is one of the verbal and thematic links between the wife and the lover that bring out their closeness.

5 **aptumne usui**: understand *sit* in this indirect question.

6 **nisi ... habere**: *nos* is plural for singular. The expression here is typically quaint and singular. The exact sense is disputed, but 'having money from an apple tree' may mean having lots of money (like our phrase about money growing on trees).

6 **quicquam**: neuter accusative singular of *quisquam* used as an adverb ('at all').

8 **frater** is here used just as an affectionate term of address.

9 **cum dicto**: 'together with the word' (i.e. so saying).

9 **delato**: from *defero*.

12 **superincurvatus** appears here only and so really highlights the lover's position bent over on top of the wife. The novelty of the word also matches and brings out the novelty of this sexual scenario.

13 **meretricio** is especially apt as she will be receiving money soon.

13 **tractabat ludicre**: i.e. she toyed with him, made a fool of him.

13–14 **hoc ... purgandum**: this is a gerundive of obligation/necessity. The pronouns indicate various spots that need cleaning, and the polysyndeton (frequency of *et*) brings out the large number of places pointed to (and perhaps simulates panting).

15 **opere** denotes the two jobs of cleaning out the jar and servicing the wife.

16 **coactus est** is from *cogo*.

APPRECIATION

9.A–C (Metamorphoses 9.4–7).

Boccaccio adapted this tale in his *Decameron* (see Hijmans and van der Paardt 1978, 212) and obviously relished the nasty, salacious humour here, as the quick-thinking and outrageously cheeky wife outsmarts her comically slow husband (who says the storage-jar is always empty and takes up space uselessly, while the lover is actually hiding in it; who does not wonder why the door is locked while his wife has a man inside with her; who calls the lover *frater*, affectionately, and without realizing quite how closely linked he is to him; who facilitates an act of adultery himself by climbing into the jar; and who personally carries that trophy of cuckoldry to the lover's home). This basically funny situation is made still funnier by context and verbal play. Ironically Lucius, who has just criticized the priests' lechery, lying and play-acting, finds all of that amusing in the case of the wife and her boyfriend (when he is not personally involved). Also the double entendre is in evidence throughout this anecdote. The obvious reference to coition in *opus* at 9.C.15 is explained in the notes. But, more subtly, before that at 9.A.17 the wife's *nervos meos contorqueo* is rather oddly applied to spinning/weaving but could easily refer to intercourse, and *cellula* was also used of a prostitute's room; while at 9.A.19 *saucia* (literally 'wounded') could denote sexual penetration. The most developed punning concerns the storage-jar. Household containers of various sorts stood for the female pudenda (see Adams 1982, 86–8), and the play on *dolio* in *dedolabat* at 9.C.12 underlines the erotic aspect of this particular storage-jar. So at 9.B.14f. the wife (while calling her husband a fool) is mockingly referring to the lover previously entering her for vigorous sex. And the lover wittily develops that idea at 9.C.3 by talking of gaping cracks and saying that the *dolium* is *quassum* (which could mean 'shaken'), and also at 9.C.5 where he wants to see if it is *aptum usui* (which could be translated as 'suitable for copulation'). Then at 9.C.9ff. there are the surreal touches of the husband entering the jar/vagina with a lamp to clean out the filth in it and the wife putting her own head into it. Can you see similar sport with *dolium* in the first paragraph of 9.B?

This tale is also given an intellectual aspect by the clever inversion of standard situations and characters of love poetry (especially Latin elegy). In such literature it is normally the lover (not his rival) who is poor, performs servile services and is described as wretched; usually the girl when she locks a man out is subject to complaint and abuse (instead of praise), and her deceit harms (rather than benefits) the lover; and often the lover's rival is rich and pays out money, and is the one inside the girl's house while the lover is locked out.

10 Ass with mill. Graffito, Rome.

The priests are finally caught with a stolen goblet and are locked up. Lucius is bought by a baker, who uses him to turn his mill-wheel. He is a good man, but his wicked wife persecutes Lucius. She has a lover, but is persuaded by her accomplice (an old woman) to take on a new and bolder one – Philesitherus. The old woman tells how he recently tricked a jealous husband. He bribed the slave guarding the man's wife and got access to her while the husband was away, but the husband suddenly returned and he had to flee. He left his slippers under the bed, and the husband found them, guessed that his wife had been entertaining a lover and dragged the slave off to the forum. Philesitherus saw this and remembered about his slippers, so rushed up and accused the slave of stealing them at the baths. The husband believed this and returned the 'stolen' slippers.

9.D On hearing this story, the baker's wife is envious and dissatisfied. The old woman promises to bring Philesitherus to her that evening.

Hactenus adhuc anicula garriente, suscipit mulier 'Beatam illam, quae tam constantis sodalis libertate fruitur! at ego misella molae etiam sonum et (ecce) illius scabiosi asini faciem timentem familiarem incidi.' ad haec anus 'Iam tibi ego probe suasum et confirmatum animi amatorem illum

alacrem vadimonium sistam.' et insuper condicta vespertina regressione,   5
cubiculo facessit. at pudica uxor statim cenas saliares comparat, vina
pretiosa defaecat, pulmenta recentia tuccetis temperat. mensa largiter
instructa, denique, ut dei cuiusdam, adventus sic exspectatur adulteri.
nam et opportune maritus foris apud naccam proximum cenitabat.

Ergo igitur (metis die propinquante) helcio tandem absolutus   10
refectuique secure redditus, non tam (hercules) laboris libertatem
gratulabar quam quod (revelatis luminibus) libere iam cunctas
facinorosae mulieris artes prospectare poteram. sol, ipsum quidem
delapsus Oceanum, subterrenas orbis plagas illuminabat, et (ecce)
nequissimae anus adhaerens lateri temerarius adulter adventat (puer   15
admodum et adhuc lubrico genarum splendore conspicuus, adhuc
adulteros ipse delectans). hunc multis admodum saviis exceptum mulier
cenam iubet paratam accumbere.

> 1 **beatam illam**: accusative of exclamation ('lucky her!').
>
> 3 **timentem** agrees with the noun *familiarem* (= her present lover) and governs the accusatives *sonum* and *faciem*.
>
> 3–4 **ad haec anus**: 'in reply to this the old woman [said]'.
>
> 4 **tibi ego**: note the intimate juxtaposition.
>
> 4 **animi**: genitive of respect ('in mind').
>
> 4–5 **amatorem...sistam**: 'I will present that eager lover as fulfilment of my promise' (the accusative *vadimonium* is predicative).
>
> 5 **regressione** appears first in Apuleius with the sense 'return'. He liked to give words new meanings.
>
> 6 **cubiculo**: local ablative ('from').
>
> 6–7 **cenas...temperat**: the fine meal and wine will be a preliminary to sex. The asyndeton is brisk in this tricolon.
>
> 8 **instructa** is from *instruo*.
>
> 8 **ut**: 'as if'.
>
> 10 **ergo igitur**: typical Apuleian fullness of expression.
>
> 10 **metis...propinquante**: i.e. as the day neared its close.
>
> 11–12 **non...quod**: 'I was glad (by god) not so much for the freedom from work as for the fact that ...'
>
> 12 **revelatis luminibus**: Lucius wore blinkers at the mill-wheel.
>
> 13–14 **Sol...illuminabat**: at the end of the day the sun set in the Ocean and then shone in the Underworld while it was night on earth.
>
> 15 **anus** is genitive singular.
>
> 16 **splendore**: ablative of cause. The advent of facial hair made boys no longer attractive to male lovers (a point alluded to in 16f.).

9.E *Philesitherus is about to start eating when the baker suddenly returns early. The wife hides her new lover under a nearby tub.*

Sed ut primum occursoriam potionem et incohatum gustum extremis
labiis contingebat adulescens, multo celerius opinione rediens maritus
adventat. tunc uxor egregia, diras devotiones in eum deprecata et crurum

ei fragium amborum abominata, exsangui formidine trepidantem
adulterum alveo ligneo (quo frumenta contusa purgari consuerant) 5
temere propter iacenti suppositum abscondit. ingenitaque astutia
dissimulato tanto flagitio, intrepidum mentita vultum, percontatur de
marito cur utique, contubernalis artissimi deserta cenula, praematurus
adforet.

At ille dolenti prorsus animo suspirans assidue, 'Nefarium' inquit 'et 10
extremum facinus perditae feminae tolerare nequiens, fuga me proripui.
hem qualis (dii boni) matrona, quam fida quamque sobria turpissimo se
dedecore foedavit! iuro per istam ego sanctam Cererem me nunc etiam
meis oculis de tali muliere minus credere.'

His instincta verbis mariti, audacissima uxor (noscendae rei cupiens) 15
non cessat obtundere, totam prorsus a principio fabulam promeret. nec
destitit donec eius voluntati succubuit maritus et sic (ignarus suorum)
domus alienae percenset infortunium.

1 **ut primum**: 'as soon as'.

1 **incohatum**: i.e. the lover had only started to eat it.

2 **multo ... opinione**: i.e. much sooner than expected (*opinione* is ablative of comparison).

3–6 **tunc ... abscondit**: the subject is *uxor egregia* (and the deponent participles *deprecata* and *abominata* agree with it); the main verb (at the end) is *abscondit*; the object is *adulterum*; *trepidantem* agrees with the object, and so does *suppositum* ('placed under'), which governs *alveo ligneo temere propter iacenti* (dative); in the parenthesis, which explains that the tub was normally used for cleaning pounded grain, *consuerant = consueverant*.

6 **ingenitaque astutia**: ablative of instrument/means.

9 **adforet**: imperfect subjunctive of *adsum*.

10 **dolenti** is ablative (for the more usual *dolente*).

11 **fuga**: ablative ('in flight').

12 **dii**: vocative plural of *deus*.

13 **per ... Cererem**: he swears by an image of Ceres (goddess of grain), which would naturally be found in a baker's establishment.

13 **nunc etiam**: 'even now'.

15 **noscendae ... cupiens**: i.e. she was keen to know about the affair (*noscendae* is gerundive, and *cupiens* + gen = 'desirous of').

16 **non cessat obtundere**: supply *eum*. *Obtundere* with the subjunctive means to assail with demands to do something.

16 **totam ... promeret**: the amplitude of expression brings out her eagerness to hear absolutely every detail, and by way of reinforcement the alliteration of *p* seems insistent.

17 **suorum**: supply *infortuniorum*.

9.F The baker explains how the fuller's seemingly respectable wife had been surprised with a young lover when the two friends arrived for dinner and hid him under a cage being used to bleach clothes.

'Contubernalis mei fullonis uxor, alioquin servati pudoris (ut videbatur)
femina, quae semper secundo rumore gloriosa larem mariti pudice

gubernabat, occulta libidine prorumpit in adulterum quempiam. cumque
furtivos amplexus obiret assidue, ipso illo denique momento quo nos
lauti cenam petebamus cum eodem illo iuvene miscebatur in venerem.   5
ergo nostra repente turbata praesentia, subitario ducta consilio, eundem
illum subiectum contegit viminea cavea, quae (fustium flexu tereti in
rectum aggerata cumulum) lacinias circumdatas, suffusa candido fumo
sulpuris, inalbabat. eoque iam (ut sibi videbatur) tutissime celato,
mensam nobiscum secura participat. interdum acerrimo gravique odore   10
sulpuris iuvenis inescatus atque obnubilatus, intercluso spiritu, diffluebat;
utque est ingenium vivacis metalli, crebras ei sternutationes commovebat.

  1 **servati pudoris**: genitive of quality/description, with *femina*.
  2 **secundo rumore** is ablative of cause, with *gloriosa*.
  3 **occulta libidine**: ablative of manner ('with hidden passion').
  3 **prorumpit in adulterum** means that she suddenly took up with a lover but suggests vividly her
leaping on to the lover.
  5 **lauti** is the perfect participle passive of *lavo*. It was usual to bathe before dinner, and here the wife
seizes her opportunity to have her lover in while the husband is off at the baths with his friend.
  5 **in venerem**: 'for the purpose of sex'.
  6–7 **eundem illum subiectum**: the reference is to the lover, and *subiectum* (from *subicio*) means
'placed under' [the cage].
  7 **viminea cavea**: ablative of instrument/means, with *contegit*.
  7–8 **fustium . . . cumulum**: 'piled up by the smooth bending of sticks so as to produce an erect
peak', i.e. made of smooth sticks bent together and rising to a peak (*tereti* is a transferred epithet: it
really belongs with *fustium* but has been transferred to *flexu*).
  11 **inescatus atque obnubilatus**: the verbs are well chosen. The first means literally 'gorged' (comically, with fumes rather than the food prepared for him), i.e. filled with. The second alludes neatly to
the clouds of sulphur fumes.
  12 **utque . . . metalli**: 'and, as is the nature of . . .' *Vivacis metalli* denotes sulphur, and it is to be
supplied as the subject of *commovebat* in 12.

*9.G At first the fuller thinks his wife is sneezing, but then he discovers the
truth. He drags out the lover and nearly kills him.*

Atque ut primum e regione mulieris pone tergum eius maritus acceperat
sonum sternutationis, quod enim putaret ab ea profectum, solito sermone
salutem ei fuerat imprecatus, et iterato rursum et frequentato saepius,
donec (rei nimietate commotus) quod res erat tandem suspicatur. et
impulsa mensa protinus remotaque cavea, producit hominem crebros   5
anhelitus aegre reflantem. inflammatusque indignatione contumeliae,
gladium flagitans, iugulare moriturum gestiebat, ni (respecto communi
periculo) vix eum ab impetu furioso cohibuissem, asseverans brevi
absque noxa nostri suapte inimicum eius violentia sulpuris periturum.
nec suadela mea sed ipsius rei necessitate lenitus, quippe iam semivivum,   10

illum in proximum deportat angiportum. tum uxorem eius tacite suasi ac
denique persuasi, secederet paululum atque ultra limen tabernae ad
quampiam tantisper familiarem sibi mulierem, quoad spatio fervens
mariti sedaretur animus (qui, tanto calore tantaque rabie perculsus, non
erat dubius aliquid etiam de se suaque coniuge tristius profecto cogitare). 15
talium contubernalis epularum taedio fugatus, larem reveni meum.'

1 **ut**: 'when'.

1 **eius** refers to the wife and goes with *tergum*.

2 **sonum sternutationis**: the sigmatism (frequency of *s*) mimics the sound of sneezing.

2 **quod...profectum**: *quod enim* (a colloquial expression) means 'because, of course'. After *putaret* the construction is accusative (understand *sonum*) and infinitive (supply *esse* with *profectum*).

2–3 **solito...imprecatus**: *fuerat imprecatus = imprecatus erat* (a sort of double pluperfect, common in later Latin). It was unlucky for someone to sneeze during a meal, so the fuller wishes his wife good health, using the customary term (*salve*; like our 'bless you!').

3 **iterato...saepius**: understand *sono sternutationis* with the two participles, and *salutem imprecatus est* with the two adverbs (the fuller keeps on wishing his wife good health as the sneezes continue).

4 **quod res erat**: 'what the situation was', i.e. what was really going on (*quod = id quod*).

7 **iugulare moriturum**: supply *eum* (referring to the lover). The future participle of *morior* means that the lover was about to die anyway, and the (rather smug) juxtaposition of the two verbs by the baker here makes the fuller seem somewhat silly.

7–8 **ni...cohibuissem**: understand before this *et iugulavisset eum* ('and he would have killed him, if I had not...'). *Communi periculo* refers to the legal danger to the fuller as a murderer and to the baker as an accomplice.

9 **noxa nostri**: 'wrongdoing on our part'.

9 **violentia...periturum**: *violentia* is ablative of cause; supply *esse* with *periturum* (future infinitive in indirect statement).

10 **ipsius rei necessitate**: i.e. the force of the circumstances.

10 **quippe iam semivivum**: *quippe* means 'as being' and the whole phrase goes with *illum* in 11 (= the lover).

12 **secederet**: the omission of *ut* with the indirect command after *persuadeo* is very rare.

12 **ultra...tabernae**: i.e. outside their home (which combines living space for them with the fuller's workshop).

13 **tantisper** goes with *quoad* (='until such time as').

13 **spatio**: ablative of instrument/means, with *sedaretur*.

14 **perculsus** is from *percello*.

14–15 **non erat dubius...cogitare**: 'he was not doubtful to be planning something' means that he was undoubtedly planning it.

16 **taedio** with the genitive means 'disgust at'.

9.H The baker's wife feigns outrage at this story, but urges him to go to bed, so she can release her lover. The baker, however, is hungry and asks for a meal. Lucius wonders how he can expose the lover.

Haec recensente pistore, iamdudum procax et temeraria mulier verbis
exsecrantibus fullonis illius detestabatur uxorem: illam perfidam, illam
impudicam, denique universi sexus grande dedecus, quae (suo pudore

postposito, torique genialis calcato foedere) larem mariti lupanari
maculasset infamia, iamque (perdita nuptae dignitate) prostitutae sibi   5
nomen asciverit. addebat et tales oportere vivas exuri feminas. et tamen
taciti vulneris et suae sordidae conscientiae commonita, quo maturius
stupratorem suum tegminis cruciatu liberaret, identidem suadebat
maritum temperius quieti decedere. at ille, utpote intercepta cena
profugus et prorsus ieienus, mensam potius comiter postulabat.   10
apponebat ei propere, quamvis invita, mulier quippini destinatam alii.

    Sed mihi penita carpebantur praecordia et praecedens facinus et
praesentem deterrimae feminae constantiam cogitanti; mecumque sedulo
deliberabam si quo modo possem (detectis ac revelatis fraudibus)
auxilium meo perhibere domino, illumque (qui ad instar testudinis   15
alveum succubabat) depulso tegmine cunctis palam facere.

> **2–3 illam . . . dedecus**: indirect statement begins here. Understand a verb of saying before these
> words, and supply *esse* as the infinitive in the three phrases (which form an outraged tricolon crescendo).
>
> **4 lupanari**: the adjective first occurs here and so is emphatic.
>
> **6 addebat** means 'she also said' and is followed by indirect statement ('it was right that . . . ').
>
> **7 vulneris** denotes the woman's passion (the image is of a wound inflicted by one of Cupid's
> arrows).
>
> **7 quo maturius**: purpose clauses containing a comparative adverb are regularly introduced by *quo*
> rather than *ut*.
>
> **9 temperius**: i.e. earlier than usual.
>
> **9 quieti**: dative of purpose ('for the purpose of sleep', i.e. to sleep).
>
> **11 apponebat**: understand as the object *cenam*, with which *quippini destinatam alii* goes. *Alii*
> (dative) refers to the lover.
>
> **12–13 mihi** is possessive dative (with *praecordia*), and *cogitanti* agrees with it. The participle governs
> two objects (linked by *et . . . et* = 'both . . . and'). *Constantiam* denotes persistence in wrongdoing. All
> the alliteration and assonance (of *-ae*) fits with indignation.
>
> **14 si quo modo**: 'whether in some way'.
>
> **15–16 illumque . . . cunctis palam facere**: 'and expose him [i.e. the lover] to all'.

*9.1 When Lucius is taken off to drink he stamps on the lover's protruding
fingers, making him give himself away. The baker calms the lover down
and announces that he will share him with his wife.*

Sic erili contumelia me cruciatum tandem caelestis respexit providentia.
nam senex claudus, cui nostra tutela permissa fuerat, universa nos
iumenta (id hora iam postulante) ad lacum proximum bibendi causa
gregatim prominabat. quae res optatissimam mihi vindictae
sumministravit occasionem. namque praetergrediens observatos   5
extremos adulteri digitos (qui per angustias cavi tegminis prominebant)
obliquata atque infesta ungula compressos usque ad summam minutiem

contero, donec intolerabili dolore commotus, sublato flebili clamore,
repulsoque et abiecto alveo, conspectui profano redditus, scaenam
propudiosae mulieris patefecit. nec tamen pistor damno pudicitiae   10
magnopere commotus exsangui pallore trepidantem puerum serena
fronte et propitiata facie commulcens incipit:

'Nihil triste de me tibi, fili, metuas. non sum barbarus, nec agresti
morum squalore praeditus; nec ad exemplum naccinae truculentiae
sulpuris te letali fumo necabo; ac ne iuris quidem severitate (lege de   15
adulteriis) ad discrimen vocabo capitis tam venustum tamque pulchellum
puellum, sed plane cum uxore mea partiario tractabo. nec herciscundae
familae, sed communi dividundo formula dimicabo, ut sine ulla
controversia vel dissensione tribus nobis in uno conveniat lectulo. nam et
ipse semper cum mea coniuge tam concorditer vixi ut ex secta   20
prudentium eadem nobis ambobus placerent. sed nec aequitas ipsa
patitur habere plus auctoritatis uxorem quam maritum.'

2 **nostra tutela**: 'custody of us' (animals).

2 **permissa fuerat** = *permissa erat.*

3 **bibendi causa**: *causa* + gerund expresses purpose.

5–10 Take this long sentence bit by bit, and in particular work out which participles go with what (looking at the endings).

6 **per**: 'on account of' (the tub is not wide enough to conceal the lover entirely, so his fingertips protrude).

7 **compressos . . . minutiem**: i.e. squashed flat (*compressos* is from *comprimo*, and *usque ad* means 'all the way to').

8 **sublato** is from *tollo.*

9 **profano** means uninitiated in the adulterous pair's secret.

10 **propudiosae** was an archaic and rare word. It is also stressed by means of alliteration.

13 **fili, metuas**: vocative plus jussive subjunctive.

14 **ad**: 'in accordance with'.

15–16 **ac . . . capitis**: i.e. he will not even resort to the law and bring the boy up on a capital charge. The ablatives are of instrument/means. According to the *lex Iulia* an adulterer who was caught in the husband's house could be put to death. The baker begins here to use legal language, partly to awe the boy, and also in a playful way, reinforced by puns in 17–19 (*tracto* can mean 'fondle'; *divido* is used of sodomizing; and *convenio* is employed of copulation).

16–17 **tam . . . puellum**: the sound and repetition of words shows the baker dwelling on and savouring the lover's charms.

17 **partiario tractabo**: i.e. I will share [you].

17–18 **nec . . . dimicabo**: 'And I will fight in an action [i.e. I will bring an action] not to split up [our] household but to share common property' [i.e. the lover]. The gerundives in the dative express purpose.

19 **tribus . . . lectulo**: 'it may be agreed by us three in one bed', i.e. an agreement may be reached by them to share one bed. *Tribus nobis* is dative of the agent.

20–1 **ex secta prudentium**: 'in accordance with the principles of the wise' (many poets and philosophers recommended such concord).

22 **patitur . . . maritum**: 'allows the wife to have greater right of ownership than the husband' (the idea is that it is only fair that they should share the lover equally as joint owners).

9.J The baker takes the young adulterer to bed. The next day he tells him off, flogs him and throws him out; then he divorces his wife.

Talis sermonis blanditie cavillatum deducebat ad torum nolentem
puerum, sequentem tamen. et pudicissima illa uxore alterorsus disclusa,
solus ipse cum puero cubans gratissima corruptarum nuptiarum vindicta
perfruebatur. sed cum primum rota solis lucida diem peperit, vocatis
duobus e familia validissimis, quam altissime sublato puero, ferula nates   5
eius obverberans, 'Tu autem,' inquit 'tam mollis ac tener et admodum
puer, defraudatis amatoribus aetatis tuae flore, mulieres appetis (atque eas
liberas), et conubia lege sociata corrumpis, et intempestivum tibi nomen
adulteri vindicas?'

His et pluribus verbis compellatum et insuper affatim plagis castigatum   10
forinsecus abicit. at ille adulterorum omnium fortissimus, insperata
potitus salute, tamen (nates candidas illas noctu diuque dirruptus)
maerens profugit. nec setius pistor ille nuntium remisit uxori, eamque
protinus de sua proturbavit domo.

> 1 **cavillatum** has a passive force here only in surviving Latin.
>
> 3 **solus . . . cubans**: this looks like a witty and wicked variation on a traditional way in which wronged husbands took revenge on adulterers (the insertion up the lover's anus of a radish or mullet).
>
> 3 **gratissima . . . vindicta**: with the extensive assonance and homoeoteleuton Lucius is dwelling on and relishing this punishment.
>
> 4 **cum primum . . . peperit**: *cum primum* means 'as soon as', and *peperit* is from *pario*. *Rota solis* refers to the chariot in which the sun god traverses the sky (*rota* 'wheel' = 'chariot', a process known as synecdoche, whereby part of an object stands for the whole). The whole phrase is poetic and rather lofty, and is comically deflated in 5–6 with the caning of the bottom (a punishment of naughty schoolboys).
>
> 5 **quam altissime**: 'as high up as possible'.
>
> 7 **defraudatis . . . flore**: i.e. such a young and pretty boy should be allowing lovers to enjoy his charms (rather than chasing women).
>
> 7–8 **atque eas liberas**: i.e. and free-born ones at that (*atque* means 'and what's more').
>
> 8 **intempestivum**: 'untimely' because the boy is too young.
>
> 12 **nates . . . dirruptus**: *nates* is accusative of respect, and the boy is split as to his buttocks by anal intercourse during the preceding night and by the caning on this day (*diu* = 'by day').
>
> 13 **nuntium remisit** is the technical term for sending notice of divorce.

9.K The wife is very angry and asks a witch to use her craft to make the baker become reconciled to her or (failing that) to murder him.

At illa, praeter genuinam nequitiam contumelia etiam, quamvis iusta,
tamen altius commota atque exasperata, ad armillum revertit, et ad
familiares feminarum artes accenditur. magnaque cura requisitam

veteratricem quandam feminam (quae devotionibus ac maleficiis quidvis
efficere posse credebatur) multis exorat precibus multisque suffarcinat   5
muneribus, alterum de duobus postulans – vel rursum mitigato conciliari
marito, vel (si id nequiverit) certe larva vel aliquo diro numine immisso
violenter eius expugnari spiritum. tunc saga illa et divini potens primis
adhuc armis facinerosae disciplinae suae velitatur, et vehementer
offensum mariti flectere atque in amorem impellere conatur animum.   10
quae res cum ei sequius ac rata fuerat proveniret, indignata numinibus et
praeter praemii destinatum compendium contemptione etiam stimulata,
ipsi iam miserrimi mariti incipit imminere capiti, umbramque violenter
peremptae mulieris ad exitium eius instigare.

    1 **contumelia** refers to the insult of being expelled by the husband and is ablative of instrument/
means, with *commota atque exasperata* in 2. The insult was justified (*iusta*) but still infuriated the wife.
    4–5 **quidvis . . . posse**: *quidvis* is the object of *efficere* (and that verb depends on *posse*).
    6–8 **conciliari . . . expugnari**: these infinitives depend on *postulans* in 6: she is asking either for
herself to be reconciled to her husband . . . or for his life to be destroyed.
    7 **nequiverit**: future perfect of *nequeo*; the witch is subject here.
    7 **larva . . . immisso**: the participle applies to *larva* as well as *numine* but agrees in gender with its
nearest noun. *Aliquo diro numine* (= a ghost, any of the gods of the Underworld etc.) is deliberately
vague (and so mysterious and unsettling).
    8 **saga . . . potens**: 'that witch who had power over the supernatural'.
    8–9 **primis . . . velitatur**: *primis* ('first') means 'preliminary' here, and the military language is
threatening.
    9–10 **vehementer . . . mariti**: these words go with *animum* in 10.
    11 **quae . . . proveniret**: 'when this went for her otherwise than she had thought' (*quae res* belongs
inside the *cum* clause; *rata fuerat* = *rata erat* and is from *reor*).
    11 **numinibus** (dative with *indignata*) denotes the magic divinities she was using (and *contemptione*
in 12 refers to their contempt).
    13 **ipsi . . . capiti**: *ipsi* is dative with *capiti* ('his very life'). The sound effects here seem both mournful
and dramatic.
    14 **peremptae** is from *perimo*.

*9.L The reader may wonder how Lucius knows what the wife and witch
were up to, so he will explain. A strange woman suddenly appears in the
bakery and takes the baker off to his bedroom. He is gone for a long
time and is later found dead there by his workers.*

Sed forsitan lector scrupulosus reprehendens narratum meum sic
argumentaberis: 'Unde autem tu, astutule asine, intra terminos pistrini
contentus, quid secreto (ut affirmas) mulieres gesserint scire potuisti?'
accipe igitur quemadmodum homo curiosus iumenti faciem sustinens
cuncta quae in perniciem pistoris mei gesta sunt cognovi.   5

Diem ferme circa mediam repente intra pistrinum mulier reatu miraque tristitie deformis apparuit, flebili centunculo semiamicta, nudis et intectis pedibus, lurore buxeo macieque foedata; et discerptae comae semicanae (sordentes inspersu cineris) pleramque eius anteventulae contegebant faciem. haec talis, manu pistori clementer iniecta, quasi   **10** quippiam secreto collocutura, in suum sibi cubiculum deducit eum et, adducta fore, quam diutissime demoratur. sed cum esset iam confectum omne frumentum quod inter manus opifices tractaverant, necessarioque peti deberet aliud, servuli (cubiculum propter astantes) dominum vocabant, operique supplementum postulabant. atque ut illis saepicule et   **15** intervocaliter clamantibus nullus respondit dominus, iam forem pulsare validius et, quod diligentissime fuerat oppessulata, maius peiusque aliquid opinantes, nisu valido reducto vel diffracto cardine, tandem patefaciunt aditum. nec uspiam reperta illa muliere, vident e quodam tigillo constrictum iamque exanimem pendere dominum; eumque nodo   **20** cervicis absolutum detractumque summis plangoribus summisque lamentationibus atque ultimo lavacro procurant; peractisque feralibus officiis, frequenti prosequente comitatu, tradunt sepulturae.

   1 **lector scrupulosus** is in apposition to the subject of *argumentaberis* ('you, as a very careful reader').

   3 **contentus**: from *contineo*.

   3 **quid … gesserint**: this is an indirect question depending on *scire*. *Gesserint* is perfect subjunctive of *gero* (*gesta sunt* in 5 is from the same verb).

   4 **homo curiosus** is in apposition to the subject of *cognovi* in 5.

   5 **cognovi**: the indicative (rather than subjunctive) in an indirect question was colloquial and common in early Comic writers.

   6–7 **reatu … tristitie**: ablatives of cause with *deformis*.

   7 **semiamicta** is the first of several rarities (also *semicanus* and the singular of *plerusque* and *anteventulae* in 9) which suit and bring out the woman's singular appearance.

   7–8 **nudis … pedibus**: ablative of description.

   8–9 People tore their hair and poured ashes over it in mourning, when somebody died and also when they had been put on trial (either or both may be to the point here – this is part of the mystery).

   11 **quippiam**: neuter accusative singular of the pronoun *quispiam,* and object of *collocutura* (future participle of *colloquor*).

   11 **suum sibi** means literally 'his own of himself'. The redundant possessive dative with *suus* was archaic and common in Apuleius.

   13–14 **necessario … aliud**: 'and other [grain] had to be asked for out of necessity' (*peti* is present infinitive passive of *peto*).

   14 **cubiculum propter**: the preposition governs *cubiculum*.

   15 **ut**: 'when'.

   16 **nullus … dominus**: the expression is well chosen as the master exists no more.

   16 **pulsare**: historic infinitive (unusually on its own among all the finite verb forms).

   17 **quod … fuerat oppessulata**: *quod* means 'because' and the verb is in the pluperfect indicative.

17–18 **maius . . . opinantes**: 'imagining something quite serious and bad' (*maius* is the comparative of *magnus*).

18 **nisu valido**: ablative of instrument/means.

20–21 **nodo cervicis**: i.e. the noose around his neck.

22 **ultimo lavacro**: i.e. the washing of the corpse before the funeral.

23 **tradunt**: understand *illum* as the object.

9.M *The baker's daughter appears, warned of what has happened by her father's ghost. After nine days of mourning she sells the estate.*

Die sequenti filia eius accurrit e proximo castello (in quod pridem denupserat), maesta atque crines pendulos quatiens et interdum pugnis obtundens ubera. quae (nullo quidem domus infortunium nuntiante) cuncta cognorat; sed ei per quietem obtulit sese flebilis patris sui facies (adhuc nodo revincta cervice), eique totum novercae scelus aperuit de 5 adulterio, de maleficio, et quemadmodum larvatus ad inferos demeasset. ea cum se diutino plangore cruciasset, concursu familiarium cohibita, tandem pausam luctui fecit. iamque nono die rite completis apud tumulum sollemnibus, familiam supellectilemque et omnia iumenta ad hereditariam deducit auctionem. tunc unum larem varie dispergit 10 venditionis incertae licentiosa fortuna. me denique ipsum pauperculus quidam hortulanus comparat.

1–2 **in . . . denupserat**: i.e. she had married someone from the *castellum* and gone to live there with him.

4 **cognorat** is the syncopated form of *cognoverat*.

4 **sed** picks up *nullo . . . nuntiante* (no person had told her; instead her father's ghost gave her the news).

4 **obtulit** is from *offero*.

8–9 **nono . . . sollemnibus**: offerings of food and drink were made at the grave on the ninth day.

10–11 **tunc . . . fortuna**: the rather pompous expression here (with chiasmus of nouns and adjectives) is undercut by the humble new owner in the next sentence.

APPRECIATION

9.D–M *(Metamorphoses 9.22–31).*

There is pervasive and diverting irony here. Most obviously the baker criticizes the fuller's wife (for being unfaithful and hiding a lover) before his own wife (who is also unfaithful and is hiding a lover), and he runs for refuge from the scandal at the fuller's house to his own equally scandalous house. All that is compounded by his wife's brazen criticism of the fuller's wife for crimes exactly the same as hers in 9.H. Less obviously, when his wife's lover is discovered, the baker (who disapproves so strongly of adultery) takes revenge for his wife's intended adultery by having an actual night of adulterous sex with the boy himself; and after she is driven out, the baker's guilty wife is actually angry and outraged, and (after scorning it) now wants her husband's love for her revived. Also more subtle is the irony at 9.F–J in connection with the coming premature death of the baker by asphyxiation (hanging). If you examine those chapters you will find various examples of this, such as the baker talking glibly about the lover of the fuller's wife having trouble with his breathing and being about to die in 9.F and 9.G, and accusing his own wife's lover of prematurity (in claiming the title of adulterer) in 9.J. Lastly there is the attitude of the narrator of this tale himself: after being amused by the adultery at 9.A–C, Lucius criticizes the baker's wife for her liaison (because she maltreated him and the baker was kind to him), and the same Lucius who was so interested in magic earlier and actually dabbled in it (hence his present form as an ass) reproaches the wife for turning to witchcraft.

As part of the entertainment we find here a complex of stories about adulterers surprised by husbands. The tale of the baker comes after those of the storage jar (9.A–C) and Philesitherus and the slippers (as passed on by the old woman to the baker's wife). On top of the comic improbability of history repeating itself like this, our inventive and ingenious author is setting himself a challenge (to give life, variety and novelty to the surprised adulterer tale when told for a third time). He rings the changes variously. For a start the baker's narrative at 9.F–G (on the fuller's wife) itself contains an anecdote of this type embedded in it (a fourth surprised adulterer story!), as told by one protagonist to another (the baker to his wife) without realizing its relevance to himself. This time Lucius is a spectator and intervenes significantly. In contrast to the earlier two accounts, here the husband is ultimately not taken in, but actually makes a fool of the lover and has sex with him himself. And at 9.Kff. there are new characters (the witch and the ghosts), a new (dark) tone, and a whole new direction (as this now becomes a tale of revenge, witchcraft and murder). You can find many more dexterous and engrossing variations like this on your own.

We have already met embedded narrative like 9.F–G (on the fuller's wife), at 7.A–B (Tlepolemus' fabricated anecdote about Haemus, which mirrored so closely the outer story). We begin to wonder if this same technique of *mise en abyme* might not be operating here too, when we see the baker telling his own unfaithful, concealing wife about the fuller's unfaithful wife concealing her lover, although the cleverness and audacity of the baker's wife and Philesitherus' dodge with the slippers mean that the baker might be taken in, so we read on eager to see how things develop. In fact the inner tale does seem to be paralleled by the outer one, as the hiding-place is exposed, the baker reacts mildly again, and his wife and her lover are unable to retrieve the situation and are ejected. As a result many will assume that the baker's story reaches its close at the end of 9.J. But there is false *mise en abyme* and false closure here, because the narrative continues with the baker killed and his wife ultimately triumphant, so that 9.Kff. come as a surprise with great impact (on surprise in Apuleius see further Anderson 1982, 77; James 1987, 235ff.; and Harrison 1999, 209).

But that is not the last of Apuleius' tricks. When we reach the real ending, we find that it is a deliberately unsatisfying and teasing close. Various questions are left unanswered in 9.L and M. For instance, why is the female ghost in 9.L sad and in mourning? How exactly was the baker hanged? Why doesn't his ghost in the dream tell his daughter about sodomizing the lover and beating his bottom (do we have an embarrassed ghost here?)? Why doesn't the daughter go after the baker's wife (a wicked stepmother guilty of adultery and terrible murder)? Is the daughter just more interested in getting the money from the auction than she is in justice? Or could she even have been set up by the baker's wife to get them the proceeds of the estate (the daughter's sudden appearance at the bakery as a sad and mourning figure recalls the female ghost of 9.L and so represents a link with the baker's wife)? This is perplexing and irritating, and if you re-examine 9.L–M, you will find more puzzles for yourselves.

Before long Lucius is stolen from the gardener by a soldier. In book 10 he sells him to two slaves (a baker and a cook), and when the ass is discovered eating their food and accepts some wine as well, their master adopts him as a guest at his table and Lucius becomes famous. A woman bribes his keeper to let her sleep with Lucius, and when his master finds out, he decides to put the ass on display in a public show, having sex with a condemned murderess. Horrified at the prospect, Lucius bolts from the show to a beach nearby, where he falls asleep. In book 11 he wakes to see the moon rise from the sea, identifies it with the Egyptian goddess Isis and prays to her.

11.A *Lucius prays for the restoration of his human form, then falls asleep and has a vision in which Isis promises that a priest of hers will have the restorative roses in her sacred procession the next day.*

'Regina caeli, tu meis iam nunc extremis aerumnis subsiste, tu fortunam collapsam affirma, tu saevis exanclatis casibus pausam pacemque tribue. sit satis laborum, sit satis periculorum. depelle quadripedis diram faciem,

11 The Capitoline Isis.

redde me conspectui meorum, redde me meo Lucio.' fusis precibus, et
astructis miseris lamentationibus, rursus mihi marcentem animum sopor   5
oppressit. ecce pelago medio (venerandos diis etiam vultus attollens)
emergit divina facies. corona multiformis sublimem destrinxerat
verticem, dextra laevaque sulcis insurgentium viperarum cohibita. tunica
multicolor nunc albo candore lucida, nunc croceo flore lutea, nunc roseo
rubore flammida. palla nigerrima splendescens atro nitore; per intextam   10
extremitatem stellae dispersae coruscabant, luna flammeos spirabat ignes.
talis ac tanta, spirans Arabiae felicia germina, divina me voce dignata est:

'En adsum, tuis commota, Luci, precibus, summa numinum, prima
caelitum. adsum tuos miserata casus, adsum favens et propitia. mitte iam
fletus et lamentationes omitte. iam tibi illucescit dies salutaris. ergo igitur   15
imperiis meis animum intende. diem qui ex ista nocte nascetur mihi
nuncupavit religio, quo (sedatis hibernis tempestatibus) navigabili iam

pelago rudem dedicantes carinam, primitias commeatus libant mei
sacerdotes. meo monitu sacerdos in procinctu pompae roseam manu
dextera sistro cohaerentem gestabit coronam. incunctanter ergo dimotis   20
turbulis alacer continuare pompam, et clementer (velut manum sacerdotis
osculabundus) rosis decerptis, beluae istius corio te protinus exue.'

Somno protinus absolutus, pavore et gaudio ac dein sudore nimio
permixtus exsurgo.

1–2 The repetition of appeals, words and sounds here makes for gravity and vehemence.

3 **sit**: jussive subjunctive ('let there be enough of . . .', i.e. let there be no more of . . .).

4 **meorum** is a noun here ('my loved ones').

4 **redde . . . Lucio**: i.e. restore me to my form as the man Lucius.

4 **fusis** is from *fundo*.

6 **pelago medio** is ablative ('from') with *emergit* in 7.

6 **venerandos . . . attollens**: *diis* is dative plural of *deus* (dative of agent with the gerundive), and *vultus* is plural for singular.

8–10 **tunica . . . flammida**: understand *erat illi* ('there was to her', i.e. she had) here (and with *palla* in line 10). Note the verbal exuberance and solemn sound here (the solemnity continues in the goddess's speech below).

12 **spirans . . . germina**: Isis' breath was as fragrant as the famous perfumes of Arabia.

16 **diem . . . nascetur**: i.e. the next day.

17 **quo**: '[the day] on which'. The reference is to a festival called the *Isidis Navigium*, which celebrated the resumption of sailing after winter ended.

18 **primitias** is in apposition to *carinam* ('offering it as first-fruits of . . .'). A new ship was dedicated to the sea, being regarded as the first-fruits (first offering) of the new sailing season.

19 **meo monitu**: 'at my command' (ablative of cause).

20 **sistro** is dative with *cohaerentem*. The garland of roses will be attached to the *sistrum* (a rattle, usually made of bronze, carried by worshippers of Isis).

21 **continuare**: second person singular of the imperative.

11.B In the procession the next day Lucius sees the priest with the roses, eats them and gets back his human form. The priest tells him to join the procession (so all can see that he has been saved by Isis).

Salutem meam gerens sacerdos appropinquat, dextera proferens sistrum
deae, mihi coronam. nec tamen inclementi me cursu proripui (verens
scilicet ne repentino quadripedis impetu religionis quietus turbaretur
ordo), sed placido gradu cunctabundus, paulatim obliquato corpore, sane
divinitus decedente populo, sensim irrepo. at sacerdos confestim restitit   5
et, ultro porrecta dextera, ob os meum coronam exhibuit. tunc ego
trepidans coronam avido ore susceptam cupidissime devoravi. nec me
fefellit caeleste promissum: protinus mihi delabitur deformis et ferina
facies. ac primo squalens pilus defluit, ac dehinc cutis crassa tenuatur,
manus non iam pedes sunt, cervix procera cohibetur, aures enormes   10

12 Lucius turns back into a human.

repetunt pristinam parvitatem, et (quae me potissimum cruciabat ante)
cauda nusquam.

Sacerdos sic effatur: 'Ad serviles delapsus voluptates, curiositatis
improsperae sinistrum praemium reportasti. sed Fortunae caecitas, dum
te pessimis periculis discruciat, ad religiosam beatitudinem improvida   15
produxit malitia. comitare pompam deae sospitatricis. videant irreligiosi,
videant et errorem suum recognoscant. ecce pristinis aerumnis absolutus,
Isidis magnae providentia gaudens, Lucius de sua Fortuna triumphat. te
iam nunc obsequio religionis nostrae dedica et ministerii iugum subi. nam
cum coeperis deae servire, tunc magis senties fructum tuae libertatis.'   20

    3 ne (meaning 'that') introduces a positive fear clause.

    3–4 religionis quietus ... ordo: 'the orderly sequence of the rite' refers to the procession consisting
of various groups of devotees parading in due order and performing various ritual acts.

    8 fefellit is the perfect indicative of *fallo*.

    12 cauda nusquam: understand *est*.

    13 serviles ... voluptates denotes Lucius' enslavement to lust for the slave Photis.

    13 curiositatis refers to his curiosity about magic ('rewarded' by the metamorphosis into an ass).

14–16 **Fortunae . . . malitia**: i.e. in spite of the blindness and malice of Fortune, her persecution of Lucius has led unintentionally to a state of religious blessedness (the connection with Isis).

16 **comitare** is the imperative.

16–17 **videant . . . recognoscant**: jussive subjunctives.

19 **obsequio** is dative ('to subservience to . . . ').

19 **ministerii** denotes service to Isis.

19 **subi**: imperative of *subeo*.

20 **libertatis**: note the paradox – service to the goddess means freedom (from malicious Fortune etc.).

APPRECIATION

11.A– B (Metamorphoses 11.2–7, 12–15).

On the overall interpretation of book 11 of the novel see Introduction section 3. We have here a series of arresting surprises, as the work now seems to take a serious turn, with Lucius' sudden religiosity (in the vehement prayer), the extraordinary vision of the majestic goddess, her solemn and compassionate words, promising release for Lucius, the fulfilment of that promise in due course (joyfully dwelled on, as his human form is finally recovered) and the priest's speech, which offers a drastic revision of all that has gone before (making it a story of redemption, about a misguided sinner who suffered grievously until rescued by the merciful goddess Isis).

That is the impression which Apuleius produces here, and works hard to produce, but actually it is all part of an elaborate tease. It becomes clear subsequently that we are being misled here, and with hindsight one can see that there are some disquieting elements which the vast majority of readers overlook. Apart from the fact that one cannot necessarily trust a vision, Isis' highly impressive speech in 11.A is immediately followed by Lucius' reaction – fear, joy and *sweat*, in fact *lots* of sweat. There is bathos there (as well as the comic picture of a heavily sweating ass). Also at 11.A.16ff. Isis tells Lucius to pay close attention: he must join her procession briskly and without hesitation, and take the restorative roses gently, as if kissing the priest's hand. But at 11.B.2ff. there is stress on the slowness with which he joins the procession, he makes no pretence of kissing the man's hand, and he gobbles down the roses very greedily (i.e. not gently). If Lucius does not have the control and intelligence to follow careful instructions on a matter of supreme importance, one must wonder how reliable he is as a reporter and interpreter of his religious experiences. Then there is the priest's speech at 11.B.13ff., which provides the edifying new direction but also, rather jarringly, makes it clear that the restored Lucius is to be made use of for propaganda purposes, to drum up converts, and suggests that he will simply exchange his earlier slavery to pleasure (13) for another form of slavery, to the goddess (18–20). Amusingly the naive Lucius fails to see any of this, even while narrating it. Can you spot any more disquieting elements in the following selections?

Lucius joins the procession and watches the consecration of the richly decorated boat filled with precious offerings. Hearing the news of his sudden appearance there, his friends arrive from home with gifts for him. He then rents a house close to Isis' temple and spends his time contemplating her statue and worshipping the goddess.

11.C *After further visions, Lucius is finally initiated into the mysteries of Isis. Then at her command he sets off for home.*

Nec fuit nox una vel quies aliqua visu deae monituque ieiuna, sed crebris imperiis me censebat initiari. sacerdotem saepissime conveneram, petens ut me arcanis initiaret. at ille anxium mihi permulcebat animum: nam diem quo quisque possit initiari deae nutu demonstrari; sumptus etiam caerimoniis necessarios simili praecepto destinari. nec me fefellit deae   5
potentis benignitas salutaris, sed noctis obscurae non obscuris imperiis monuit advenisse diem mihi semper optabilem, quantoque sumptu deberem procurare supplicamentis. discussa quiete, protinus ad receptaculum sacerdotis contendo. et senex comissimus ducit me protinus ad fores aedis. de opertis adyti profert libros litteris ignorabilibus   10
praenotatos. indidem mihi praedicat quae forent ad usum teletae necessario praeparanda. ea protinus naviter et aliquanto liberalius (partim ipse, partim per meos socios) coemenda procuro.

   Iam dies aderat divino destinatus vadimonio, et me sacerdos deducit ad sacrarii penetralia. accessi confinium mortis et, calcato Proserpinae   15
limine, remeavi; nocte media vidi solem candido coruscantem lumine; deos inferos et deos superos accessi coram et adoravi. mane factum est, et perfectis sollemnibus processi, et umeris dependebat pretiosa chlamyda. exhinc suaves epulae.

   Tandem deae monitu pro meo modulo supplicue gratis persolutis   20
domuitionem comparo. complexus sacerdotem, veniam postulabam quod eum condigne munerari nequirem. tandem digredior et recta larem revisurus meum contendo.

> 3 **nam** introduces the priest's words in indirect statement.
> 5 **simili**: i.e. by Isis.

5 **fefellit** is from *fallo*.

6 **noctis obscurae** ('of' = 'during') goes with *imperiis*.

7 **quantoque sumptu**: the construction changes here from indirect statement to indirect question.

11–12 **quae . . . praeparanda**: i.e. the necessary preparations for the rite of initiation (*forent* is imperfect subjunctive of *sum*).

12 **aliquanto liberalius**: 'rather extravagantly'.

13 **coemenda**: *procuro* + gerundive = arrange for a thing to be done.

15–17 **accessi . . . adoravi**: this is a mysterious and exalted account of the experience of initiation, in which the initiate underwent rebirth and encountered various Egyptian divinities (including the sun god). Proserpina (line 15) was the queen of the Underworld.

17 **mane factum est**: *mane* is a noun here, and *factum est* acts as the perfect tense of *fio*.

20 **monitu**: ablative of cause ('at the command').

20 **gratis** is an alternative form for the ablative plural *gratiis*.

23 **revisurus**: future participle of *revideo*.

11.D *A few days later Isis sends Lucius to Rome and he becomes a worshipper in her shrine there. Then he is told by means of visions that he must be initiated into the rites of the god Osiris as well.*

Paucisque post diebus (deae potentis instinctu) nave conscensa Romam versus profectionem dirigo. sacrosanctam istam civitatem accedo. nec ullum tam praecipuum mihi exinde studium fuit quam cotidie supplicare summo numini reginae Isidis. eram cultor denique assiduus, fani quidem advena, religionis autem indigena.

Ecce sol annum compleverat, et quietem meam rursus interpellat numinis benefici cura pervigilis, et rursus teletae commonet. mirabar quid temptaret, quid pronuntiaret. quidni? plenissime iamdudum videbar

5

13 Procession of Isis worshippers.

initiatus. ac dum religiosum scrupulum partim apud meum sensum
disputo, partim sacratorum consiliis examino, novum mirumque   10
comperior: deae me tantum sacris imbutum, at magni dei Osiris necdum
sacris illustratum. proxima nocte vidi quendam de sacratis qui denuntiaret
epulas. is, ut agnitionem mihi scilicet certo signo sumministraret, sinistri
pedis talo paululum reflexo, cunctabundo incedebat vestigio. sublata est
post tam manifestam deum voluntatem ambiguitatis tota caligo. et, deae   15
matutinis perfectis salutationibus, de pastophoris unum conspexi statim
praeter indicium pedis cetero statu nocturnae imagini congruentem,
quem Asinium Marcellum vocitari cognovi postea. nec moratus conveni
protinus eum, sane nec ipsum futuri sermonis ignarum. nam sibi visus est
quiete proxima, dum magno deo coronas exaptaret, de eius ore audisse   20
mitti Madaurensem admodum pauperem, cui statim sua sacra deberet
ministrare; nam ipsi grande compendium sua comparari providentia.

1 **post** is the adverb.
1 **instinctu**: ablative of cause.
2 **versus** (the preposition) governs *Romam*.
2 **sacrosanctam**: because the cult of Isis was prominent there.
2–4 **nec . . . Isidis**: i.e. his chief occupation there was worship of Isis.
4–5 **quidem . . . autem**: these two words mark the contrast (he was a stranger to Isis' shrine in Rome but no stranger to her cult generally).
8 **videbar**: understand *mihi* (i.e. he thought that he had long since been fully initiated).
11 **tantum**: 'only'.
11–12 **imbutum . . . illustratum**: supply *esse* (these are infinitives in indirect statement). The Egyptian god Osiris was the husband of Isis, and his cult was connected to (but still distinct from) hers. *Necdum* here = *nondum*.
12 **vidi**: in a dream.
12 **denuntiaret**: the subjunctive (instead of indicative) here is odd.
14 **sublata est** is from *tollo* ('remove').
15 **deum**: genitive plural.
17 **cetero statu**: ablative of respect.
19 **sane . . . ignarum**: i.e. he knew what Lucius was going to say (because he had dreamed about him).
20 **proxima**: i.e. on the previous night.
20 **audisse** is followed by indirect statement.
21 **sua** here and in 22 refers to Osiris, while *ipsi* denotes Asinius.

11.E *Lucius has to sell his clothes to pay for this initiation. Then he is told to undergo a third initiation, and has his doubts, but acquiesces after more visions and finally is enrolled among the priests at Rome.*

Desponsus sacris, sumptuum tenuitate contra votum meum retardabar.
tamen identidem numinis premebar instantia. iamque saepicule

stimulatus, postremo iussus, veste ipsa mea (quamvis parvula) distracta,
sufficientem corrasi summulam. ergo principalis dei nocturnis orgiis
illustratus, plena iam fiducia germanae religionis obsequium divinum   5
frequentabam. quae res summum peregrinationi meae tribuebat solacium
nec minus etiam victum uberiorem sumministrabat, quaesticulo forensi
nutrito.

  Post pauculum tempus inopinatis et usquequaque mirificis imperiis
deum rursus interpellor et cogor tertiam quoque teletam sustinere. nec   10
levi cura sollicitus, mecum ipse cogitationes exercitius agitabam:
'Nimirum perperam vel minus plene consuluerunt in me sacerdos
uterque.' et hercules iam de fide quoque eorum opinari coeptabam
sequius. quo me cogitationis aestu fluctuantem sic instruxit nocturna
divinatione clemens imago: 'Assidua numinum dignatione laetus, capesse   15
gaudium, et exsulta ter futurus quod alii vel semel vix conceditur.'
instructum teletae comparo largitus; nec hercules me sumptuum paenituit
(liberali deum providentia iam stipendiis forensibus bellule fotum).

  Denique post dies pauculos Osiris me per quietem recipere visus est. ac
in collegium me pastophorum suorum allegit. denique, quaqua raso   20
capillo, collegii vetustissimi et sub illis Sullae temporibus conditi munia
(non obumbrato vel obtecto calvitio, sed quoquoversus obvio) gaudens
obibam.

---

  1 **sumptuum:** *sumptus* in the sense of 'resources' is very rare and so the word directs the reader's
attention to the financial aspect.

  5 **plena . . . fiducia:** ablative of manner.

  5 **germanae:** i.e. related to the cult of Isis.

  7 **nec minus** = 'and furthermore'.

  7–8 **quaesticulo . . . nutrito:** i.e. Osiris ensured that Lucius was successful in the job of advocate
that he took on while in Rome, so that he made some money at it.

  10 **deum:** genitive plural (look out for this genitive form below).

  10–11 **nec levi** = *et magna* (litotes).

  12–13 **vel . . . uterque:** *minus* = *non*; *consuluerunt* is plural because its subject (*sacerdos
uterque*), although singular, implies plurality; and *in me* means 'in my case'.

  15 **dignatione** is ablative of cause.

  16 **ter . . . conceditur** refers to the three initiations. *Futurus* is the future participle of *sum*; *quod* =
id quod ('something which'), and *alii* is dative singular.

  18 **providentia:** ablative of cause ('thanks to').

  18 **fotum** is from *foveo*.

  20–21 **raso capillo:** ritual shaving of the head was customary for priests of Isis and Osiris.

  21 **Sullae:** the famous Roman dictator was born round about 138 BC and died in 79 BC.

  22 **quoquoversus obvio:** i.e. openly shown to people wherever he went (some Romans despised
this ritual baldness).

APPRECIATION

11.C–E (Metamorphoses 11.19, 21–30).

In 11.C the elaborate tease (even longer in the original) continues. There is a solemn and reverent build-up to the awesome initiation, and then with the return home of Lucius, who has now done all that Isis and her priest asked of him, we now seem to have reached the obvious and logical end of the narrative, especially as the *Onos* (on which see Introduction section 3) closes with the hero going home and thanking the gods. However, this is in fact not the conclusion; and with hindsight one can see some disquieting elements in 11.C too (e.g. the emphasis on expenditure and the frequency of visions, both of which are expanded in the following chapters).

The tease is finally and clearly exposed at 11.D–E, as Apuleius has more fun at our expense. At 11.D.1–5 Lucius goes off to Rome and becomes established there as a worshipper of Isis, and again we seem to have arrived at the end. But then after further visions he is initiated into the cult of Osiris too and is helped by the god to earn a living at Rome, so again the story seems complete. But then after yet more visions Lucius undergoes a third initiation, and the book really does conclude, at last. One becomes more and more irritated by all the false endings and extra initiations. One also becomes more and more suspicious: Lucius has so many (very convenient) visions; the financial aspect of the cults is often mentioned; Lucius himself expresses misgivings, twice (11.D.7ff., 11.E.9ff.); and the priest Asinius (whose name suggests *asinus*, meaning 'ass' and 'dolt'!) is a dubious character (crippled people were not normally admitted to Egyptian priesthoods; and he incorrectly intimates that the Greek Lucius comes from Madaura in north Africa). One is led by all of this to conclude that the novel's foolish and gullible hero is being deceived by others and is deceiving himself, and that he has become the victim of a pair of mercenary and exploitative cults. Once you see the point, you also see how funny it is for Lucius to act as he does and to pass on so glibly an account of his naive actions. The final sentence sends us away with a picture of him with the shaven head of a priest, and of a buffoon too (see Winkler 1985, 225ff.), and enrolled in a priesthood founded in the days of Sulla, who was famous for being rapacious, venal and deceitful, and (in line with the faking here) was said to have associated with actors and to have loved the theatre (see Murgatroyd 2004, 321).

VOCABULARY

~

[Words marked with an asterisk should be known by or intelligible to a student after two years of Latin, so memorize any that you have to look up more than twice.]

*a(b) (+ abl) by, from, in respect of, as a result of

*abeo -ire -i(v)i -itum go away

*abicio -cere -eci -ectum throw off, throw out, give up, drop

abigo -igere -egi -actum drive away, fend off

abluo -uere -ui -utum wash

abnuo -ere -i deny, repudiate

abominor -ari -atus sum (+ dat) wish on

*abrumpo -umpere -upi -uptum break

abscido -dere -di -sum amputate, cut off

abscondo -ere -i -itum hide

absolvo -vere -vi -utum release (from), open

absonus -a -um harsh, discordant

absque (+ abl) without

abstergeo -gere -si -sum wipe away

*absum abesse afui be away, be off, be removed

*absurdus -a -um ridiculous

*abundans -antis abounding (with), crammed (with)

*ac and, than

accedo -dere -ssi -ssum go up to, come, arrive at

*accendo -dere -di -sum kindle, light, incite

*accessus -us (m) access, opportunity

accingo -gere -xi -ctum gird; accingor (reflexive) get ready

*accipio -ipere -epi -eptum accept, hear, receive, greet

accommodo -are -avi -atum lend

accumbo -mbere -bui -bitum recline at

accurate meticulously, carefully

*accurro -rrere -rri -rsum run up to, rush up

*acer acris acre keen, shrewd, penetrating, fierce, acrid

*acies -ei (f) line (of soldiers)

acquiesco -escere -evi rest, sleep

Actiacus -a -um at Actium (on west coast of Greece)

actor -oris (m) steward, manager

actutum at once

acus -us (f) pin

*ad (+ acc) to, into, up to, towards, to the house of, with regard to, for, for the purpose of, until, in response to, in, in accordance with, so as to agree with, against

addico -icere -ixi -ictum assign, doom

additamentum -i (n) increase

*addo -ere -idi -itum add

*adduco -cere -xi -ctum bring to, close, attract (to)

adedo -edere -edi -esum eat away

*adeo -ire -i(v)i -itum go to join

adhaereo -rere -si -sum (+ dat) cling to

adhibeo -ere -ui -itum apply (to), put into practice, indulge

adhinnio -ire -ivi -itum whinny (to)

*adhortor -ari -atus sum urge

*adhuc still, as yet

*aditus -us (m) attack, entrance, access

adiuro -are -avi -atum swear by

admodum very, rather, quite, altogether, completely

admolior -iri -itus sum apply (to), lay (hands) on (+ dat)

admoveo -movere -movi -motum move to, apply, move close

*adorno -are -avi -atum decorate, adorn, dress

*adoro -are -avi -atum plead, pray, worship

*adripio -ere -ui adreptum seize, grab

*adsum adesse adfui be present (in), be there, be here, be available

*adulescens -entis (m) young man

*adulter -eri (m) adulterous lover, adulterer

adulterinus -a -um counterfeit

*adulterium -(i)i (n) adultery

adusque (+ acc) right up to

advena -ae (m) stranger, newcomer

*advenio -venire -veni -ventum arrive

advento -are -avi -atum approach, arrive

adventor -oris (m) customer

adventus -us (m) arrival

adversus (+ acc) against, in opposition to, in criticism of

adytum -i (n) sanctuary, innermost part of a temple

*aedes -is (f) house, temple; aedes (pl) house

*aedificium -(i)i (n) building

aegerrime with great distress, with great difficulty, very reluctantly

aegre with difficulty, with great effort

*Aegyptius -a -um Egyptian

aemulus -a -um rival

aemulus -i (m) rival, imitator

aequitas -atis (f) principle of equality

aerumna -ae (f) trouble, hardship, suffering

aerumnabilis -is -e distressing, miserable

*aes aeris (n) bronze, money

aestuo -are -avi -atum be agitated, vacillate

aestus -us (m) surge, rough sea

*aetas -atis (f) age, youth

*aeternus -a -um everlasting, permanent

Aetolia -ae (f) Aetolia (a region in north-west Greece)

affatim amply, thoroughly

affecto -are -avi -atum try to get

affingo -ngere -nxi -ctum make up, devise, forge, simulate

*affirmo -are -avi -atum maintain, strengthen, support

afflo -are -avi -atum blow upon, burn

aggero -are -avi -atum pile up

agglutino -are -avi -atum attach, fasten

*aggredior -di -ssus sum attempt, proceed (to), attack

*aggressio -ionis (f) attack

*aggressura -ae (f) attack, assault

agito -are -avi -atum turn over

agminatim in hordes

agnitio -onis (f) recognition

*ago agere egi actum do, conduct, be busy, proceed, render, drive along

agrestis -is -e of a peasant, uncivilized

*aio (2nd person sing ais; 3rd person sing ait) say

alacer -cris -cre moving nimbly, brisk, eager

alacritas -atis (f) enthusiasm

alacriter eagerly, briskly

albus -a -um white

Alcimus -i (m) Alcimus

alias at other times

*alienus -a -um not one's own, belonging to another, another's, separate, of another country, unsuitable (to)

alioquin otherwise, as a general rule

aliorsum elsewhere

aliquantisper for a while

aliquanto rather

aliquantus -a -um a certain (amount), a considerable

aliqui -qua -quod some, a, a single

*aliquis -quis -quid some, some or other, someone, something

*alius -a -ud other, another, else; alius . . . alius one . . . another

allego -egere -egi -ectum admit

allibesco -ere be roused

alligo -are -avi -atum tie to (+ dat)

allubentia -ae (f) inclination

*alte deeply

*alter -era -erum one (of two), the other (of two); alter . . . alter the one . . . the other

alterco -are argue, argue with (+ dat)

alterno -are -avi -atum share

alterorsus elsewhere, in another room

*altus -a -um deep, profound, high, advanced, loud

alveus -i (m) tub

alvus -i (f) belly, bowels

amaritudo -inis (f) bitterness, acidity

amarus -a -um bitter

*amator -oris (m) lover

*ambiguitas -atis (f) ambiguity, uncertainty

*ambo -ae -o both

ambulo -are -avi -atum walk, go about, stroll

amens -entis mad, frantic

*amicitia -ae (f) friendship

*amicus -i (m) friend

amitto -ittere -isi -issum lose, let go

*amo -are -avi -atum love

amoenus -a -um attractive

*amor -oris (m) love, passion, desire

amoveo -overe -ovi -otum move away, keep (from)

amplector -cti -xus sum embrace

amplexus -us (m) embrace

amplius more

amputo -are -avi -atum cut through

an whether, or, really

anceps -itis twofold, double

ancillula -ae (f) slave girl, maid

angiportus -us (m) alley

angulus -i (m) corner

angustia -ae (f) narrowness

anhelitus -us (m) gasp, pant

anicula -ae (f) old woman

*****anima -ae** (f) life, soul, spirit

*****animal -alis** (n) animal, creature

*****animalis -is** (f) creature, animal

*****animus -i** (m) mind, heart, spirits, courage, frame of mind, attitude, emotions, anger

annosus -a -um long-lasting

annumero -are -avi -atum pay out

*****annus -i** (m) year

ansula -ae (f) hook

*****ante** previously, before; (+ acc) in front of

antecello -ere outstrip, surpass

antelucio before dawn

anteluculo before dawn

antependulus -a -um hanging down in front (of the face)

*****antequam** before

antesignanus -i (m) leader, frontline fighter

anteventulus -a -um hanging down in front

anteverto -tere -ti forestall, prevent

Anticthones -um (m pl) people of the southern hemisphere

anus -us (f) old woman

*****anxie** anxiously, meticulously

*****anxius -a -um** anxious, worried

apage (+ acc) be off (with), get away with (you)

aper apri (m) boar

aperio -ire -ui -tum open, reveal

appareo -ere -ui -itum appear

apparo -are -avi -atum prepare

appello -are -avi -atum address, greet, call

appello -ellere -uli -ulsum put in at

appendix -icis (m) appendage, attachment

appeto -ere -i(v)i -itum chase after

applaudo -dere -si -sum (+ dat) knock to

applico -are -avi -atum lead (to), attach (to)

appono -onere -osui -ositum serve

approno -are -avi -atum lean forwards

appropinquo -are -avi approach

*****aptus -a -um** suitable (for)

*****apud** (+ acc) at the home of, at, on, in

*****aqua -ae** (f) water, stream

*****Arabia -ae** (f) Arabia

arbitrium -(i)i (n) settlement, deciding, wishes

*****arbitror -ari -atus sum** observe, consider, judge

*****arbor -oris** (f) tree

arcanum -i (n) secret rite, mystery

arcessitor -oris (m) summoner

arcula -ae (f) box, casket

arcus -us (m) bow

*****ardens -entis** fiercely hot, burning, intense, ardent

*****ardor -oris** (m) fire, passion, enthusiasm

arenosus -a -um sandy

argentum -i (n) silver

argumentor -ari -atus sum reason, argue

Argus -i (m) Argus (a guardian with many eyes)

aries -etis (m) ram

Aristomenes -is (m) Aristomenes

*****arma -orum** (n plural) weapons

armillum -i (n) wine-jar; **ad armillum revertere** get up to one's old tricks

*****armo -are -avi -atum** arm

arrepo -pere -psi creep up

arrigo -igere -exi -ectum stir, rouse

arripio -ere -ui arreptum seize, grab

*****ars artis** (f) art, craft, trick

arto -are -avi -atum constrict, contract

artus -a -um close, dear

arvum -i (n) field, countryside

*****ascendo -dere -di -sum** mount, climb up on to

ascisco -iscere -ivi -itum adopt, claim, take over

asellus -i (m) ass

Asinius -a -um Asinius

asinus -i (m) ass

*****aspectus -us** (m) sight, stare, glare

*****asper -era -erum** harsh, angry, bitter

aspergo -gere -si -sum spatter, stain, sully, besmirch

aspergo -inis (f) spattering, spray

aspernor -ari -atus sum push away, spurn, reject

*****aspicio -icere -exi -ectum** examine, watch, see

asporto -are -avi -atum carry off

assevero -are -avi -atum assert emphatically, affirm, make serious

*****assidue** continually, constantly

*****assiduus -a -um** continual, incessant, constant

assisto -ere astiti take up a position, stand, stand nearby

assumo -ere -psi -ptum take as a companion

assurgo -gere -rexi -rectum stand up

ast but

asto -are -iti stand (by)

astruo -ere -xi -ctum add

astus -us (m) cunning, guile

*astutia -ae (f) cunning, cleverness

*astutulus -a -um crafty, clever

*at but

ater atra atrum dark

*atque and, and what's more

atratus -a -um dressed in black, in mourning

atrium -ii (n) entrance hall

*attentus -a -um attentive, attending (to)

attiguus -a -um adjacent, neighbouring

attingo -tingere -tigi -tactum touch

attollo -ere raise, lift

attraho -here -xi -ctum drag

attritus -us (m) grinding, whetting

*auctio -onis (f) auction

auctor -oris (m) originator, person responsible, proposer

auctoritas -atis (f) right of ownership

auctus -us (m) growth

*audax -acis bold, audacious

*audeo -dere -sus sum dare, dare to perform

*audio -ire -i(v)i -itum hear

*aufero -ferre abstuli ablatum take away, steal

*aufugio -fugere -fugi run away, flee

*augustus -a -um venerable, majestic

aula -ae (f) court

aureus -a -um golden, of gold

aureus -i (m) gold coin

*auris -is (f) ear

*aurum -i (n) gold

ausculto -are -avi -atum (+ dat) listen to, obey

auspicor -ari -atus sum start on

autem but, on the other hand, and, actually (in a surprised question)

autumo -are -avi -atum affirm, say

*auxilium -(i)i (n) help, assistance

avello -ellere -elli -ulsum tear away

*avide greedily, eagerly, impatiently

*avidus -a -um greedy, eager

*avis -is (f) bird

avius -a -um pathless, remote

avus -i (m) grandfather

bacchatim like Bacchantes (female worshippers of Bacchus)

bacchor -ari -atus sum rave, wander

baculum -i (n) stick

balbuttio -ire murmur, stammer

barathrum -i (n) abyss, Underworld

*barbarus -a -um barbaric, uncivilized, savage

*barbarus -i (m) barbarian

basio -are -avi -atum kiss

beate happily

beatitudo -inis (f) blessedness, bliss

beatus -a -um fortunate, happy

bellule nicely

bellus -a -um handsome, smart, fine

belua -ae (f) beast, animal, monster

*bene well, pleasantly, thoroughly

*beneficium -(i)i (n) benefit; beneficio (+ gen) thanks to

*beneficus -a -um kindly, beneficent

*benignitas -atis (f) benevolence, kindness

*bestia -ae (f) animal, beast

*bibo -ere bibi drink

bilis -is (f) bile, anger

blandities -ei (f) sweetness (of a speech)

*bonum -i (n) good

*bonus -a -um good, virtuous, kind, efficient, reliable, worthy

borrio -ire swarm

bos bovis (m) bull

*bracchium -(i)i (n) arm

brevi soon

breviculus -a -um very small

brevitas -atis (f) scarcity

bulla -ae (f) locket, amulet

buxans -antis of box-wood (i.e. pale, like the box-tree)

buxeus -a -um like box-wood (i.e. pale, like the box-tree)

cacumen -inis (n) top

*cadaver -eris (n) corpse

*caecitas -atis (f) blindness

*caecus -a -um blind

*caedes -is (f) murder

*caedo -ere cecidi caesum strike, beat

*caeles -itis (m + f) heavenly one, divinity

*caelestis -is -e heavenly, divine

*caelum -i (n) sky, heaven

caerimonia -ae (f) rite, ceremony

*Caesar -aris (m) Caesar, the emperor

*calamitosus -a -um wretched, unfortunate

calceus -i (m) shoe

calco -are -avi -atum trample underfoot, spurn, tread on

caliculus -i (m) small cup-shaped blossom

*calida -ae (f) hot water

*calidus -a -um hot, warm

caligo -inis (f) blackness, obscurity

calix -icis (m) drinking-cup

callenter skilfully, cleverly

callidus -a -um expert, ingenious, crafty

callosus -a -um tough

*calor -oris (m) heat, anger

calumnior -ari -atus sum accuse falsely

calvitium -ii (n) baldness

calx calcis (f) back part of the hoof, heel

Calypso -onis (f) Calypso (a sea nymph)

*candeo -ere -ui be white, gleam

*candidus -a -um white, bright

*candor -oris (m) brilliance, radiance

cani -orum (m pl) grey hairs

*canis -is (m + f) dog

canities -ei (f) grey hair

*cantamen -inis (n) incantation

*cantatio -ionis (f) singing, song

*cantatrix -icis employing incantations, sorcerous

*cantio -ionis (f) magical incantation

capella -ae (f) goat

capesso -ere -i(v)i start on, enter on, take (the road)

*capillus -i (m) hair

*capio capere cepi captum seize, get

caprea -ae (f) roe deer

captiose so as to take in, beguilingly

captiosus -a -um ensnaring, beguiling

*captivitas -atis (f) capture, captivity

*captivus -a -um captured, captive

capulus -i (m) hilt, coffin

*caput -itis (n) head, life

cardo -inis (m) hinge

carina -ae (f) ship

cariosus -a -um rotten

caro carnis (f) flesh

carpo -ere -si -tum seize, sample, select, torment

*carus -a -um dear, beloved

caseus -i (m) cheese

cassus -a -um groundless, needless

castellum -i (n) fortified town

castigo -are -avi -atum punish

castor -oris (m) beaver

*casus -us (m) fall, misfortune, disaster, danger, death, situation

*caterva -ae (f) pack, throng

cauda -ae (f) tail

caupo -onis (m) (male) innkeeper

caupona -ae (f) (female) innkeeper, landlady

*causa -ae (f) cause, reason, motive, case; causam agere conduct a case; causa (abl) for the purpose of

cautes -is (f) crag, cliff

*cautio -ionis (f) caution

cavea -ae (f) cage

*caveo -ere cavi cautum beware, make sure, prevent, be on guard against

cavillor -ari -atus sum mock, make fun of

cavillum -i (n) jesting, banter

*cavus -a -um hollow, enclosing

*cedo -dere -ssi -ssum yield, give way (to)

*celer -eris -ere quick, speedy

*celeritas -atis (f) speed

*celeriter quickly

*celerrime very quickly

cella -ae (f) small room

cellula -ae (f) small room, humble apartment

celo -are -avi -atum conceal

*cena -ae (f) dinner

cenito -are dine, have dinner

censeo -ere -ui -um propose, recommend

centunculus -i (m) cloak, rags

cenula -ae (f) little dinner, dinner

cera -ae (f) wax

Cerberus -i (m) Cerberus

Ceres -eris (f) Ceres (goddess of grain)

cereus -i (m) wax taper

cerno -ere crevi cretum see

cernuo -are fall head first

*certe certainly, at least

*certus -a -um sure, convinced, definite

cerva -ae (f) hind, doe

cervix -icis (f) neck

*cesso -are -avi -atum cease, subside

*ceterus -a -um other, rest (of)

Charite -es (f) Charite

chlamyda -ae (f) cloak

Chryseros -otos (m) Chryseros

*cibatus -us (m) food

*cibus -i (m) food

cicatrix -icis (f) scar

cieo ciere civi citum call on, summon

*cingo -gere -xi -ctum surround, encircle

cinis -eris (m) ash

*circa (+ acc) round about

*circum around, round about

circumdo -dare -dedi -datum place around, hang around

*circumfluo -ere -xi surge around, crowd around

*circumfundo -undere -udi -usum pour around; circumfundor (reflexive) spread around

circumplector -cti -xus sum embrace

*circumsto -stare -steti stand around
circumtorqueo -ere twist around, pull around
citro to this side; ultro citro back and forth
*civis -is (m) citizen
*civitas -atis (f) town, city
*clades -is (f) disaster
*clamito -are -avi -atum shout repeatedly,
    invoke/summon repeatedly
*clamo -are -avi -atum shout, cry out, proclaim
*clamor -oris (m) shout, shouting
*clamosus -a -um shouting, noisy
*clandestinus -a -um secret
*claresco -escere -ui become illuminated
*clarus -a -um famous, clear, bright
claudo -dere -si -sum shut up, confine, close
claudus -a -um lame
claustrum -i (n) bolt, bar
clavis -is (f) key
clavus -i (m) nail, spike
*clemens -entis kindly
*clementer gently, in a kindly manner
clunis -is (m + f) buttocks, hind quarters
coaequo -are -avi -atum make equal, equate
coarguo -ere prove a charge, show to be guilty
coemo -emere -emi -emptum buy
*coepi -isse -tum begin, commit
*coepto -are -avi -atum begin
coeptum -i (n) enterprise; coepta (pl) enterprise
coerceo -ere -ui -itum confine, check
coetus -us (m) meeting, group, crowd
*cogitatio -onis (f) thought
*cogito -are -avi -atum think, think of,
    contemplate, plan
*cognosco -oscere -ovi -itum find out, learn of
*cogo -ere coegi coactum collect, knot,
    compress, compel
cohaereo -rere -si -sum (+ dat) be attached to,
    be bound to
cohibeo -ere -ui -itum restrain, control, confine,
    lock in, bind, keep in place, shrink
*cohors -ortis (f) cohort, armed force
cohortor -ari -atus sum urge, rouse, sick on
coitus -us (m) (sexual) intercourse
collabor -bi -psus sum collapse, fall, fail
collegium -(i)i (n) guild, band, college
collis -is (m) hill
colloquor -qui -cutus sum discuss
colluctatio -ionis (f) struggle, combat
*collum -i (n) neck
*colo -ere -ui cultum live in, cultivate
colonus -i (m) farmhand, tenant-farmer

*color -oris (m) colour
*coma -ae (f) hair
comburo -urere -ussi -ustum burn, destroy
    with fire
comes -itis (m) companion
comis -is -e kind
comissor -ari -atus sum revel, have a party
comitatus -us (m) crowd, escort
comiter good-humouredly, genially, courteously
comitor -ari -atus sum accompany, join
commasculo -are screw up (courage)
commeatus -us (m) convoy, voyaging,
    navigation
commeo -eare -eavi -eatum travel, go, move
commilito -onis (m) fellow soldier
comminisco -ere think up
comminiscor -inisci -entus sum think up,
    devise
comminus at close quarters
committo -ittere -isi -issum entrust, commit
commodum a short time ago, just
commodum -i (n) advantage, benefit, interest
commoneo -ere -ui -itum remind (of)
commoror -ari -atus sum delay
*commoveo -overe -ovi -otum stir up, rouse,
    move, produce, upset, disturb
commulceo -ere soothe
*communis -is -e shared, joint, common
compareo -ere -ui be seen, be in evidence
comparo -are -avi -atum prepare (for), get
    ready, make, buy
compello -are -avi -atum address, rebuke
*compello -ellere -uli -ulsum force, impel,
    whet
compendium -(i)i (n) gain, profit, acquisition
comperior -eri -ertus sum discover
complector -cti -xus sum embrace, hug
compleo -ere -evi -etum complete, fill, fill out,
    run through
comprimo -imere -essi -essum reduce, squeeze,
    crush, subdue
computo -are -avi -atum count up, reckon up
concedo -dere -ssi -ssum leave, grant, allow
concido -dere -di -sum cut to pieces
concilio -are -avi -atum (+ dat) reconcile (to)
concito -are -avi -atum spur, hurl
concitus -a -um fast
*conclamo -are -avi -atum shout for, call up
conclave -is (n) room
*concorditer harmoniously
concubitus -us (m) (sexual) intercourse

concurro -rrere -rri -rsum hurry together, come running up

concursus -us (m) crowd, gathering

condico -icere -ixi -ictum fix up

condigne fittingly, worthily

condo -ere -idi -itum close, establish, found

conduco -cere -xi -ctum gather together

confero -ferre contuli collatum take, contribute, give, compare, bring together; sermonem conferre converse; vestigium conferre engage

confertus -a -um crowded together, closely packed, in close formation

confestim at once

conficio -icere -eci -ectum kill, complete, finish, process

confinium -(i)i (n) boundary, border, interval before (+gen)

*confirmo -are -avi -atum strengthen, stiffen

confluo -ere -xi flock together, gather

conformo -are -avi -atum make to correspond

confoveo -overe -ovi -otum care for, sustain

confundo -undere -udi -usum disconcert, dismay, confuse

confuto -are -avi -atum confound, take aback

congero -rere -ssi -stum heap up, throw, shower, wield repeatedly

congressus -us (m) act of sexual intercourse

congruens -entis suitable, fitting, corresponding

*coniuga -ae (f) wife

*coniunctio -ionis (f) union, relationship

*coniunx -ugis (m + f) spouse, husband, wife

coniveo -vere -vi close the eyes, go to sleep

*conor -ari -atus sum try, attempt

conquiesco -escere -evi settle down, cease, halt

conquiro -rere -si(v)i -situm look for

conscendo -dere -di -sum go up to, board

*conscientia -ae (f) guilty conscience

*conscius -a -um aware (of), privy (to), accomplice (of)

consector -ari -atus sum make for, seek, pursue, try (to)

*consentio -tire -si -sum agree

consequor -qui -cutus sum acquire, follow

consero -erere -evi -itum plant

*conserva -ae (f) fellow-slave

*conservus -i (m) fellow-slave

*considero -are -avi -atum contemplate, hold an investigation

consido -sidere -sedi sit down, take up position, encamp

consigno -are -avi -atum seal

consiliator -oris (m) adviser

*consilium -(i)i (n) plan, planning, strategy, advice

consisto -sistere -stiti stop, be (in a place or state)

consone in unison, (sounding) together

consonus -a -um harmonious

*conspectus -us (m) sight

*conspicio -icere -exi -ectum catch sight of, see

*conspicor -ari -atus sum catch sight of, see

*conspicuus -a -um distinguished, illustrious, conspicuous

*constans -antis steadfast

*constantia -ae (f) persistence

constituo -uere -ui -utum establish, locate, place, set

consto -are -iti take up a position, stand one's ground

constringo -ngere -nxi -ctum string up, squeeze, tie up

consuesco -escere -evi -etum become accustomed; consuevi be accustomed

consuetus -a -um usual

consulo -ere -ui -tum consult, (+ dat) protect, see to; boni consulo do well

*consumo -ere -psi -ptum devour

consurgo -rgere -rrexi -rrectum stand up

contego -gere -xi -ctum cover, dress, conceal

*contemptio -onis (f) contempt, scorn

contendo -dere -di -tum strive, struggle, make for, hurry

*contentus -a -um content

contero -terere -trivi -tritum grind, crush

continentia -ae (f) self-control, restraint, repression of passions

contineo -inere -inui -entum keep, confine

contingo -ingere -igi -actum touch

continuor -ari -atus sum join

*continuus -a -um ceaseless, continuous

contorqueo -quere -si -tum contort, hurl

*contra (+ acc) opposite, facing, in opposition to, contrary to, against, to meet

contraho -ahere -axi -actum enter into, bring on oneself

contrecto -are -avi -atum caress, fondle

*controversia -ae (f) dispute, controversy

contrunco -are -avi -atum tear to pieces, gobble up

contubernalis -is (m) intimate friend

contumelia -ae (f) insult, affront

contumulo -are -avi -atum bury

contundo -undere -udi -usum pound, crush

conubium -(i)i (n) marriage

*convallis -is (f) valley

convector -oris (m) fellow traveller

convenio -venire -veni -ventum agree, tally, be consistent with (+ dat), approach, come; convenit (impersonal) it is agreed

*conversatio -ionis (f) intimacy, moving around, association

converto -tere -ti -sum turn, change, turn around; convertor turn

convolo -are -avi -atum rush in together

convolvo -vere -vi -utum wrap, enfold

*convulnero -are -avi -atum pierce, gouge

copia -ae (f) body of men

*copiosus -a -um numerous, abundant

*cor cordis (n) heart

coram face to face

corium -(i)i (n) hide (thick skin of an animal)

cornu -us (n) horn

corolla -ae (f) garland

corona -ae (f) crown, garland

*corpus -oris (n) body, corpse

corrado -dere -si -sum scrape together

*corrumpo -umpere -upi -uptum ruin, violate

corruo -ere -i collapse

corusco -are -avi glitter

cotidie every day

crapula -ae (f) intoxication, drunkenness

crasso -are -avi -atum make thick; crassor thicken

crassus -a -um thick

crastino tomorrow

crastinus -a -um of tomorrow

*creber -bra -brum frequent

*crebriter frequently, repeatedly

*credo -ere -idi -itum believe, imagine, trust (+ dat)

*credulitas -atis (f) belief

*cremo -are -avi -atum burn

crepusculum -i (n) dusk

cresco -ere crevi cretum grow, increase

*crimen -inis (n) charge, accusation

crinalis -is -e worn in the hair, hair-

crinis -is (m) hair

croceus -a -um saffron-coloured, yellow

*cruciabilis -is -e tortured, painful

*cruciatus -us (m) torture, agony

*crucio -are -avi -atum torture

*crudelis -is -e cruel

crudus -a -um raw

cruentus -a -um bloody, involving bloodshed, blood-stained, cruel

cruor -oris (m) blood

*crus cruris (n) leg

*crux crucis (f) cross, crucifixion

cubiculum -i (n) bedroom, room

cubile -is (n) bed

cubito -are -avi -atum lie down, sleep

cubo -are -ui -itum lie down, go to bed

cucurbita -ae (f) gourd

*culpa -ae (f) blame, guilt, crime

cultor -oris (m) worshipper

*cum when, since; (+ abl) with, together with, along with; cum primum as soon as

cumulatus -a -um abundant, great

cumulo -are -avi -atum increase, crown

cumulus -i (m) peak

cunctabundus -a -um moving slowly, delaying

cunctatio -ionis (f) hesitation

*cunctus -a -um all, every

*cupide eagerly, with alacrity

*cupido -inis (f) desire, lust

*Cupido -inis (m) Cupid (god of love)

*cupiens -entis desirous (of)

*cupio -ire -i(v)i -itum want, desire

*cupressus -us (f) cypress

*cur why

*cura -ae (f) care, anxiety, worry, concern, carefulness

*curiositas -atis (f) curiosity

*curiosus -a -um inquisitive, meddlesome

currulis -is -e belonging to chariots; currulis equus racehorse

cursus -us (m) gallop, run, rush, speed, course

custodela -ae (f) custody, guarding

custodia -ae (f) guarding, protection

custodio -ire -i(v)i -itum guard, protect

custos -odis (m) guard

cutis -is (f) skin, hide

dammula -ae (f) deer

damno -are -avi -atum condemn, doom

damnum -i (n) loss, deprivation, damage

Daphne -es (f) Daphne

*de (+ abl) from, from being, of, out of, concerning, about, by, originating with, in accordance with, over

*dea -ae (f) goddess

*debeo -ere -ui -itum ought, should, have to

debilitatio -ionis (f) mutilation

decedo -dere -ssi -sum depart, retire, give way to

*decem ten

decerno -ernere -revi -retum decide, decree

decerpo -ere -si -tum remove, cut off, bite off

decido -ere -i fall down

*decimus -a -um tenth

*decipio -ipere -epi -eptum deceive

decipulum -i (n) trap, snare

decorus -a -um beautiful

decrepitus -a -um worn out, enfeebled

decurro -rrere -rri -rsum run down, come running

decus -oris (n) source of glory, glory, ornament

dedecus -oris (n) repulsive appearance, misbehaviour, disgraceful conduct, disgrace

dedico -are -avi -atum dedicate, consecrate

dedolo -are -avi -atum hew into shape, copulate with

deduco -cere -xi -ctum lead off, take away

defaeco -are -avi -atum decant, strain

*defectus -a -um enfeebled, defective

defero -ferre -tuli -latum take down, lower down, convey

deficio -icere -eci -ectum fail, weaken; deficior lack, am lacking

definio -ire -i(v)i -itum determine, define, finish off

defleo -ere -evi -etum weep, mourn (as dead)

defluo -ere -xi -xum fall off, disappear

*deformis -is -e disfigured, ugly, ghastly

*deformo -are -avi -atum deform, disfigure, transform

defraudo -are -avi -atum (+ abl) cheat of, rob of

*defunctus -i (m) dead man

dehinc from now on, next, then

dehisco -ere gape, yawn

dehortor -ari -atus sum advise against a course of action, dissuade

deicio -icere -ieci -iectum let grow down, let droop

deiero -are -avi -atum swear, take an oath

*dein then

delabor -bi -psus sum plunge down, be shot down, slip down (from), sink into, slip away, disappear

*delecto -are -avi -atum delight, entice

*delibero -are -avi -atum ponder, consider

*delicatus -a -um pretty, amorous, delicate, luxurious

Delphicus -a -um of Delphi (in Greece)

deluo -ere wash away

demeo -are -avi -atum go down, descend

demergo -gere -si -sum bury, plunge down

demigro -are -avi -atum go away

*demitto -mittere -misi -missum send down, stick down

Demochares -is (m) Demochares

*demonstro -are -avi -atum point out, indicate

demoror -ari -atus sum detain, linger

demorsico -are -avi -atum bite pieces off

*denarius -ii (m) denarius (a Roman coin)

*denique finally, in short, in fact

denoto -are -avi -atum point out, indicate

dens dentis (m) tusk

*densus -a -um dense, closely packed

denubo -bere -psi -ptum marry (away from home)

denuntio -are -avi -atum announce

deorsus downwards, down, down below

deosculor -ari -atus sum kiss warmly

depello -ellere -uli -ulsum push aside, dislodge, remove, get rid of

dependeo -ere -i hang down (from)

depingo -ngere -nxi -ctum depict, represent

depono -onere -osui -ositum hold in deposit (until a job's completion)

deporto -are -avi -atum carry out

deprecor -ari -atus sum pray (for), entreat, call down (on)

*deprehendo -dere -di -sum catch, pounce on

depromo -ere -psi -ptum fetch from (+ abl), bring out, take out

derigo -igere -exi -ectum direct (one's forces)

deruo -ere -i -tum fall off

*descendo -dere -di -sum descend, climb down

descisco -iscere -i(v)i -itum turn away, defect

deseco -are -ui -tum cut off

*desero -ere -ui -tum forsake, abandon, leave

*desiderium -(i)i (n) desire, longing

*desidero -are -avi -atum desire, need

desino -inere -i(v)i -itum cease, stop

*desisto -istere -titi cease, desist, leave off

desolo -are -avi -atum leave all alone, abandon

despicio -icere -exi -ectum look down on

despolio -are -avi -atum strip someone (acc) of something (abl)

despondeo -dere -di -sum pledge, promise

destino -are -avi -atum tie, intend, agree on, designate, appoint

destituo -uere -ui -utum fix

destringo -ngere -nxi -ctum unsheathe, draw, be rested lightly on

desum -esse -fui be lacking (to), not be forthcoming, fail to support (+ dat)

detego -gere -xi -ctum expose, reveal

*deterreo -ere -ui -itum deter, frighten off

deterrimus -a -um horrible, very wicked

*detestabilis -is -e abominable, detestable

*detestor -ari -atus sum curse, loathe, express abhorrence for

detineo -inere -inui -entum take up

detorqueo -quere -si -tum deflect, direct (away)

detraho -here -xi -ctum take down

detrunco -are -avi -atum behead, mutilate, eat pieces from

*deus -i (m) god

*devasto -are -avi -atum ravage, lay waste

deverto -tere -ti -sum turn aside (for lodging), put up

devolvo -olvere -olvi -olutum roll down, fall down, roll off

*devoro -are -avi -atum gobble up, gulp down

devotio -onis (f) curse, spell

devoveo -overe -ovi -otum pledge, vow, devote

*dexter -tera -terum right

*dextera -ae (f) right hand

*dextra on the right

*dextrorsum to the right

dicacitas -atis (f) mockery

*dico -ere dixi dictum speak, say

*dictum -i (n) word

*dies diei (m + f) day, daylight

diffamo -are -avi -atum slander, spread news

differo -rre distuli dilatum put off, defer

*difficultas -atis (f) difficulty, trouble

diffluo -ere -xi -ctum pass out

diffringo -ingere -egi -actum break, shatter

diffundo -undere -udi -usum dissolve, cheer

*digitus -i (m) finger

*dignatio -onis (f) esteem

*dignitas -atis (f) esteem, honour, dignity

*dignor -ari -atus sum (+ abl) deem worthy of

*dignus -a -um worthy, deserving

digredior -gredi -gressus sum depart

dilabor -bi -psus sum slip away

dilectus -us (m) discrimination, distinction

*diligenter carefully, thoroughly

*diligentia -ae (f) diligence, carefulness

dilorico -are -avi -atum pull open

diluo -uere -ui -utum dissolve, wash away

dimico -are -avi -atum fight

dimitto -mittere -misi -missum hurl

dimoveo -movere -movi -motum move about, turn, part, wrench open

dinosco -ere discern, determine

dirigo -igere -exi -ectum point, direct at, direct, guide

diripio -ipere -ipui -eptum steal, loot

dir(r)umpo -umpere -upi -uptum split, break

*dirus -a -um dreadful, frightening

discedo -dere -ssi -ssum depart, get away

discerno -ernere -revi -retum distinguish, decide

discerpo -pere -psi -ptum tear apart, rend

*disciplina -ae (f) discipline, craft

discludo -dere -si -sum keep apart, lock up

discrimen -inis (n) danger

*discrucio -are -avi -atum torment

discurro -rrere -rri -rsum run about

discus -i (m) dish

discutio -tere -ssi -ssum dispel, dissipate, shake off

dispergo -gere -si -sum disperse, scatter

dispono -ponere -posui -positum organize, arrange

disputo -are -avi -atum reason out, debate

*dissensio -onis (f) disagreement

dissimulanter dissemblingly, secretly

dissimulo -are -avi -atum conceal

*dissonus -a -um confused, dissonant

distendo -dere -di -tum swell, distend, spreadeagle

distinguo -guere -xi -ctum resolve, dispel

distraho -here -xi -ctum tear, sell off

*diu for a long time

diu by day

diurnus -a -um daytime, done by day

diutine for a long time

diutinus -a -um long-lasting

diuturnus -a -um long-lasting

*diverse variously, in various places/ways

*diversus -a -um different, opposite

*dives -itis rich

*divido -idere -isi -isum share, divide

*divinatio -onis (f) prophecy

divinitus through divine agency

*divinus -a -um divine, supernatural, connected with a deity

*do dare dedi datum give, provide, cause to go, attribute

*doceo -ere -ui -ctum tell, inform

*doctus -a -um learned

documentum -i (n) proof

*doleo -ere -ui -itum grieve, be upset

dolium -ii (n) vat, storage-jar

*dolor -oris (m) pain, grief

*domina -ae (f) mistress, madam

*dominus -i (m) master, owner, sir

domuitio -onis (f) return home

domuncula -ae (f) little house, cottage

*domus -us (f) home, house, property, household

*donec until

*dono -are -avi -atum give

*dormio -ire -i(v)i -itum sleep

dorsum -i (n) back

draco -onis (m) snake

*dubito -are -avi -atum hesitate

*dubius -a -um doubtful

*duco -cere -xi -ctum draw, lead

*ducto -are -avi -atum lead

*ductor -oris (m) leader, driver

*dulcedo -inis (f) sweetness

*dulcis -is -e sweet

*dum while, until

*duo -ae -o two

duro -are -avi -atum harden, solidify; duror harden

*dux ducis (m) leader, general

*e (+ abl) out of, from

ebullio -ire -i(v)i burst out

*ecce look, see, lo and behold, suddenly

editus -a -um high; ex edito from on high

edo -ere -idi -itum bring forth, give birth to

efficio -icere -eci -ectum cause to become, make, render, achieve

efflictim passionately, to distraction

efflo -are -avi -atum breathe forth

effluo -uere -uxi flow out

effor -ari -atus sum speak

effrico -are (-ui) -atum rub away

*effugio -ugere -ugi escape

*effundo -undere -udi -usum pour out, emit, throw

*ego mei I, myself

*egredior -di -ssus sum go out through

egregius -a -um excellent, outstanding

*egressio -ionis (f) departure

eiulatus -us (m) wailing, shrieking

elementum -i (n) element (a substance, like water, from which matter is made up)

elido -dere -si -sum expel, crush

eluvies -iei (f) crust

emeditor -ari -atus sum contrive carefully

*emergo -gere -si -sum emerge, come forth

eminus at a distance, from long range

emolior -iri -itus sum heave out

emptor -oris (m) buyer

*en look

*enarro -are -avi -atum relate fully, tell in detail

Endymion -onis (m) Endymion (a handsome hero)

*enim for, of course

*enormis -is -e huge

*eo ire i(v)i itum go, advance, make one's way

epulae -arum (f pl) banquet, dinner

*equester -tris -tre of a horse

*equus -i (m) horse

erado -dere -si -sum scrape off

ergo therefore, so

erilis -is -e to one's master

eripio -ipere -ipui -eptum snatch (away), rescue

*error -oris (m) error, mistake, moral lapse

eruptio -ionis (f) rush, spout

essito -are -avi -atum devour

*et and, also, even; et . . . et both . . . and

*etenim for

*etiam also, even, actually

*etsi even if

Europa -ae (f) Europa

evado -dere -si -sum go away, escape (from), leave, depart from

evello -ellere -elli (or -ulsi) -ulsum tear away

eventus -us (m) event, fate

evigilo -are -avi -atum wake up

*ex (+ abl) out of, from, to the extent of, in accordance with

examino -are -avi -atum consider, examine

examussim exactly in place, making a perfect fit

exanclo -are -avi -atum endure, go through

exanimatus -a -um dead

exanimis -is -e dead

exapto -are -avi -atum place (on)

exaspero -are -avi -atum roughen, make rough, rouse, set on, incense

excarnifico -are -avi -atum torture, torment

excio -ire -i(v)i -itum rouse, stir into action, call out

excipio -ipere -epi -eptum collect, receive, greet

excubo -are -avi -atum keep watch

excutio -tere -ssi -ssum shake off, knock off, shake out of, shoot out

*exemplum -i (n) example; exemplo in the
    manner (of)
exercitatus -a -um practised, active
exercite anxiously
exhibeo -ere -ui -itum produce, provide, display
exhinc after that
exigo -igere -egi -actum complete
*exiguus -a -um small, short
*exilium -(i)i (n) exile
eximie especially, perfectly, exceptionally
exinde subsequently, after that
*exitium -(i)i (n) destruction, killing
exobruo -uere -ui -utum dig out
exoculo -are -avi -atum deprive of eyes, blind
exonero -are -avi -atum discharge, unload
exopto -are -avi -atum long for
exoro -are -avi -atum persuade, win over
expedio -ire -i(v)i -itum unravel, unwind,
    disentangle, provide
expergiscor -i experrectus sum wake up
expergite vigilantly
expergo -gere -gi -gitum awaken
*experior -iri -tus sum experience, undergo
expleo -ere -evi -etum fill, satisfy
*exploro -are -avi -atum reconnoitre, keep an
    eye on
expono -onere -osui -ositum expose
expostulo -are -avi -atum remonstrate,
    complain
expugno -are -avi -atum storm, plunder, destroy
exsanguis -is -e bloodless, pale
exsculpo -ere -si -tum chip off, hack away
exsecror -ari -atus sum curse, abhor
exsertus -a -um watchful
*exspecto -are -avi -atum wait for
*exstinguo -guere -xi -ctum extinguish,
    darken, kill
*exsulto -are -avi rejoice, exult
*exsurgo -gere -rexi get up, rise up, emerge
extermino -are -avi -atum remove, expel
extimus -a -um outermost, edge of
extorqueo -quere -si -tum wrench away from
    (+ abl), constrain, compel
extorris -is -e exiled, banished
extrarius -a -um not belonging to the household
extremitas -atis (f) border
*extremus -a -um extreme, utmost, outermost,
    edge of, extremely distressing, worst, very
    disgusting
exuo -uere -ui -utum take off, strip, set free
    (from)

exuro -rere -ssi -stum burn, kill
    by fire

faber -bri (m) workman
fabrilis -is -e as a workman
*fabula -ae (f) conversation, tale, story
facesso -ere -i(v)i -itum depart, be off
*facies -iei (f) face, appearance, sight, form,
    figure
*facile easily, readily
*facilis -is -e easy, agile, deft
facinerosus -a -um evil, wicked
facinorosus -a -um wicked, criminal
facinus -oris (n) crime, act, deed, feat
*facio facere feci factum do, produce, perform,
    make, render, ensure, provide
factio -onis (f) band, gang
*factum -i (n) action, deed
faetidus -a -um foul-smelling
fallacia -ae (f) trickery, deceit, trick
fallo fallere fefelli falsum mislead, cheat,
    disappoint
*Fama -ae (f) Rumour
fames -is (f) hunger
famigerabilis -is -e famous, notorious
*familia -ae (f) household, slaves of a
    household, group of slaves, estate
familiaris -is -e friendly (to), well-known,
    habitual
familiaris -is (m) close friend, servant
*famosus -a -um famous, infamous
famulitium -(i) i (n) household, domestic staff
famulus -i (m) servant
fanum -i (n) shrine
fasciola -ae (f) bandage
*fatigo -are -avi -atum weary, tire out
*fatum -i (n) fate, doom
*fatuus -a -um silly, foolish
fauces -ium (f pl) jaws
*faveo -ere favi fautum be favourably inclined,
    be propitious
fax facis (f) torch, firebrand
*felix -icis fortunate, lucky, rich, blessed
*femina -ae (f) woman
feminal -alis (n) private parts, female
    pudendum
*femininus -a -um female, as worn by a woman
femus -oris (n) thigh
*fenestra -ae (f) window
*fera -ae (f) wild creature, beast, wild animal
feralis -is -e funeral, funerary, of the dead, fatal

feriae -arum (f pl) holiday

ferinus -a -um bestial, of a wild animal, of/by
    wild animals

ferio -ire strike

feritas -atis (f) wildness

ferme approximately, roughly

*fero ferre tuli latum bring, take; feror be
    borne, go

*ferocitas -atis (f) ferocity, savagery

*ferreus -a -um made of iron, of iron

*ferrum -i (n) iron, steel, weapon

ferula -ae (f) cane, stick

ferus -a -um wild, fierce

fervens -entis seething, inflamed

fervidus -a -um excited, angry, savage

*festinatio -ionis (f) haste

*festino -are -avi -atum be in a hurry,
    hasten (to)

festive delightfully, attractively

ficulneus -a -um fig-, fig-bearing

*fidelis -is -e faithful, reliable

fidens -entis self-confident, assured

fidenter with confidence, boldly

*fides -ei (f) good faith, fidelity, honesty,
    honour, protection, loyalty

fiducia -ae (f) confidence

fidus -a -um faithful

*filia -ae (f) daughter

*filius -(i)i (m) son

fimum -i (n) excrement

finitimus -a -um neighbouring, nearby

*fio fieri factus sum be done, become,
    arrive

*firmiter stubbornly, firmly, securely

*firmo -are -avi -atum strengthen, fasten
    securely

fistulatim in a spray, in a jet

flagitium -(i)i (n) outrage, sexual misconduct,
    disgrace, sin

flagito -are -avi -atum demand, call for

flagrantia -ae (f) scorching

flagro -are -avi burn, be inflamed

*flamma -ae (f) flame

*flammeus -a -um fiery, flaming

*flammidus -a -um flaming, fiery, radiant

flebilis -is -e tearful, plaintive, lamentable,
    causing tears, wretched

flecto -ctere -xi -xum bend, modify, prevail on,
    soften

*fleo flere flevi fletum weep, lament

*fletus -us (m) weeping, tears

flexus -us (m) bending

*flos floris (m) flower, bloom, brightness,
    choicest part, youthful beauty

fluctuo -are -avi -atum be tossed

*flumen -inis (n) river

*fluvialis -is -e belonging to a river

*fluvius -(i)i (m) river

fluxus -us (m) discharge, flux

foculus -i (m) oven, hearth

foedo -are -avi -atum pollute, disgrace,
    dishonour, disfigure

foedus -eris (n) bond, relationship

foetor -oris (m) stench

folium -(i)i (n) leaf, trifle, elementary part

follis -is (m) bag, sack

fomentum -i (n) poultice, remedy

*fons fontis (m) spring, stream

foramen -inis (n) hole, chink

forensis -is -e in the forum, derived from the
    law-courts

forinsecus out, away

foris elsewhere, out

*foris -is (f) door, one of the leaves of a double
    door; fores (pl) door

*forma -ae (f) form, appearance, shape

formica -ae (f) ant

formido -inis (f) acute fear, terror

formido -are -avi -atum be terrified

*formo -are -avi -atum shape, mould, fashion

formosus -a -um handsome

formula -ae (f) action

forsitan perhaps

forte by chance

*fortis -is -e brave, strong, powerful

*fortiter vigorously, bravely

*fortuna -ae (f) fortune, chance, bad luck,
    condition, wealth

*Fortuna -ae (f) Fortune (the goddess)

*forum -i (n) the forum

fovea -ae (f) pit

foveo -ere fovi fotum support, provide for

fragium -(i)i (n) breaking, fracture

*frango -ere fregi fractum break, shatter

*frater fratris (m) brother

*fraus fraudis (f) deceit, trickery

fremitus -us (m) roar, growling

fremo -ere -ui -itum roar

frequens -entis populous, well-populated, large,
    frequent, regular

*frequenter often, repeatedly

frequentia -ae (f) mass, multitude

frequento -are -avi -atum make frequently, attend, perform

***frigidus -a -um** cold

frondosus -a -um leafy, wooded

frons frontis (f) forehead, brow, expression

fructus -us (m) fruit, benefit, advantage

frumentum -i (n) corn, grain

fruor -i fructus sum (+ abl or acc) enjoy

***frustra** in vain, futilely, to no purpose, uselessly

frutex -icis (m) bush, shrub

***fuga -ae** (f) flight, desertion

***fugio -ere fugi** flee, go into exile

***fugo -are -avi -atum** drive off

fulgens -entis flashing, glittering

fullo -onis (m) fuller

fulmineus -a -um like a lightning-flash, flashing

fumus -i (m) vapour, fumes

funditus completely

fundo -undere -udi -usum pour, pour out, shed

funestus -a -um connected with death/mourning, of death, of mourning, fatal, murderous, lamentable

funiculus -i (m) a thin rope, rope

funis -is (m) rope

funus -eris (n) funeral, corpse

***furens -entis** mad, enraged

***furibundus -a -um** frenzied, delirious

***furiosus -a -um** mad, wild

***furtim** secretly, stealthily

***furtivus -a -um** secret, furtive

fuscus -a -um dark

fustis -is (m) club, cudgel, stick

***futurus -a -um** future, coming, imminent

gannitus -us (m) murmur, whisper

garrio -ire -ivi chatter

***gaudeo -dere gavisus sum** rejoice, take pleasure (in)

***gaudium -(i)i** (n) joy, delight

gena -ae (f) cheek

genialis -is -e of marriage, marriage-

genitalia -ium (n pl) the sexual organs

genu -us (n) knee

***genuinus -a -um** natural, innate

***genus -eris** (n) type

germanus -a -um related, kindred

germen -inis (n) perfume, fragrance

***gero -ere gessi gestum** carry, bear, contain, do

gestio -ire -i(v)i have a strong desire (for), long (to), be set on

gesto -are -avi -atum carry

gestus -us (m) gesture, movement

***gladiatorius -a -um** gladiatorial

***gladius -(i)i** (m) sword

glisco -ere increase

***gloria -ae** (f) renown, glory

***gloriosus -a -um** glorious, illustrious

gnarus -a -um knowing

grabatulus -i (m) (little) bed

gracilis -is -e thin, that makes thin, grinding

***gradus -us** (m) step, pace

***grandis -is -e** large, great, serious

grassor -ari -atus sum advance, rampage

***gratia -ae** (f) profit, agreeableness, thanks, favour; **gratias ago** give thanks; **gratias persolvo** repay/render thanks

Gratia -ae (f) a Grace (minor goddess)

***gratuitus -a -um** free of charge

***gratulor -ari -atus sum** be glad, congratulate

***gratus -a -um** welcome, pleasant

***gravis -is -e** heavy, strong, oppressive, grievous, harsh

***graviter** heavily

***gravo -are -avi -atum** weigh down, burden

gregatim in a herd

guberno -are -avi -atum manage

gurgustiolum -i (n) hovel

gustulum -i (n) titbit, delicacy, appetiser

gustus -us (m) hors-d'oeuvre, appetiser

***habeo -ere -ui -itum** have, display

habitus -us (m) appearance, get up, style of dress

hactenus up to this point

Haemus -i (m) Haemus (an invented robber)

Harpyia -ae (f) a Harpy (female monster)

haud not

haurio -rire -si -ritum scoop up, drink

helcium -ii (n) halter, rope for hauling

hem ah!, what's this?

heptapylos -on seven-gated, with seven city-gates

***herbula -ae** (f) herb

herciscor -i split up

***hercules** by Hercules, by god

***hereditarius -a -um** inherited, consisting of an inheritance, of one's inheritance

***heres -edis** (m) heir, successor

heus hey

hibernus -a -um of winter

***hic** here

***hic haec hoc** this, he, she, it, this man

hilaro -are -avi -atum cheer, gladden, lighten

hilarus -a -um cheerful

hio -are -avi gape

hispidus -a -um shaggy, bristly

historia -ae (f) story

hodiernus -a -um of today, today's

*__homo -inis__ (m) human being, person, man

homuncio -onis (m) little man

*__honor -oris__ (m) honour

*__hora -ae__ (f) hour

hordeacius -a -um of barley

horreo -ere -ui shudder at

horresco -ere shudder at, fear

horreum -i (n) storehouse, granary, storeroom

horridus -a -um prickly, dreadful

horripilo -are become hairy

*__hortor -ari -atus sum__ incite, urge (on)

hortulanus -i (m) gardener

hortulus -i (m) small garden, garden

hospes -itis (m) arrival, guest

hospitium -(i)i (n) inn, lodgings, home

*__humanus -a -um__ human, of a human

humilitas -atis (f) lowness of birth, status etc.

*__humus -i__ (f + m) ground, earth; **humi** on the ground

*__iaceo -ere -ui -itum__ lie, lie helpless, lie dead

iacto -are -avi -atum propel, kick, throw

iaculatio -ionis (f) throwing, hurling

iaculum -i (n) spear

*__iam__ already, by now, now, soon; **iam nunc** right now; **non iam** no longer

iamdudum for a long time now, long since, some time ago

*__ianitor -oris__ (m) porter, doorkeeper

*__ianua -ae__ (f) door

*__ibi__ there

ibidem there and then, at that very moment

ictus -us (m) thrust, stroke, blow

*__idem eadem idem__ same

identidem repeatedly, again and again

ieiunus -a -um empty, hungry, (+ abl) devoid of

ientaculum -i (n) breakfast

*__igitur__ therefore, well then

*__ignarus -a -um__ unaware, not knowing what one is doing, ignorant

*__igniculus -i__ (m) little fire

*__ignis -is__ (m) fire

ignorabilis -is -e undecipherable, unknown

*__ignoro -are -avi -atum__ be ignorant of, not know

ilico immediately

illac by that route

*__ille -a -ud__ that, he, she, it, that famous, that man

illibatus -a -um kept entire, undiminished

*__illinc__ from there, from that group

illo to that place

*__illuc__ to that place, into that place

illucesco -cescere -xi dawn

*__illumino -are -avi -atum__ illuminate, light up, reveal

illunius -a -um moonless

illustro -are -avi -atum enlighten

*__imago -inis__ (f) apparition, vision, representation, picture, statue

imber -bris (m) shower, rain

imbuo -uere -ui -utum initiate

immanis -is -e huge, savage, frightful

immaturitas -atis (f) prematureness

immergo -gere -si -sum insert, plunge in

immerito unjustly, without cause

immineo -ere (+ dat) threaten

immisceo -scere -scui -xtum merge, mix (with)

*__immitto -ittere -isi -issum__ send (in), insert, insert into (+ dat)

immo rather, no rather, worse still; **immo vero** no rather, or rather

immodice excessively

immodicus -a -um immoderate, excessive

impatiens -entis (+ gen) unable to bear

impatienter unbearably

impedimentum -i (n) hindrance, obstruction

impedio -ire -i(v)i -itum hamper, impede

impello -ellere -uli -ulsum impel, drive, thrust away

*__imperium -(i)i__ (n) command

*__impero -are -avi -atum__ give an order, make demands

impetro -are -avi -atum obtain, secure

*__impetus -us__ (m) violent onward movement, impetus, attack, charge, violence, fit (of passion etc.)

impigre briskly, energetically

impleo -ere -evi -etum fill

implico -are -ui -itum entangle, envelop

*__imploro -are -avi -atum__ beg for

*__impono -onere -osui -ositum__ place, place on (+ dat)

importunus -a -um inappropriate

imprecor -ari -atus sum call on (in prayer), wish on (+ dat)

improbo -are -avi -atum reject

improbus -a -um wicked, shameless, wanton

improsperus -a -um unfortunate

improvide unwarily, without forethought

improvidus -a -um thoughtless, unwary, unforeseeing

improvisus -a -um unexpected(ly)

*imprudentia -ae (f) imprudence, thoughtlessness

impudicus -a -um immoral

*impurus -a -um dirty, disgusting

*imus -a -um lowest, bottom of, depths of

*in (+ acc) into, to, in respect of, on, on to, so as to form, for the sake of, for, up to, against; (+ abl) in, in the midst of, among, on, in the guise of, in the case of

inacidatus -a -um vinegar-soaked

inalbo -are -avi -atum whiten, bleach

inanimis -is -e lifeless

inanis -is -e illusory, groundless

incanto -are -avi -atum (+ dat) sing on

incedo -dere -ssi proceed, walk

*incendium -(i)i (n) fire, conflagration

*incertus -a -um inarticulate, not certain (to happen), unpredictable, of uncertain outcome

incido -dere -di incasum fall (into), chance to find

incinctus -a -um girt, wrapped round (with clothes etc.)

incingo -ngere -nxi -nctum gird, arm

*incipio -ipere -epi -eptum begin, begin to speak

*incito -are -avi -atum arouse, excite, spur on

*inclamo -are -avi -atum shout out, call out to

inclemens -entis impetuous, violent

inclino -are -avi -atum cause to lean, bend forwards

includo -dere -si -sum shut in, lock in

inclutus -a -um renowned, famous

incohatus -a -um unfinished

incola -ae (m) inhabitant

incolo -ere -ui live in, live on

incolumis -is -e uninjured, intact, unharmed

incomitatus -a -um unaccompanied, on one's own

inconivus -a -um open, unsleeping

incrementum -i (n) growth

incubo -are -ui -itum stay at, sleep on, keep watch over

incunctanter without hesitation

incursio -ionis (f) attack

incutio -tere -ssi -ssum strike something (in acc) into someone (in dat), dash something (in acc) against someone (expressed by in + acc)

indagatus -us (m) tracking down

indago -inis (f) ring of huntsmen, hunt

indago -are -avi -atum track down

inde from there

*indicium -(i)i (n) sign, token, evidence, indication, disclosure

*indico -are -avi -atum make known, disclose, reveal

indidem from the same place, from them

indigena -ae (m) native

indigeo -ere -ui (+ abl) be in need of

*indignatio -ionis (f) indignation, resentment

indignor -ari -atus sum (+ dat) be angry with

indipiscor -i indeptus sum catch up with

indoctus -a -um uneducated

*induco -cere -xi -ctum lead

induo -uere -ui -utum put on, put head into, assume the form of, dress in (+ abl)

*industria -ae (f) diligence, hard work

inedia -ae (f) starvation

ineffabilis -is -e unspeakable

*ineptia -ae (f) foolishness, nonsense

*ineptus -a -um foolish

inermis -is -e unarmed

inesco -are -avi -atum gorge

*infamia -ae (f) notoriety, stigma

infantulus -i (m) baby boy

infaustus -a -um ill-omened

*infelix -icis unhappy, poor, unlucky

inferi -orum (m pl) the dead, the Underworld

inferialis -is -e funereal, funeral

inferus -a -um of the world below, of the Underworld

*infesto -are -avi -atum infest, make unsafe

infestus -a -um hostile, warlike, furious, aggressive

inficio -ficere -feci -fectum immerse, impregnate, taint, stain

infimo -are -avi -atum bring down

infit he/she begins (to speak)

*inflammo -are -avi -atum make fiery, incense

*infortunium -(i)i (n) misfortune, trouble

*infundo -undere -udi -usum pour into (+ dat)

ingenitus -a -um innate, natural

*ingenium -(i)i (n) temperament, spirit, nature

*ingredior -di -ssus sum go, travel, start

*inhabito -are -avi -atum inhabit, live there, live in (+ dat)

inhaereo -rere -si -sum hold on, get entangled in, cling to (+ dat)

*inhibeo -ere -ui -itum hinder, prevent

inhorreo -ere bristle, stand on end

inhortor -ari -atus sum incite something (acc) to attack someone (dat)

inibi there

inicio -icere -ieci -iectum throw on/into (+ dat), place on (+ dat), throw over, pour in, superimpose

inigo -igere -egi -actum push forward

*inimicus -i (m) enemy

*initio -are -avi -atum initiate

*initium -(i)i (n) beginning, start

*iniuria -ae (f) injury, physical hurt

innato -are -avi swim in (+ dat or abl)

inoculo -are -avi -atum spangle, decorate

inopinatus -a -um unexpected

inquam (3rd person sing inquit) say

*inquietus -a -um sleepless, disturbed

inquilinus -i (m) inhabitant

*inquiro -rere -si(v)i -situm inquire about

*insanus -a -um insane, crazed

inscendo -dere -di -sum mount, climb on to

insecutio -ionis (f) pursuit

insequor -sequi -secutus sum pursue, attack, follow on

insiciatus -a -um stuffed (with finely chopped meat)

insigniter conspicuously

insilio -ire -ui leap on, attack

insimulo -are -avi -atum accuse

insinuo -are -avi -atum insert, put inside

insisto -ere institi (+ acc or dat) stand on, be on top of

insomnis -is -e unsleeping

*insperatus -a -um unexpected, unhoped for

inspersus -us (m) sprinkling on

*instabilis -is -e fickle, shifting

instans -antis present, insistent

instantia -ae (f) insistence, importunity

instar (n) equivalent; ad instar after the fashion (of)

instigo -are -avi -atum incite, impel

instinctus -a -um excited, roused

instinctus -us (m) prompting, instigation

insto -are -iti be imminent, threaten

instringo -ingere -inxi -ictum rouse, incite

instructus -us (m) equipment, apparatus

*instrumentum -i (n) instrument, device

instruo -ere -xi -ctum plan, set up, equip, set, instruct

insumo -ere -psi -ptum employ, spend

insuo -uere -ui -utum sew up someone (in acc) in something (in dat)

insuper above, on top, in addition; (+ acc) on top of, down into

insurgo -gere -rexi rear up, (+ dat) stand up on

intectus -a -um uncovered

integer -gra -grum undamaged, unharmed, entire

*intellego -gere -xi -ctum understand, comprehend

intemeratus -a -um unsullied, unimpaired

intemperans -antis unrestrained, headstrong

intempestivus -a -um untimely

intempestus -a -um unseasonable; nox intempesta dead of night

intendo -dere -di -tum direct; animum intendo pay attention to

intentus -a -um intense, drawn

*inter (+ acc) among, between, in the midst of

intercipio -cipere -cepi -ceptum interrupt

intercludo -dere -si -sum block, stifle

interdum from time to time, meanwhile

*interea meanwhile

intereo -ire -ivi -itum be destroyed

interficio -ficere -feci -fectum kill

interpello -are -avi -atum interrupt, accost

interstinguo -guere -xi -ctum kill

intervocaliter with cries at intervals

intexo -ere -ui -tum weave together, plait, embroider

*intime deep inside

*intimus -a -um inmost

intingo -gere -xi -ctum dip in, insert

*intolerabilis -is -e unbearable

intorqueo -quere -si -tum stir, wiggle

intra (+ acc) within, inside

intrepidus -a -um fearless, undaunted, untroubled

intrinsecus inside

intro inside, in

introduco -cere -xi -ctum bring in

introeo -ire -i(v)i -itum enter

introrepo -pere -psi slink in, creep in

introrumpo -rumpere -rupi burst in, break in

intueor -eri -itus sum observe, see

inurgueo -ere press (on someone)

*invado -dere -si -sum seize, invade, enter
  boldly, attack
inversus -a -um inverted, turned upside down
Invidia -ae (f) Envy
invisitatus -a -um unseen, never seen before,
  strange
invitus -a -um unwilling, involuntary
involvo -volvere -volvi -volutum wrap up, cover
*iocus -i (m) joke, jest, sport
*ipse -a -um oneself, myself, yourself, himself,
  herself, itself, the very, the actual, by oneself
*irreligiosus -a -um irreligious, unbelieving
irrepo -pere -psi creep into, creep inwards
*is ea id this, that, he, she, it
Isis -idis (f) Isis (Egyptian goddess)
*iste ista istud this, that, your, he, she, it
istic in that matter of yours
*ita in such a way
*itaque and so
*iter itineris (n) journey, travel, road
itero -are -avi -atum repeat
iuba -ae (f) mane
*iubeo -bere -ssi -ssum order, tell
iugulo -are -avi -atum kill by cutting the
  throat, kill
iugulum -i (n) throat
iugum -i (n) yoke
iumentum -i (n) baggage animal, working
  animal
*Iuppiter Iovis (m) Jupiter
iuro -are -avi -atum swear, take an oath
*ius iuris (n) law, legal system, bonds
*iustus -a -um just, justified
*iuvenis -is -e young
*iuvenis -is (m) young man
*iuventus -utis (f) young men
iuxta (+ acc) near

labes -is (f) defect, slip
labia -ae (f) lip
labium -ii (n) lip
*labor -oris (m) work, labour, task, job, toil,
  hardship
labor -bi -psus sum fail, collapse, faint
*laboriosus -a -um toiling, harassed
*laboro -are -avi -atum suffer (from), be
  distressed
lac lactis (m) milk
*lacero -are -avi -atum rend, mangle, rip
laciniae -arum (f pl) garments, clothes, rags
*lacrima -ae (f) tear

*lacrimo -are -avi -atum weep
lacteus -a -um milky
*lacus -us (m) lake, pond
*laetor -ari -atus sum rejoice, be delighted
*laetus -a -um happy, delighted
*laeva on the left
Lamachus -i (m) Lamachus
*lamentatio -onis (f) lamentation, wailing
*lamentor -ari -atus sum grieve, mourn
lamia -ae (f) female monster, hag
*lancea -ae (f) lance
laniena -ae (f) butchery, mutilation
lanificium -(i)i (n) spinning, weaving
lanio -are -avi -atum tear, mutilate, wound
  savagely
lanius -(i)i (m) butcher
lapis -idis (m) rock
laqueus -i (m) noose, trap, trouble
lar laris (m) home, household; lares (pl)
  property
largior -iri -itus sum give generously, grant
largiter generously, abundantly
largitus without stint, munificently
larva -ae (f + m) ghost, evil spirit
larvalis -is -e of a ghost, spectre-like
larvatus -a -um possessed by a ghost
*lascivia -ae (f) lust, lasciviousness
*lassitudo -inis (f) weariness, exhaustion
*lassus -a -um tired, weary
latebra -ae (f) subterfuge, means of concealment
latenter stealthily, secretly, in concealment
lateo -ere -ui lurk, be concealed, escape the
  notice of
latex laticis (m) water
latibulum -i (n) hiding-place
latratus -us (m) barking, bark
*latrina -ae (f) latrine
latro -onis (m) robber, bandit
latrocinor -ari -atus sum engage in brigandage,
  plunder
latus -eris (n) side, flank
*laudo -are -avi -atum praise, commend
laureus -a -um resembling laurel; laurea rosa
  laurel rose
lavacrum -i (n) bath
lavo -are lavi lautum wash; lavor bathe
lector -oris (m) reader
lectulus -i (m) bed, funeral bier
*legitimus -a -um legally required, legitimate
lenio -ire -i(v)i -itum calm down, mollify
lenis -is -e gentle, placid

leniter quietly
lepidus -a -um charming, amusing
letalis -is -e lethal, poisonous
levis -is -e slight
levo -are -avi -atum lessen, relieve, relieve of
  (+ abl)
*****lex legis** (f) law, statute
Liber -eri (m) Bacchus (the god of wine)
*****liber libri** (m) book
*****liber -era -erum** free, free-born
*****liberalis -is -e** magnanimous, generous
*****liberalitas -atis** (f) generosity
*****liberaliter** extravagantly
*****libere** freely
*****liberi -orum** (m pl) children
*****libero -are -avi -atum** set free, save, rescue
*****libertas -atis** (f) freedom, boldness
*****libido -inis** (f) desire, sexual desire, lust,
  longing
libo -are -avi -atum pour a libation on, make an
  offering on, offer
libro -are -avi -atum poise (in flight)
licentiosus -a -um capricious, wanton
liceor -eri -itus sum make a bid, negotiate
licet it is permitted, although
ligneus -a -um wooden
lima -ae (f) file, filing
limen -inis (n) threshold, doorway
limus -a -um glancing sideways
*****lingua -ae** (f) tongue
linteolum -i (n) linen bandage
linteus -a -um of linen
*****liquor -oris** (m) liquid
lito -are -avi -atum make a propitiatory offering
*****littera -ae** (f) letter; **litterae** (pl) epistle, letter
litus -oris (n) coast, shore
loco -are -avi -atum position, place
locuples -etis well supplied, rich
*****locus -i** (m) place, spot, room, space, situation
*****longe** far off, by far, greatly; (+ acc) far from
*****longus -a -um** lengthy, long
*****loquor loqui locutus sum** speak
lorica -ae (f) earthwork (mound of earth used as
  a defence)
lorum -i (n) leather strap
lotium -(i)i (n) urine
lubricus -a -um slippery, smooth
luceo -ere luxi shine, give light
lucerna -ae (f) lamp
lucidus -a -um bright
Lucius -(i)i (m) Lucius

lucrum -i (n) profit
luctuosus -a -um sorrowful, mournful
luctus -us (m) grief, mourning
luculentus -a -um beautiful
lucus -i (m) grove
ludicre playfully
lugeo -ere luxi luctum mourn
lumen -inis (n) light, lamp, eye
*****luna -ae** (f) moon
lupanaris -is -e of a brothel
lupus -i (m) wolf
luror -oris (m) sallowness, sickly pallor
luteus -a -um yellow
*****lux lucis** (f) light, daylight, dawn
Lynceus -ei (m) Lynceus (a keen-sighted
  Argonaut)

Macedonia -ae (f) Macedonia (a region in north
  Greece)
macies -ei (f) leanness, thinness, emaciation
maculo -are -avi -atum defile, disgrace
Madaurensis -is (m) a man from Madaura (in
  north Africa)
madeo -ere be wet, be drunk (with)
mador -oris (m) wetness, liquid
maereo -ere mourn, be sad
maeror -oris (m) grief, sorrow, lamentation
*****maestus -a -um** sad, mourning
*****magicus -a -um** magic
*****magis** more
magnanimus -a -um noble-spirited, brave, bold
*****magnificus -a -um** magnificent, splendid
*****magnitudo -inis** (f) size, great size
*****magnopere** greatly, particularly, earnestly
*****magnus -a -um** large, great, considerable,
  mighty
*****maior -or -us** greater, quite serious
*****male** wickedly, immorally, wrongfully
maleficium -(i)i (n) sorcery
*****malitia -ae** (f) malice, wickedness
*****malo malle malui** prefer, choose rather
malum -i (n) apple-tree
*****malum -i** (n) trouble, wrongdoing, harm
*****malus -a -um** bad, evil, unpleasant, hostile
mancipo -are -avi -atum surrender
mando -are -avi -atum entrust, commit
mando -dere -di -sum chew, bite
manduco -onis (m) glutton
mane in the morning; **as noun** morning
manes -ium (m pl) the dead, ghosts, ghost
*****manifestus -a -um** clear, obvious

mansio -ionis (f) stopping-place, dwelling

*manus -us (f) hand, lower arm, band, gang, power

Marcellus -i (m) Marcellus

marceo -ere droop, flag, be enfeebled

marcidus -a -um enfeebled, exhausted

*mare -is (n) sea

margo -inis (f) edge, lip

marito -are -avi -atum marry; passive get married

maritus -i (m) husband

Mars Martis (m) Mars (god of war)

*masculinus -a -um masculine, of a man

*masculus -a -um masculine, of a man

*mater matris (f) mother; mater familias mistress of the household

*matrona -ae (f) matron, married woman

mature at an early time, early, quickly

*maturesco -escere -ui mature

matutino in the early morning

matutinus -a -um in the early morning

*maximus -a -um very great, very large, abundant

medela -ae (f) remedy, cure

*medicus -i (m) doctor

*mediocris -is -e moderate, slight

*medius -a -um middle, mid, (in) the middle of

mel mellis (n) honey, sweetness

mellitus -a -um honeyed, delicious as honey

*membrum -i (n) limb; membra (pl) body

*memini -isse remember

memorabilis -is -e memorable, remarkable

*memoria -ae (f) memory

memoro -are -avi -atum say, relate, recall

*mensa -ae (f) table, meal

*mensis -is (m) month

mentior -tiri -titus sum feign, make a show of, play deceitfully

mentum -i (n) chin

merces -edis (f) wage, pay

mereo -ere -ui -itum earn

mereor -eri -itus sum deserve

meretricius -a -um typical of a prostitute, a prostitute's

merito naturally, deservedly, with good cause

Meroe -es (f) Meroe

merum -i (n) neat wine

merus -a -um mere, simple

meta -ae (f) limit, end, goal

metallum -i (n) mineral

*metuo -ere -ui -utum fear

*metus -us (m) fear

*meus -a -um my

*miles -itis (m) soldier

*militaris -is -e military, of soldiers

*mille a thousand

milvinus -a -um kite-like

minax -acis threatening

mineus -a -um having the colour of cinnabar, bright red

minister -tri (m) assistant, accomplice

ministerium -(i)i (n) support, agency, service

ministro -are -avi -atum provide, administer

*minor -or -us smaller, less

minus less, not

*minuties -ei (f) smallness, flatness

*mirabundus -a -um wondering, astonished (at)

*miraculum -i (n) miracle

*mire marvellously, amazingly

*mirificus -a -um astonishing

*miror -ari -atus sum marvel at, be amazed at, wonder

*mirus -a -um marvellous, amazing, extraordinary

misceo -ere -ui mixtum be physically joined, throw into confusion, fill with confused noise

misellus -a -um poor, wretched, pitiable

*miser -era -erum wretched, unhappy, distressing, poor, pitiful

misere pitifully

misereo -ere -ui feel pity; miseret me + gen I feel sorry for

misereor -eri -itus sum have pity

misericordia -ae (f) pity, compassion

*miserinus -a -um wretched, unhappy

*miseriter pathetically

miseror -ari -atus sum pity

mitella -ae (f) turban

mitigo -are -avi -atum relax, relieve, soften, mollify

mitis -is -e gentle

*mitto -ere misi missum send, throw out, give up, cease

modice slightly

modicus -a -um moderate, little

modo only, only provided that; non modo ... sed/verum etiam not only ... but also

modulus -i (m) unit; pro meo modulo within my limitations, as best I could

modus -i (m) type, manner, way; in modum in the manner (of)

mola -ae (f) millstone, mill

mollis -is -e soft, effeminate

*****momentum -i** (n) moment

*****moneo -ere -ui -itum** warn, tell

monile -is (n) necklace, jewellery

monimentum -i (n) monument, tomb

*****monita -orum** (n pl) warning, advice

*****monitio -ionis** (f) advice, warning

*****monitus -us** (m) command, admonition

*****mons montis** (m) mountain

monstro -are -avi -atum point to

*****monumentum -i** (n) tomb, sepulchral
monument

mora -ae (f) delay

*****morior mori mortuus sum** die

moror -ari -atus sum delay

*****mors mortis** (f) death

morsico -are nibble

morsiuncula -ae (f) little bite

morsus -us (m) bite, biting

*****mortalis -is** (m + f) mortal, human

*****mortifer -era -erum** deadly

*****mortuus -a -um** dead; **as noun** dead
person

mos moris (m) character, morals

motus -us (m) movement

*****mox** soon, next

mucro -onis (m) sword-point, sword

mugio -ire -ivi -itum moo

mugitus -us (m) growl, roar

*****muliebris -is -e** a woman's

*****mulier -eris** (f) woman

*****multicolor -oris** of many colours

multifariam in many places

multiformis -is -e of many designs, intricate

multiiugus -a -um multifarious, of many parts

*****multitudo -inis** (f) host, large number,
large group

*****multo** much

*****multus -a -um** numerous, many, much

muneror -ari -atus sum present with a
gift, reward

munia (n pl) duties, functions

munio -ire -i(v)i -itum protect, guard, man

munus -eris (n) task, duty, gift, show

mus muris (m) mouse

mustela -ae (f) weasel

*****muto -are -avi -atum** change, transform

*****mutuo** mutually, one another

*****mutuus -a -um** mutual, given in return

Myrrhine -es (f) Myrrhine (a maid)

nacca -ae (m) fuller (someone who cleanses and
thickens cloth)

naccinus -a -um of the fuller

*****nam** for

*****namque** for

nanciscor -i na(n)ctus sum get, acquire

nares -ium (f pl) nostrils, nose

*****narratus -us** (m) narrative, account

*****narro -are -avi -atum** talk, relate, recount, tell

*****nascor nasci natus sum** be born

nasus -i (m) nose

nates -ium (f pl) buttocks

natura -ae (f) penis

*****navigabilis -is -e** navigable, able to be sailed

*****navis -is** (f) ship

naviter actively, zealously, completely, briskly

***** -ne** whether, really (introducing a question)

*****ne** in order that not, lest, for fear that, that (in a
fear clause), that not, not; **ne . . . quidem** not
even; **ne . . . saltem** not even

nebula -ae (f) cloud

*****nec** and not, neither, but not, not even; **nec . . .
nec** neither . . . nor

necdum not yet, and not yet

*****necessario** of necessity

*****necessarius -a -um** necessary, requisite

*****necessitas -atis** (f) constraint, compulsion

neco -are -avi -atum kill

necto -ere nexi nectum attach to (+ dat), bind

nefandus -a -um wicked, heinous

*****nefarius -a -um** evil, abominable

negotiator -oris (m) trader, businessman

negotium -(i)i (n) business

*****nemo -inis** (m) nobody

nemus -oris (n) wood, grove

nepos -otis (m) grandson

*****neque** and not, neither; **neque . . . neque**
neither . . . nor

*****nequeo -ire -i(v)i** be unable (to), be unable
to do

nequissimus -a -um thoroughly evil, absolutely
useless

nequitia -ae (f) wickedness, depravity

nervus -i (m) bowstring, muscle

*****nescio -ire -i(v)i -itum** not know

*****nescius -a -um** not knowing, unknown,
inexplicable

*****neve** and that not

nexus -us (m) embrace

*****ni** if not

Nicanor -oris (m) Nicanor

nidificium -(i)i (n) nest
nidor -oris (m) stink, smell
*****niger -gra -grum** black
*****nihil** (n) nothing; **as adverb** not at all
*****nimietas -atis** (f) excess
nimirum no doubt
*****nimis** too, very
*****nimium -(i)i** (n) excess, abundance
*****nimius -a -um** excessive, very great, copious
*****nisi** if not, unless, except
nisus -us (m) effort, heave
nitor -oris (m) brightness, glitter, sheen
nitor niti nisus sum strive, direct efforts
  (towards)
noctu by night
*****nocturnus -a -um** nocturnal, at night
nodus -i (m) noose
*****nolo nolle nolui** not wish, not want, be
  unwilling; **noli** + **infin** don't
*****nomen -inis** (n) name, title
*****nominatim** by name
*****non** not
*****nondum** not yet
nonnumquam sometimes, on various occasions
nonus -a -um ninth
*****nos nostrum/nostri** we, ourselves, I
*****nosco -ere novi notum** find out
*****noster -tra -trum** our, my
novalia -ium (n pl) park
noverca -ae (f) stepmother
*****novi novisse notum** know, (+ infin) know
  how to
*****novus -a -um** new
*****nox noctis** (f) night
noxa -ae (f) harm, wrongdoing
*****noxius -a -um** harmful, deadly
*****nudo -are -avi -atum** strip of (+ abl),
  strip, empty
*****nudus -a -um** bare, naked, unsheathed, exposed
nugae -arum (f pl) trifle, bagatelle
*****nullus -a -um** none, no, not; **as noun** nobody
numen -inis (n) supernatural power, god,
  divinity
*****numero -are -avi -atum** count, reckon
*****numerosus -a -um** numerous
*****numerus -i** (m) number, plurality, company,
  band
nummatus -a -um moneyed, wealthy
nummularius -(i)i (m) banker
nummus -i (m) coin, sesterce (Roman unit of
  money)

*****nunc** now; **nunc . . . nunc** at one point . . . at
  another point
nuncupo -are -avi -atum call, name, consecrate,
  dedicate
*****nuntio -are -avi -atum** bring word of, report
*****nuntius -(i)i** (m) message, notice of divorce
nupta -ae (f) bride, married woman
nuptiae -arum (f pl) marriage
nusquam nowhere
nutrio -ire -i(v)i -itum nourish, nurse, feed,
  support, increase
nutrix -tricis (f) nurse
nutus -us (m) nod (of approval or command)

*****o** oh
*****ob** (+ acc) on account of, with a view to, in
  front of
*****obarmo -are -avi -atum** arm
obdo -dere -didi -ditum push home, fasten
obeo -ire -i(v)i -itum visit, go to, approach,
  view, perform, accept, take on
*****obesus -a -um** bulky, plump
obicio -icere -ieci -iectum throw
obliquo -are -avi -atum bend, move to the side,
  edge in
*****obliquus -a -um** sidelong, sideways
*****obliviscor -livisci -litus sum** (+ gen) forget
obnixus -a -um determined, resolute
obnubilo -are -avi -atum becloud, render
  unconscious
obruo -ere -i -tum smother, overwhelm
obsaepio -ire -si -tum hem in
*****obscurus -a -um** obscure, dark
obsequium -(i)i (n) obedience, subservience,
  service
obsero -are -avi -atum bolt
observito -are -avi -atum have regard to, pay
  attention to
observo -are -avi -atum notice
obsideo -idere -edi -essum beset, attack, occupy,
  blockade, besiege
obtego -gere -xi -ctum cover, conceal
obtero -terere -trivi -tritum crush, annihilate
obtestor -ari -atus sum invoke, implore
obtundo -undere -udi -usum pound, batter,
  assail, assail with demands
obumbro -are -avi -atum cover
obverbero -are -avi -atum beat, strike
obvius -a -um in the way, meeting, placed so as
  to meet, put in a line of vision
*****occasio -onis** (f) opportunity, chance

occido -dere -di -sum kill

occipio -ipere -epi -eptum begin

occludo -dere -si -sum lock, bolt

*occulto -are -avi -atum hide

*occultus -a -um hidden, secret

occurro -rrere -rri -rsum run up, confront, crop up

occursorius -a -um welcoming, of welcome

Oceanus -i (m) Ocean (great river surrounding earth's land mass)

ocius quickly

*oculus -i (m) eye

*odiosus -a -um hateful

*odium -(i)i (n) hatred

*odor -oris (m) smell, stink

*odorus -a -um fragrant

oenophorum -i (n) a large jug of wine

offendo -dere -di -sum offend, annoy

offero -ferre obtuli oblatum reveal, provide, bring on, present, give

officinator -oris (m) foreman, manager

officiosus -a -um dutiful, attentive

officium -(i)i (n) service, kind act, rite, post, observance, function

offigo -gere -xi -xum fasten, nail

offulcio -cire -si -tum stop up

oleum -i (n) oil

*olim long since, long ago

olla -ae (f) pot

ollula -ae (f) little pot

olus -eris (n) vegetable

*omen -inis (n) omen

omitto -ittere -isi -issum stop, abandon

ommisceo -ere combine something (acc) with something (dat)

omnino at all

*omnis -is -e all, every

onustus -a -um loaded, laden (with)

opera -ae (f) service, assistance

operor -ari -atus sum work hard (in), busy oneself (with)

operose painstakingly

opertum -i (n) secret place

opertus -a -um obscure, secret

operulae -arum (f pl) slender earnings

opifex -icis (m) workman

opilio -onis (m) herdsman

opimus -a -um fine, plump

*opinio -ionis (f) belief, expectation

*opinor -ari -atus sum imagine, think

opitulor -ari -atus sum give help

oportet -ere -uit it is proper, it is right that (+ acc and infin)

opperior -iri -tus sum await

oppessulo -are -avi -atum bolt, bar

oppido absolutely, altogether, exceedingly

*opportune conveniently

*opportunus -a -um timely, opportune, convenient, useful

opprimo -imere -essi -essum catch, overwhelm

ops opis (f) help, wealth

optabilis -is -e desirable, desired

optatus -a -um desired

*optimus -a -um best

optutus -us (m) gaze

*opulens -entis prosperous, rich

*opulentia -ae (f) wealth

*opus -eris (n) work, job, sexual intercourse

*orbis -is (m) the world

Orcus -i (m) Orcus (god of the Underworld), the Underworld

ordior -diri -sus sum begin (to speak)

ordo -inis (m) sequence

orgia -orum (n pl) secret rites, mysteries

*orno -are -avi -atum furnish, adorn, add lustre to

*os oris (n) face, features, mouth, lips

*os ossis (n) bone

osculabundus -a -um kissing

osculum -i (n) kiss

Osiris -is (m) Osiris (Egyptian god)

ostium -(i)i (n) door

otiose at ease, in a leisurely manner

otiosus -a -um not at work, leisurely, doing nothing, idle

otium -(i)i (n) leisure, ease, relaxation

ovicula -ae (f) sheep

paelicatus -us (m) existence of a rival, a liaison

paene almost

paenissime very nearly

paeniteo -ere -ui make someone (in acc) feel regret for something (in gen)

paganus -i (m) villager

pagus -i (m) village

palam openly; palam facere expose

palla -ae (f) cloak

palliastrum -i (n) a poor cloak

pallor -oris (m) paleness, pallor

*palmula -ae (f) palm (of the hand)

pango -ere pepigi pactum arrange, agree

*panis -is (m) bread

pannosus -a -um dressed in rags, tattered

pannulus -i (m) ragged clothes, rags

Panthia -ae (f) Panthia (a witch)

papilla -ae (f) breast

*paratus -a -um ready, prepared

*parco -ere peperci (+ dat) spare, refrain from
    injuring

*parens -entis (m + f) parent

pareo -ere -ui -itum be visible, be seen

pario -ere peperi partum produce, give birth to

*paro -are -avi -atum prepare, make available,
    get, provide

parricidium -(i)i (n) murder of a close
    relative/friend

*pars partis (f) part, portion

partiario on the basis of sharing

particeps -ipis (f) sharer

participo -are -avi -atum share

*partim partly

partio -ire -ivi -itum split up

*parvitas -atis (f) smallness

*parvulus -a -um small, scant; (as noun) little
    one, child

*parvus -a -um small, a little, scant

pasco -ere pavi pastum graze

passer -eris (m) sparrow

passim everywhere, all over the place

pastophorus -i (m) priest (of Isis or Osiris)

pastor -oris (m) shepherd, herdsman

patefacio -facere -feci -factum open up, expose

*pater patris (m) father

*paternus -a -um of the father, paternal

patibulum -i (n) gibbet, cross

patior pati passus sum allow

patrius -a -um ancestral

patulus -a -um open

pauculus -a -um little, short, few

*paucus -a -um few

paulatim gradually, bit by bit

paulisper for a short while

paulo by a small amount, a little

paululum a little, a bit, for a short while

*pauper -eris poor

*pauperculus -a -um poor

*pauperies -iei (f) poverty

*paupertas -atis (f) poverty

*paupertinus -a -um poor

*pausa -ae (f) pause, respite; pausam facere
    (+ dat) desist from

paveo -ere be frightened, be terrified

pavor -oris (m) fear, terror

*pax pacis (f) peace

pectus -oris (n) breast, heart, chest

*pecunia -ae (f) money

pecus -oris (n) livestock, (farm and domestic)
    animal

*peior -ior -ius worse, quite bad

pelagus -i (n) sea

pello -ere pepuli pulsum rouse, drive along

pendeo -ere pependi hang

pendulus -a -um sagging, drooping,
    loose-hanging

penetrale -is (n) inmost part, inner shrine

penitus deep inside (adv)

penitus -a -um inmost, the depths of

*per (+ acc) through, through the length of,
    across, along, by means of, thanks to, during,
    by, on account of

perago -agere -egi -actum perform, complete

perastutulus -a -um very artful, very astute

percello -ellere -uli -ulsum strike, overcome

percenseo -ere -ui recount, give a full
    account of

percieo -iere -ii -itum propel, stir

percitus -a -um panicked, alarmed

percolo -ere -ui percultum worship

percontor -ari -atus sum ask; percontor de
    (+ abl) ask of

percrebresco -rescere -rui become widespread

percuro -are -avi -atum cure, fix up

percussor -oris (m) murderer

percutio -tere -ssi -ssum strike, stagger, impinge
    on

perditus -a -um depraved, abandoned

perdius -a -um throughout the day

*perdo -ere -idi -itum lose, abandon, destroy,
    kill, affect severely

perduco -cere -xi -ctum lead, take

peregrinatio -ionis (f) foreign travel, staying
    abroad

peregrinus -i (m) foreigner, stranger

peremptor -oris (m) killer

*pereo -ire -i(v)i -itum perish, die

perfero -ferre -tuli -latum convey, take, tell

perficio -icere -eci -ectum complete

*perfidia -ae (f) disloyalty, treachery

*perfidus -a -um unfaithful

perflabilis -is -e airy, well-ventilated

perfluo -ere -xi -xum stream (with)

perfrico -are -ui -atum rub all over

perfringo -ingere -egi -actum break, burst
    through, break into

perfruor -frui -fructus sum (+ abl) enjoy thoroughly

perfundo -undere -udi -usum drench, suffuse

perfungor -gi -ctus sum go through

pergo -gere -rexi -rectum move on, proceed (to)

perhibeo -ere -ui -itum present, give

***periculum -i** (n) danger, endangerment

perimo -imere -emi -emptum kill, murder

perlino -linere (-levi) -litum smear all over (with)

perlucidus -a -um clearly intelligible

perluo -uere -ui -utum bathe, drench

permetior -tiri -nsus sum travel over, cover

permisceo -scere -scui -xtum mix in, add, mingle with (+ dat), steep in, cover with

***permitto -ittere -isi -issum** allow, entrust

permulceo -cere -si -sum calm down, soothe, charm

pernicies -ei (f) destruction

pernicitas -atis (f) speed, nimbleness

pernox -octis throughout the night

perperam incorrectly

perpes -etis the whole, continuous

***perpetuo -are -avi -atum** perpetuate, immortalize

***perpetuus -a -um** everlasting

perquiesco -ere rest

persentisco -ere become fully conscious of

persolvo -lvere -lvi -lutum perform, repay, discharge

***persona -ae** (f) role, character

personatus -a -um masking one's real feelings, playing a part

***perspicax -acis** keen-sighted, perceptive

***perspicio -icere -exi -ectum** inspect, scrutinize, see through, discern

***persuadeo -dere -si -sum** (+ acc or dat) persuade

***perterreo -ere -ui -itum** terrify

pertracto -are -avi -atum pass the hand over, finger

perveho -here -xi -ctum convey, carry

***pervenio -enire -eni -entum** come, arrive

pervicax -acis steadfast, persistent

pervigil -ilis awake all night long, ever-vigilant

pervigilis -is -e ever-vigilant

pervoluto -are -avi -atum roll; **pervolutor** roll over, writhe

***pes pedis** (m) foot

***pessimus -a -um** worst, thoroughly evil, most distressing

pessulus -i (m) bolt

pestilens -entis unhealthy, noxious, pernicious

petitio -ionis (f) courting

petitor -oris (m) suitor, wooer

***peto -ere -i(v)i -itum** make for, be on one's way to, ask for, ask, seek, chase, want, attack

Photis -idis (f) Photis (a servant)

Phrixus -i (m) Phrixus

***pietas -atis** (f) devotion, dutifulness

piget -ere -uit it affects with horror for something (gen)

pigre slowly, reluctantly

pilus -i (m) hair, bristles

pinnula -ae (f) little wing

pistor -oris (m) baker

pistrinum -i (n) bakery

***placeo -ere -ui/-itus sum** be pleasing, be attractive, appeal

placidus -a -um kind, coaxing, quiet, calm, gentle, friendly

plaga -ae (f) blow, stroke, wound

plaga -ae (f) area, region

plagosus -a -um battered, mangled

plane clearly, quite, completely

plango -gere -xi -ctum beat the breast, mourn

plangor -oris (m) lamentation, shriek, beating the breast

Plataea -ae (f) Plataea (town in central Greece)

platanus -i (f) plane-tree

platea -ae (f) street

***plene** fully, completely

***plenus -a -um** full, complete

***plerusque -aque -umque** most of; (in plural) very many, most

Plotina -ae (f) Plotina

plumula -ae (f) little feather

***plures -es -a** more

plurifariam extensively

***plurimus -a -um** very many

***plus -ris** (n) more, a greater amount

plusculum -i (n) a fairly large amount

poculum -i (n) drink, drinking-cup

***poena -ae** (f) punishment

***poenalis -is -e** of punishment, punitive

pompa -ae (f) procession

pone (+ acc) behind

poples -itis (m) back of knee, hock

popularis -is -e local

***populosus -a -um** crowded

*populus -i (m) the people

porrigo -igere -exi -ectum stretch out, offer,
   direct

*porta -ae (f) city gate

possessio -onis (f) estate

*possideo -idere -edi -essum possess, engulf

*possum posse potui be able, may, bring oneself
   to, have the courage to

post later; (+ acc) after

*postea later, subsequently

posterior -ior -ius rear

postpono -onere -osui -ositum disregard, treat
   as unimportant

postremo finally

postremus -a -um lower, extreme, rear, hind

*postulo -are -avi -atum ask for, request,
   demand, require

*postumus -a -um posthumous

potatio -ionis (f) drinking party

*potens -entis powerful, possessing the ability to
   (+ infin), having power over (+ gen)

potio -onis (f) drink

potior -iri -itus sum (+ abl) acquire, obtain

potissimum in particular

potius rather, in preference

potus -us (m) drink

prae (+ abl) on account of, in comparison with,
   ahead of

praebeo -ere -ui -itum offer

praecedo -edere -essi -essum precede

praeceps headlong (adv)

praeceps -ipitis headlong, impetuous

praeceptum -i (n) instruction, order

praecingo -gere -xi -ctum gird, surround;
   (passive) tuck up one's clothes

praecipio -ipere -epi -eptum order (+ dat),
   command, advise

praecipito -are -avi -atum hurl down

praecipue especially, in particular

praecipuus -a -um chief, outstanding

praecisio -ionis (f) severing, amputation

praeco -onis (m) crier, one who makes public
   announcements

praecordia -orum (n pl) heart, midriff,
   entrails

*praeda -ae (f) booty, spoil

praedico -are -avi -atum proclaim, declare

praedico -dicere -dixi -dictum prophesy,
   warn of

praeditus -a -um endowed (with)

praedo -onis (m) robber, brigand, plunderer

*praefero -ferre -tuli -latum give precedence
   to one person or thing
   (in acc) over another (in dat)

praegrandis -is -e very large, huge

praematurus -a -um very early

praemineo -ere stick out, protrude

praeminor -ari -atus sum threaten (with), hold
   out as a threat

*praemium -(i)i (n) payment, reward

praenobilis -is -e very distinguished, well-born

praenoto -are -avi -atum write down, inscribe

*praeparo -are -avi -atum prepare

*praesens -entis present, imminent

praesentarius -a -um in effect immediately,
   immediate

*praesentia -ae (f) presence

praesertim especially

praesidium -(i)i (n) security, safety, protector

praestino -are -avi -atum buy

praesto -are -iti -atum give, supply, afford,
   provide

praestolor -ari -atus sum be waiting, be ready

praesum -esse -fui (+ dat) be in command of

praeter (+ acc) in addition to, besides, beyond,
   except

praetereo -ire -i(v)i -itum pass by

praeterfluo -ere flow past

praetergredior -di -ssus sum pass by

prandium -(i)i (n) lunch

pratens -entis meadowy, belonging to a meadow

pratum -i (n) meadow

*prehendo -dere -di -sum grasp, take hold of

*premo -mere -ssi -ssum press, urge, suppress

pressim firmly, closely

pretiosus -a -um expensive

*pretium -(i)i (n) price, wages

*prex precis (f) prayer, entreaty

pridem some time ago, previously

primarius -a -um leading, of the highest
   importance

primitiae -arum (f pl) first-fruits, first offering

*primo first, firstly

*primum at first, in the first place, firstly, the
   first time

*primus -a -um first; in primis above all, chiefly

*princeps -ipis (m) leader

*principalis -is -e major, foremost

principium -(i)i (n) beginning

*prior -ior -ius earlier, previous, first

pristinus -a -um original, former

prius sooner, first, earlier

privo -are -avi -atum (+ abl) strip, rob (of),
    deprive (of)

*pro (+ abl) for the sake of, for, in place of,
    according to, in front of

probe well, satisfactorily

probo -are -avi -atum examine, test

probrum -i (n) abuse, insult

procax -acis impudent, headstrong, bold

procedo -dere -ssi -ssum come out, go forward

procella -ae (f) storm

procerus -a -um tall, long

procinctus -us (m) equipment

*proclamo -are -avi -atum call out, appeal
    noisily

*procul in the distance, far away

procuro -are -avi -atum (+ acc or dat) look
    after, see to, arrange

procurro -currere -(cu)curri -cursum run
    forward, rush ahead

procus -i (m) suitor, wooer

prodo -dere -didi -ditum betray, forsake

*produco -cere -xi -ctum bring forward, bring
    out, lead out, lead

*proelior -ari -atus sum fight, struggle

*proelium -(i)i (n) fight, battle

profanus -a -um uninitiated

profectio -onis (f) departure, setting out

profecto certainly, undoubtedly

profero -ferre -tuli -latum bring out, display,
    hold out

*proficiscor -ci profectus sum set out, depart,
    come

profor -fari -fatus sum speak out

*profugio -ugere -ugi run away, make one's
    escape

*profugus -a -um fleeing, fugitive, making one's
    escape

profundo -undere -udi -usum pour out, spill

*profundus -a -um deep, intense, extreme

prognascor -asci -atus sum be born (from)

*prohibeo -ere -ui -itum restrain (from),
    prevent

proicio -icere -ieci -iectum fling, dump,
    cast out

prolabor -labi -lapsus sum slip out

prolixe wholeheartedly

prolixus -a -um extended, widened, lengthy

proluo -uere -ui -utum wash away

promineo -ere -ui protrude

promino -are -avi -atum drive out

*promissum -i (n) promise

promo -mere -mpsi -mptum reveal

promoveo -overe -ovi -otum move forward,
    advance

prompte readily, eagerly

*pronuntio -are -avi -atum announce,
    relate, say

*pronus -a -um headlong, eager, leaning
    forward, inclined (to)

*propello -ellere -uli -ulsum drive out

propere quickly

*propheta -ae (m) prophet

propinquo -are -avi (+ dat) draw near to,
    approach

*propitio -are -avi -atum win over, propitiate,
    make benevolent

*propitius -a -um well-disposed, propitious

*propter (+ acc) near; (as adverb) nearby

propudiosus -a -um shameful

prorepo -pere -psi -ptum crawl out

proripio -ipere -ipui -eptum hurl forward

prorsus absolutely, thoroughly, totally, precisely

prorumpo -rumpere -rupi -ruptum rush forth,
    lapse, burst out, break out

proseco -are -ui -tum sever, amputate

prosectus -us (m) cut, gash

prosequor -sequi -secutus sum escort, attend

Proserpina -ae (f) Proserpina (queen of the
    Underworld)

proserpo -ere creep out

prosilio -ire -ui rush forward

prospecto -are -avi -atum look out, observe

*prospicio -icere -exi -ectum see before one,
    view, look after (+ dat), overlook, look
    around for

prosterno -ernere -ravi -ratum knock to the
    ground, knock over, stretch out, bring
    down

*prostituta -ae (f) prostitute

prosum prodesse profui (+ dat) be of use to

protelo -are -avi -atum beat off

proterreo -ere -ui -itum frighten off

protinus immediately

protraho -here -xi -ctum drag out

proturbo -are -avi -atum drive out

provectus -a -um advanced, late

provenio -enire -eni -entum occur, go

*providentia -ae (f) care, providence
    (sometimes personified as a prescient
    controlling force)

*provincia -ae (f) province

proximo -are approach

*proximus -a -um close (to), adjacent, next, previous, nearby, neighbouring; **de proximo** at close quarters

*prudens -entis wise

*pubes -is (f) private parts

*publicus -a -um public

pudice decently, respectably, virtuously

pudicitia -ae (f) chastity, virtue

pudicus -a -um chaste, virtuous

pudor -oris (m) shame, chastity, decency

*puella -ae (f) girl

*puellus -i (m) boy

*puer -eri (m) boy

pugnus -i (m) fist

*pulchellus -a -um pretty

*pulcher -chra -chrum beautiful, fine, noble

*pulchre prettily, attractively

pulmentum -i (n) stew

pulpa -ae (f) flesh, fleshy part of the body

pulso -are -avi -atum knock on, beat, strike

pulsus -us (m) shove

pulvereus -a -um turned to dust, dusty

punicans -antis bright red

*punio -ire i(v)i -itum punish

*punior -iri -itus sum punish

pupula -ae (f) pupil (of the eye)

purgo -are -avi -atum clean

pusio -onis (m) boy

puteus -i (m) well (for water)

*puto -are -avi -atum think, consider

putor -oris (m) rottenness, stench

putris -is -e rotten

pyxis -idis (f) jar

qua where

*quadripes -edis four-footed; (as noun) four-footed animal

quadrupes -edis (m) horse

*quaero -rere -sivi -situm seek, hunt for, obtain

quaesticulus -i (m) small source of income

quaestus -us (m) gainful occupation, profit, income

*qualis -is -e how fine

*qualitas -atis (f) nature, character

*quam than, as, how, to the highest degree possible, what!

*quamquam although

*quamvis although, however (much)

*quantum -i (n) how much, as much as

*quantus -a -um how great, how much, how many

quaqua completely

*quartus -a -um fourth

*quasi as if

quasso -are -avi -atum shake

quatio -tere -ssum shake, move vigorously, fracture

-que and

quemadmodum how

queo quire qui(v)i be able (to)

queror -i questus sum complain

*qui quae quod who, which, any

*quicumque quaecumque quodcumque whoever, whatever

quid why

quidam quaedam quoddam a certain, some, a kind of, a particular, a certain person, someone

quidem certainly, really, in fact, indeed, to be sure, on the one hand

quidni why not?, naturally

*quies -etis (f) sleep, rest

*quiesco -ere quievi quietum fall asleep, be asleep, rest

*quietus -a -um asleep, orderly, peaceful

quin why not

quinam quaenam quodnam just who, just what

*quinque five

quippe as is to be expected, for, as being

quippini of course, because

Quirites -tium (m pl) citizens

quirito -are cry out in protest, make an outcry over

*quis quis quid who, what

*quis qua(e) quid anyone, anything

quispiam quaepiam quippiam someone, something

quispiam quaepiam quodpiam a certain, one, some

*quisquam quisquam quicquam anyone, anything

*quisque quaeque quidque each, every, each person

*quisquis quisquis quidquid (quicquid) whoever, whatever

quivis quaevis quidvis anyone at all, anything at all

quivis quaevis quodvis any you please, any at all

quo to which place, so that thereby

quoad until, until such time as

*quod because, on the grounds that, the fact that

quodsi but if

*quoniam since
*quoque also
quoquoversus in every direction, everywhere
quorsum to what a point, to what an action
quotiens whenever, as often as

*rabidus -a -um frenzied, raging, mad
*rabies -ei (f) ferocity, frenzy
radix -icis (f) root
rado -dere -si -sum shave off
ramus -i (m) branch
rana -ae (f) frog
*rapina -ae (f) booty, loot
*rapio -ere -ui -tum seize, rob
raptim hurriedly, hastily
*rarus -a -um rare, uncommon
ratio -ionis (f) account, financial record
*raucus -a -um hoarse
reatus -us (m) condition of being accused, state
    as a defendant
rebullio -ire bubble up
recedo -dere -ssi -ssum retire, withdraw
*recens recently (adv)
*recens -entis fresh, recently cooked
recenseo -ere -ui -um enumerate, recount
*receptaculum -i (n) repository, container,
    lodging
recido -cidere -c(c)idi fall back, fall to the
    ground
recipio -ipere -epi -eptum welcome, admit,
    receive, withdraw; me recipio retire
reciprocus -a -um alternating, see-sawing
recognosco -oscere -ovi -itum examine, inspect,
    recognize
recondo -ere -idi -itum return, store
recordor -ari -atus sum think, reflect
recta directly, straight
recte rightly, properly, well, thoroughly
rectus -a -um erect
recupero -are -avi -atum restore, revive
recuro -are -avi -atum tend, cure
*recurro -rrere -rri -rsum run back
*reddo -ere -idi -itum pay, hand over, return,
    restore, surrender, give, produce
*redeo -ire -ii -itum return
redintegro -are -avi -atum renew, revive
*reditus -us (m) return, recall
reduco -cere -xi -ctum draw back, bring back,
    bend back, check
redux -ucis returning
refectio -ionis (f) refreshment

refectus -us (m) refreshment, rest
refercio -cire -si -tum cram, stuff (with)
refero -ferre rettuli relatum mention, tell of,
    take away, bring back
reficio -icere -eci -ectum refresh, revive
reflecto -ctere -xi -xum twist, deform
reflo -are -avi -atum blow out, pant
*reformatio -ionis (f) transformation,
    reshaping
*reformo -are -avi -atum transform
refoveo -overe -ovi -otum revive, refresh,
    restore
*regina -ae (f) queen
*regio -ionis (f) area, region, direction
regressio -onis (f) return
*religio -onis (f) religion, religious feeling,
    religious practice, rite, cult
*religiosus -a -um of devotion, connected with
    duty, religious
*relinquo -inquere -iqui -ictum leave, leave
    behind
*reliquiae -arum (f pl) remains, remnants
*reliquus -a -um remaining, rest (of)
relucto -are (+ dat) struggle against, resist
remaneo -ere -si remain, stay behind
remedium -(i)i (n) remedy, solution
remeo -are -avi -atum come back, return
reminiscor -i (+ gen) recall
*remitto -mittere -misi -missum send
*removeo -movere -movi -motum remove
renideo -ere shine
renitor -ti -sus sum resist, struggle
*renudo -are -avi -atum uncover, lay bare, strip
    of (+ abl)
*renuntio -are -avi -atum report
*reor reri ratus sum think, imagine
repando -ere open wide
repello -ere reppuli repulsum push back
repente suddenly
repentino suddenly
repentinus -a -um sudden
reperio -ire repperi repertum find
repeto -ere -i(v)i -itum return to
repigro -are -avi -atum retard, diminish
replaudo -ere strike, beat
replico -are -avi -atum turn over (a thought),
    retrace
repono -onere -osui -ositum put to bed, make
    dependent (on)
reporto -are -avi -atum carry back, transport,
    gain

repraesento -are -avi -atum make available, present to view

*reprehendo -dere -di -sum find fault with, criticize

repugno -are -avi -atum (+ dat) fight back against

*repulsa -ae (f) rejection, rebuff

reputo -are -avi -atum reflect on, think over

requiro -rere -si(v)i -situm look for, ask about, ask for

*res rei (f) thing, object, property, fact, act, situation, circumstances, affair; re vera in fact

rescula -ae (f) article of small value, trifle

reseco -care -(cui) -ctum cut open

resero -are -avi -atum unbar, open

*reservo -are -avi -atum keep (for), reserve (for)

resideo -ere resedi squat, settle down, sit on (+ dat or acc)

resido -ere resedi sit down, settle down

*resisto -istere -stiti (+ dat) resist, withstand, stay, make a stand, halt

respicio -icere -exi -ectum look round at, take into account, show concern for, have a bearing on

*respondeo -dere -di -sum reply

restis -is (f) rope

*restituo -uere -ui -utum give back, restore

*resurgo -rgere -rrexi -rrectum rise again

retardo -are -avi -atum delay, hold back

*retineo -ere -ui -entum hold, grasp

retiolum -i (n) net

retorqueo -quere -si -tum twist around, change, reverse

retrorsum back, backwards

revalesco -escere -ui recover, revive

revello -ellere -elli -ulsum tear

revelo -are -avi -atum uncover, reveal

*revenio -venire -veni -ventum return

reverto -tere -ti return

revertor -ti -sus sum return

revideo -idere -isum revisit

revincio -cire -xi -ctum bind, tie

revinco -incere -ici -ictum win over

revoco -are -avi -atum call back

rigor -oris (m) tautness, rigidity

rima -ae (f) crack

rimor -ari -atus sum examine, scrutinize, look around to see

ripa -ae (f) bank

*risus -us (m) laughter

rite duly, in accordance with religious procedure

ritus -us (m) practice

*rivus -i (m) river, torrent

*robur -oris (n) strength

*rogo -are -avi -atum ask, call on, beg for

Roma -ae (f) Rome

roncus -i (m) croak

ros roris (m) dew, liquid, water

*rosa -ae (f) rose

*rosarius -a -um rosy, connected with roses

*roseus -a -um rosy, rose-coloured, consisting of roses

*rota -ae (f) wheel

rubor -oris (m) redness

rudis -is -e new, simple

ruina -ae (f) ravine

*rumor -oris (m) gossip, report, reputation

*rumpo -ere rupi ruptum break, snap

*ruo -ere -i rush

*rurestris -is -e of the countryside, rural

*rursum again, back

*rursus again

*rusticanus -i (m) rustic, peasant

saccaria -ae (f) a job as a porter

sacerdos -otis (m) priest

sacramentum -i (n) oath of allegiance

sacrarium -ii (n) sanctuary, shrine

sacratus -i (m) an initiate

*sacrilegus -a -um impious, sacrilegious

*sacrosanctus -a -um inviolable, sacred

*sacrum -i (n) rite

*saepe frequently

saepicula -ae (f) hedge

saepicule often

saepio -ire -si -tum surround, enclose

*saepius more frequently

*saevio -ire -ii -itum rage, behave ferociously, be savage

*saevitia -ae (f) savagery

*saevus -a -um savage, cruel, violent

saga -ae (f) witch

*sagaciter perceptively, acutely

*sagax -acis keen, perceptive

sagino -are -avi -atum stuff full (with food)

sagitta -ae (f) arrow

sagus -a -um practising witchcraft

salebrosus -a -um rough, rugged

saliaris -is -e sumptuous (like the banquets of the Salii priests)

saltem at least; ne . . . saltem not even

*saluber -bris -bre beneficial, salutary

*salus -utis (f) safety, life, salvation, welfare,
    well-being

*salutaris -is -e salutary, rescuing, of salvation

salutatio -onis (f) greeting, salutation

salvus -a -um intact, undamaged

*sanctus -a -um upright, virtuous, sacred

sane doubtless, obviously, certainly

*sanguis -inis (m) blood

sanies -ei (f) gore

*sanus -a -um healthy

sarcina -ae (f) load, burden

sarcinosus -a -um loaded down, burdened

sarcinula -ae (f) little bag, small pack

sarcio -cire -si -tum mend, make good

*satio -are -avi -atum satisfy, fill

*satis satisfactorily, properly, quite, fairly, pretty;
    as noun enough

saucius -a -um wounded, afflicted, befuddled

savior -ari -atus sum kiss

savium -ii (n) kiss

*saxum -i (n) rock

scabies -ei (f) roughness, crust

scabiosus -a -um mangy

scabo -ere scabi scratch

scaena -ae (f) spectacle, charade, performance,
    setting, staging

scaevus -a -um unlucky

scapulae -arum (f pl) haunches

scaturrigo -inis (f) stream

*scelestus -a -um criminal, wicked

*scelus -eris (n) crime, something terrible

schema -ae (f) posture

scilicet of course, naturally, no doubt

*scio -ire -i(v)i -itum know

sciscitor -ari -atus sum inquire, find out by
    inquiry

scissilis -is -e torn, tattered

scitulus -a -um pretty

scitus -a -um clever, nice

scolasticus -i (m) schoolboy

scorteus -a -um leathery, resembling hide in
    texture

scortum -i (n) prostitute

scrupulosus -a -um very careful

scrupulus -i (m) worry, problem

scrutor -ari -atus sum probe, search out

*se sui himself, herself, itself, themselves

sebacium -ii (n) tallow candle

secedo -dere -ssi -ssum withdraw, go away

*secreto secretly, in private

*secretum -i (n) secret

secta -ae (f) principles

secundum (+ acc) in pursuance of

*secundus -a -um second, satisfactory,
    favourable

*secure unconcernedly, with an easy mind,
    without a care

*securus -a -um untroubled, carefree

secus differently, otherwise

secutor -oris (m) attendant

*sed but, now

*sedeo -ere sedi sessum sit

sedes -is (f) home, residence

*sedo -are -avi -atum calm down

*sedulo carefully, attentively

*sedulus -a -um attentive, painstaking

semel once

semesus -a -um half-eaten

semiamictus -a -um half-covered, scantily clad

semianimis -is -e half-alive, half-dead

semicanus -a -um greying, half-grey

*semimortuus -a -um half-dead

semiobrutus -a -um half-buried

semisopitus -a -um half-asleep

semita -ae (f) path

semitrepidus -a -um half-afraid

semivivus -a -um half-alive

*semper always, continuously

*senex -is (m) old man

*senilis -is -e old

sensim gradually, bit by bit

sensus -us (m) consciousness, mind

*sententia -ae (f) opinion, verdict

*sentio -tire -si -sum feel, perceive, believe

sepelio -elire -eli(v)i -ultum bury

*septem seven

*sepulcrum -i (n) tomb

*sepultura -ae (f) burial, grave

*sequens -entis following, subsequent

sequius otherwise, unfavourably

*sequor -i secutus sum follow, come away

*serenus -a -um calm, serene

*sermo -onis (m) conversation, talk, remark,
    speech, expression

sero at a late period of time, late

servilis -is -e servile

*servio -ire -i(v)i -itum (+ dat) serve, be a
    slave to

*servo -are -avi -atum guard, preserve, keep
    intact

*servulus -i (m) worthless slave, slave

*servus -i (m) slave

*sese = se

seta -ae (f) bristle

setius less readily; non setius none the less

seu or

*severitas -atis (f) severity, strictness

*severiter sternly, severely

*sexus -us (m) sex

*si if, whether

sibilus -i (m) whistle

*sic so, like this, in this way, as follows, in the
same way

sidus -eris (n) star

*signum -i (n) signal, sign, indication

*silentium -(i)i (n) silence

*sileo -ere -ui say nothing, be silent

*similis -is -e similar; (+ gen or dat) similar to

*similiter in a similar manner

*similitudo -inis (f) similarity, resemblance

simul at the same time, as soon as

simulacrum -i (n) likeness, image, ghost

simulanter in pretence, apparently

simulatio -ionis (f) pretence

simulo -are -avi -atum feign, simulate

*sine (+ abl) without

*singularis -is -e remarkable, unusual

singuli -ae -a each, individual, single, every
single

singultus -us (m) sob

sinister -tra -trum left, harmful, bitter

sinus -us (m) breast, fold of a garment over the
breast

siqui if anyone

sis please

sisto -ere steti statum cause to appear (in
court), present, position

sistrum -i (n) sistrum, rattle

sitio -ire be thirsty

situs -a -um situated, built

*sobrius -a -um sober, staid

*socia -ae (f) sharer, partner

*socio -are -avi -atum form, make, link,
attach, share

*socius -(i)i (m) comrade, friend

Socrates -is (m) Socrates (friend of
Aristomenes)

sodalis -is (m) companion, boyfriend

sol solis (m) sun; Sol the Sun (god)

solacium -(i)i (n) consolation, relief, solace,
comfort

*soleo -ere -itus sum be accustomed to

*soliditas -atis (f) solidity

solidus -a -um entire, complete

*solitarius -a -um living on one's own, solitary

*solitudo -inis (f) solitude, loneliness, wasteland

solitus -a -um usual, customary

sollemne -is (n) ceremony, ritual

sollers -ertis clever

sollerter cleverly, skilfully

sollertia -ae (f) cleverness

sollicite anxiously, carefully

sollicitus -a -um troubled

solum -i (n) ground, earth

solum only; non solum . . . sed/verum etiam not
only . . . but also

*solus -a -um alone, on one's own, only

somnio -are -avi -atum dream

somnior -ari -atus sum dream

somnium -(i)i (n) dream

somnolentus -a -um of sleep

*somnus -i (m) sleep

*sonax -acis noisy

*sonus -i (m) sound

*sopio -ire -i(v)i -itum overcome with sleep

*sopor -oris (m) sleep

*soporifer -era -erum soporific, inducing sleep

sordeo -ere be dirty, be soiled

sordes -is (f) filth, dirt

*sordidus -a -um foul, shabby, dirty

*soror -oris (f) sister

sospes -itis safe and sound, unscathed

sospitatrix -icis saving, saviour

spatium -(i)i (n) period, interval, span, extent

*species -ei (f) likeness

*spectaculum -i (n) show, performance, sight

*spectamen -inis (n) sight, spectacle

spectatus -a -um tried and tested

*specto -are -avi -atum see, look

spelunca -ae (f) cave

*sperno -ere sprevi spretum reject, disdain

*spes spei (f) hope

spica -ae (f) ear (of grain)

spiculum -i (n) javelin

spina -ae (f) spine, backbone

*spiritus -us (m) breath, breathing, soul, spirit,
life, consciousness

*spiro -are -avi -atum breathe forth, exhale, give
off

splendesco -ere gleam, be glossy

*splendor -oris (m) brightness, sheen

spoliatio -ionis (f) plundering, robbing

spolium -ii (n) spoil, booty

spongea -ae (f) sponge

spongia -ae (f) sponge

sponsus -i (m) fiancé

sponte of one's own accord, voluntarily, at one's
own request

spumeus -a -um foam-covered

spurcus -a -um filthy, foul

*squaleo -ere -ui be dirty, be coarse

*squalidus -a -um dirty

*squalor -oris (m) uncouthness

stabularius -(i)i (m) innkeeper

stabulum -i (n) inn, stable

*statim immediately, at once

statuo -uere -ui -utum decree, decide upon,
make up one's mind

status -us (m) state, condition, physical
appearance

stella -ae (f) star

*sterilis -is -e barren, sterile, not endowed

sternutatio -ionis (f) sneeze, sneezing fit

sterto -ere (-ui) snore

stilus -i (m) pen

stimulo -are -avi -atum incite, spur on, goad

stipendium -(i)i (n) payment, income

stipes -itis (m) trunk

stipo -are -avi -atum make compact, pack tight

*sto stare steti statum stand

stragulus -a -um for bedding; vestis stragula
bed-clothes

strenuus -a -um vigorous, keen

strepitus -us (m) noise, din

stridor -oris (m) squeal, hiss

studiose in concern, vigorously

*studium -(i)i (n) enthusiasm, eagerness,
occupation

*stupor -oris (m) bewilderment, stupefaction

stuprator -oris (m) adulterous lover

suadela -ae (f) persuasion, persuasive argument

suadeo -dere -si -sum urge, advise

suapte of his own accord

suavis -is -e attractive, delightful

*sub (+ abl) beneath, in front of, during;
(+ acc) up into

subdo -ere -idi -itum place below, insert

subeo -ire -i(v)i -itum be joined to, go up to, go
under, submit oneself to

subicio -icere -ieci -iectum place under

subitarius -a -um hastily formed

sublevo -are -avi -atum lift up (off hinges)

sublimis -is -e high up, lofty, heroic, illustrious,
sublime

sublimo -are -avi -atum raise, bring up from the
Underworld

subsidium -(i)i (n) help

subsilio -ire -ui bounce, jump up and down

subsisto -istere -titi (+ dat) help

*subterrenus -a -um beneath the earth,
subterranean

subtraho -trahere -traxi -tractum (+ dat)
remove from

subvenio -enire -eni -entum help

succubo -are lie under

succumbo -mbere -bui -bitum give in (to)

sudor -oris (m) sweat

suffarcino -are -avi -atum stuff, load down

*sufficiens -entis sufficient

*sufficio -icere -eci -ectum suffice, be
adequate (for)

suffigo -gere -xi -xum fasten (to)

suffundo -undere -udi -usum permeate

sulcus -i (m) furrow, coil

Sulla -ae (m) Sulla (Roman dictator)

*sulpur -uris (n) sulphur

*sum esse fui be, exist

sumministro -are -avi -atum supply, furnish

summula -ae (f) small sum

*summus -a -um topmost, the top of, surface of,
extreme, greatest, supreme, closest

*sumo -mere -mpsi -mptum pick up, adopt,
assume, take, consume, put on

sumptus -us (m) expenditure, expenses, sum,
resources

supellex -ectilis (f) furniture

*super (+ acc) on top of, above, over, on, upon;
(+ abl) concerning, about

supercubo -are -avi (+ dat) recline on
top of

superi -orum (m pl) gods above

superincurvatus -a -um arching over

*superior -ior -ius higher up, previous

supernato -are -avi -atum (+ dat) ride on the
back of (something swimming)

superruo -ere collapse on top of

supersum -esse -fui survive, remain alive

superus -a -um of the heavens above

supervivo -vivere -vixi (+ dat) remain alive
longer than, survive

*supino -are -avi -atum lay (a person) on his
back

suppetior -ari -atus sum bring help

supplementum -i (n) additional material,
supplies

supplicamentum -i (n) propitiatory offering or
  ceremony
supplico -are -avi -atum (+ dat) do worship,
  supplicate
supplicue humbly
suppono -ponere -posui -positum place,
  (+ dat) place under
*__supremus -a -um__ final, critical, extreme
surrideo -ere -si -sum smile
suscipio -ipere -epi -eptum take, adopt,
  conceive, take on, undertake, give birth to,
  continue (speaking), reply
suscito -are -avi -atum wake up, stir to action,
  incite
suspendo -dere -di -sum hang; **suspendere se**
  lean out
suspensus -a -um on tenterhooks
*__suspicor -ari -atus sum__ suspect
suspiritus -us (m) sigh
suspiro -are -avi -atum sigh
*__sustineo -ere -ui__ endure, suffer, shoulder, put
  up with, undergo, sustain
susurrus -i (m) whisper
sutilis -is -e stitched together, patched
*__suus -a -um__ his, hers, its, their (own)

taberna -ae (f) workshop
tabernula -ae (f) inn
tabula -ae (f) a writing-tablet, document,
  record, painting, panel (of a door)
*__taceo -ere -ui -itum__ be silent
*__tacite__ quietly, privately
*__tacitus -a -um__ silent, secret
taeda -ae (f) torch
taedium -(i)i (n) disgust
*__talis -is -e__ such, like that, looking like that
talus -i (m) ankle
*__tam__ so, so much
*__tamen__ however, yet, nevertheless
*__tandem__ at length, at last, finally, really
tantillulus -a -um so small
tantisper in the meanwhile, for the present, for
  such time as
tantum only
*__tantum -i__ (n) so much, such a large amount
*__tantus -a -um__ so great, so big, so much
Tartara -orum (n pl) Tartarus (in the
  Underworld), the Underworld
Tartarus -i (m) Tartarus (part of the
  Underworld), the Underworld
taurus -i (m) bull

tectum -i (n) roof
tegmen -inis (n) cover, covering
tego -gere -xi -ctum cover, conceal
teleta -ae (f) rite of initiation
telum -i (n) weapon
temerarius -a -um rash, reckless, impetuous
temere by chance, as it happened
temeritas -atis (f) rashness
temero -are -avi -atum commit an act of
  violation
temperius earlier
tempero -are -avi -atum (+ dat) exercise
  moderation in, season, blend
tempestas -atis (f) storm
tempestivus -a -um given at the right time
tempto -are -avi -atum test, try, attempt
*__tempus -oris__ (n) time, period, duration
*__tenaciter__ tenaciously, stubbornly
*__tenax -acis__ clinging tight, tenacious
tendo -dere tetendi tentum stretch, insist on (a
  viewpoint)
tenebrae -arum (f pl) darkness, shadows
tenebro -are make dark
tenellus -a -um tender, soft
*__teneo -ere -ui -tum__ keep, maintain, possess,
  hold on to, embrace, have intercourse with
*__tener -era -erum__ tender, immature, sensuous,
  weak, effeminate
tenuis -is -e thin, poor
tenuitas -atis (f) scarcity, shortage
tenuo -are -avi -atum make thin
tenus (+ abl) as far as
tepeo -ere be warm
ter three times
teres -etis smooth
tergum -i (n) back
terminus -i (m) end, confine, limit, boundary,
  city limit
*__terra -ae__ (f) earth, ground
*__terreo -ere -ui -itum__ frighten, terrify
*__terror -oris__ (m) terror
tertius -a -um third
testa -ae (f) jar
testimonium -(i)i (n) validating testimony,
  witness
testis -is (m) witness
testudo -inis (f) tortoise
Thebae -arum (f pl) Thebes (town in central
  Greece)
Thessalia -ae (f) Thessaly (an area in northern
  Greece)

Thrasyleon -onis (m) Thrasyleon

Thrasyllus -i (m) Thrasyllus

tigillum -i (n) small beam

*timeo -ere timui fear

*timide fearfully

*timor -oris (m) fear

titubo -are -avi -atum stagger, totter

Tlepolemus -i (m) Tlepolemus

*tolero -are -avi -atum endure, put up with

*tollo -ere sustuli sublatum send up, lift up,
    raise, remove

tondeo -dere tonsum trim, cut off

tonitrus -us (m) thunder

tormentum -i (n) torture

torus -i (m) bed, marriage bed, funeral bier,
    muscle

*totus -a -um all, whole, entire

tracto -are -avi -atum treat, fondle, handle,
    work on

*trado -ere -idi -itum hand over (to), deliver,
    consign, let into

*traho -here -xi -ctum drag, take along with one

*tranquillus -a -um quiet, tranquil

transabeo -ire -i(v)i get away, move away beyond

transadigo -igere -egi -actum thrust (through),
    transfix

transeo -ire -i(v)i -itum cross over, pass, make
    one's way

transfero -ferre -tuli -latum transport, convey

transigo -igere -egi -actum complete, commit

*trepidatio -ionis (f) alarm, nervousness

*trepido -are -avi -atum tremble, be frightened,
    be excited

*trepidus -a -um fearful, shaky

*tres tres tria three

tribuo -uere -ui -utum grant, give

*tristis -is -e sad, grim, dreadful

*tristities -ei (f) sadness, grief

*triumpho -are -avi -atum triumph; triumpho
    de (+ abl) be victorious over

trivium -(i)i (n) crossroads (place where three
    roads meet)

trucido -are -avi -atum slaughter, butcher

truculentia -ae (f) ferocity, savagery

*tu tui you, yourself

tubero -are form a rounded swelling,
    protuberate

tuccetum -i (n) savoury meat, sausage

tuguriolum -i (n) small hut

*tum then

tumor -oris (m) swell, swelling

*tumultus -us (m) commotion, fuss, uproar

tumulus -i (m) mound, grave, hill

*tunc then

tundo -ere tutudi tunsum strike, beat

*tunica -ae (f) tunic, robe

*turba -ae (f) crowd

*turbela -ae (f) group, bunch

*turbo -are -avi -atum disturb, upset, alarm

turbula -ae (f) group of people

*turpis -is -e disgraceful, shameful

tutela -ae (f) protection, care, guardianship

tuto safely, securely

*tuus -a -um your

uber -eris copious, abundant, rich

uber -eris (n) breast

ubertim copiously

*ubi when, where

Ulixes -i (m) Ulysses (Latin name for the hero
    Odysseus)

*ullus -a -um any

*ultimus -a -um final

ultio -ionis (f) revenge

ultra (+ acc) beyond

ultro to a point further off, spontaneously; ultro
    citro back and forth

ultroneus -a -um voluntary

ululabilis -is -e howling

ululatus -us (m) howl, yell, shriek

umbilicus -i (m) navel

umbra -ae (f) ghost

umbrosus -a -um dark, shadowy

umerus -i (m) shoulder

umidus -a -um moist, wet

umor -oris (m) liquid, fluid

*unde whence, from where, from what cause,
    how

*undique on all sides

ungula -ae (f) hoof

*unicus -a -um single, sole, singular, unique

unio -ire -ii -itum share, unite

*universus -a -um all, whole

*unus -a -um one, a single

*urina -ae (f) urine, piss

uro -ere ussi ustum burn, sear

ursa -ae (f) bear

ursus -i (m) bear

uspiam anywhere

usquam anywhere

usque all the way

usquequaque completely

*usus -us (m) use, performance, need

*ut that, so that, with the result that, so as to, in order that, when, how, as, as if; ut primum as soon as

utcumque somehow or other

uterque utraque utrumque each (of two)

uterus -i (m) womb, belly

utique exactly, on earth

*utor uti usus sum (+ abl) use, employ

utpote because

utriculus -i (m) small leather bottle

*uxor -oris (f) wife

*uxorcula -ae (f) little wife, wife

vacuefacio -acere -eci -actum (+ abl) empty of

*vacuo -are -avi -atum empty out

*vacuus -a -um empty, idle

vadimonium -(i)i (n) guarantee, fulfilment of a promise, pledge

vado -ere go; vadere in sententiam support someone's opinion

valens -entis in a healthy condition

valetudo -inis (f) health, condition

valide forcefully, vigorously, powerfully

validus -a -um strong, powerful, drastic

valvae -arum (f pl) door

vapor -oris (m) heat

varicus in a straddling posture

*varie in various directions

*varius -a -um various, varied, conflicting

vasto -are -avi -atum plunder, ravage

*vastus -a -um huge, very loud

vecordia -ae (f) madness, derangement

vegetus -a -um vigorous, active

*vehementer violently, strongly, immensely

*veho -here -xi -ctum carry; vehor ride

*vel or, even; vel . . . vel either . . . or

velitor -ari -atus sum skirmish

*velocitas -atis (f) speed

*velox -ocis swift

velut as if

venabulum -i (n) hunting spear

venaticus -a -um used in hunting, hunting

venatio -onis (f) hunt

venator -oris (m) huntsman

venatus -us (m) hunt, game, prey

venditio -onis (f) sale

vendito -are -avi -atum offer for sale

vendo -ere -idi -itum sell

venenum -i (n) poison, drug, substance

*venerabilis -is -e august, awesome

venerius -a -um sexual, erotic

*veneror -ari -atus sum pay homage to, venerate

venia -ae (f) pardon

*venio -ire veni ventum come, go

venter -tris (m) belly

Venus -eris (f) Venus (goddess of love)

*venus -eris (f) love, sex

venus -us (m) sale

venustus -a -um attractive, charming

*verbum -i (n) word

*vere really, truly, genuinely

*vereor -eri -itus sum fear

*veritas -atis (f) truth

vermis -is (m) worm, maggot

vero however

versipellis -is (f) shape-shifter, someone who alters her form

versus (+ acc) towards

vertex -icis (m) peak, head

*verto -tere -ti -sum turn

verum but

*verum -i (n) the truth

*verus -a -um true; re vera in fact

vesanus -a -um mad, insane

vesica -ae (f) bladder

vespera -ae (f) evening

vespertinus -a -um in the evening

*vester -tra -trum your, of you, on your part (= you in the plural)

vestigium -(i)i (n) step, footstep

*vestio -ire -i(v)i -itum clothe, dress

*vestis -is (f) clothing, dress, robe, cloth, bed-clothes

veteratrix -icis practised, skilful

*vetus -eris old

*vetustus -a -um old, ancient

vexillarius -(i)i (m) standard-bearer

vexillatio -ionis (f) detachment

*via viae (f) road, journey, way

viaticulum -i (n) travelling-money

*viator -oris (m) traveller

*vicarius -a -um vicarious, substitute

vicina -ae (f) neighbour

vicinia -ae (f) neighbourhood

vicinus -i (m) neighbour

vicis (gen) (f) situation; vice after the manner (of)

*vicissitudo -inis (f) change, reversal

*victima -ae (f) victim, sacrificial offering

victus -us (m) livelihood

*video -dere -di -sum see, observe, take care;
    videor seem, seem good

viduo -are -avi -atum (+ abl) deprive of,
    strip of

*vigilia -ae (f) watch (a division of the hours of
    the night), vigil, vigilance, wakefulness

*vigilo -are -avi -atum stay awake, wake up

*vigor -oris (m) vigour

*vigorate vigorously

*villa -ae (f) villa, house in the country,
    country estate

villico -are -avi -atum oversee, manage

vimineus -a -um wicker, made of wickerwork

vincio -cire -xi -ctum bind

vinculum -i (n) chain

vindico -are -avi -atum inflict punishment (on),
    take revenge (on), avenge, claim

vindicta -ae (f) revenge, punishment

*vinum -i (n) wine

*violenter violently

*violentia -ae (f) force, violence, powerful
    effect

*vipera -ae (f) viper, snake

*vir viri (m) man, lover, husband, true man,
    soldier

virectum -i (n) greenery

*virginalis -is -e of a girl

*virgo -inis (f) virgin, girl

*virilis -is -e manly, brave as a man's; virilia
    -ium (n pl) private parts

*virtus -utis (f) potency, bravery, virtue

*vis vis (f) violence, violent attack

viscera -um (n pl) insides, entrails, flesh

visito -are -avi -atum see

*viso -ere -i go to see, view, see

*visus -us (m) vision

*vita -ae (f) life, livelihood

*vivax -acis enduring, long-lived

*vivo -ere vixi victum be alive, live

*vivus -a -um living, alive

*vix scarcely, hardly, only just, with difficulty

*vocito -are -avi -atum call, name

*voco -are -avi -atum call, summon, invite,
    bring

vocula -ae (f) gentle word

*volo velle volui be willing, wish, want

*voluntas -atis (f) will, wishes, desire

*voluptas -atis (f) pleasure

voluto -are -avi -atum roll; volutor roll about,
    wallow

*vomo -ere -ui -itum vomit

*voracitas -atis (f) voracity, ravenous appetite

*vos vestrum/vestri you (plural)

votum -i (n) desire, wishes

*vox vocis (f) voice, speech, words

*vulgus -i (n) crowd, mob

*vulnero -are -avi -atum wound

*vulnus -eris (n) wound

*vultur -uris (m) vulture

*vultus -us (m) face, expression, countenance,
    appearance, shape

Zatchlas -ae (m) Zatchlas (a priest)

zona -ae (f) belt

LIST OF WORKS CITED

~

(I list here only works which are cited by me. Many other works, especially commentaries, have also been consulted and exploited, but have not been specifically referred to in my book.)

Adams, J. N. (1982). *The Latin Sexual Vocabulary*. London.

Anderson, G. (1982). *Eros Sophistes*. Chico, CA.

Balme, M. G. and Morwood, J. H. W. (1976). *Cupid and Psyche*. Oxford.

Courtney, E. (2001). *A Companion to Petronius*. Oxford.

Finkelpearl, E. D. (1998). *Metamorphosis of Language in Apuleius*. Ann Arbor, MI.

Frangoulidis, S. A. (1992). 'Epic inversion in Apuleius' tale of Tlepolemus/Haemus', *Mnemosyne* 45: 60–74.

    (1994). 'Self-imitation in Apuleius' tales of Tlepolemus/Haemus and Thrasyleon', *Mnemosyne* 47: 337–48.

Hägg, T. (1983). *The Novel in Antiquity*. Oxford and Berkeley.

Haight, E. H. (1927). *Apuleius and his Influence*. London.

Harrison, S. J. (1990). 'Some Odyssean scenes in Apuleius', *Materiali e Discussioni* 25: 193–201.

    ed. (1999). *Oxford Readings in the Roman Novel*. Oxford.

    (2000). *Apuleius: A Latin Sophist*. Oxford.

Hijmans, B. L. and van der Paardt, R. Th., eds. (1978). *Aspects of Apuleius' Golden Ass*. Groningen.

James, P. (1987). *Unity in Diversity*. Hildesheim.

Jones, P. V. and Sidwell, K. C. (1986). *Reading Latin*. Cambridge.

Kennedy, B. H. (1962). *The Revised Latin Primer*. London.

Kenney, E. J. (1990). *Apuleius – Cupid and Psyche*. Cambridge.

    (1998). *Apuleius – The Golden Ass*. Harmondsworth.

Krabbe, J. K. (1989). *The Metamorphoses of Apuleius*. New York.

    (2003). *Lusus Iste: Apuleius' Metamorphoses*. Lanham, MD.

Mason, H. J. (1994). 'Greek and Latin versions of the Ass-story', *Aufstieg und Niedergang der römischen Welt* II 34.2: 1665–1707. Berlin and New York.

Morwood, J. (1999). *A Latin Grammar*. Oxford.

Murgatroyd, P. (1997). 'Three Apuleian openings', *Latomus* 56: 126–33.

(2001a). 'Foreshadowing in Apuleius' *Metamorphoses*, I–III', *Latomus* 60: 647–52.

(2001b). 'Embedded narrative in Apuleius' *Metamorphoses* 1.9–10', *Museum Helveticum* 58: 40–6.

(2004). 'The ending of Apuleius' *Metamorphoses*', *Classical Quarterly* 54: 319–21.

Penwill, J. L. (1990). 'Ambages reciprocae: Reviewing Apuleius' *Metamorphoses*', *Ramus* 19: 1–25.

Reardon, B. P., ed. (1989). *Collected Ancient Greek Novels*. Berkeley and Los Angeles.

Sandy, G. (1997). *The Greek World of Apuleius*. Leiden.

Schlam, C. S. (1992). *The* Metamorphoses *of Apuleius*. Chapel Hill, NC.

Schmeling, G., ed. (1996). *The Novel in the Ancient World*. Leiden.

Shumate, N. (1996). *Crisis and Conversion in Apuleius'* Metamorphoses. Ann Arbor, MI.

Smith, W. S. (1994). 'Style and character in The Golden Ass', *Aufstieg und Niedergang der römischen Welt* II 34.2: 1575–99. Berlin and New York.

Sullivan, J. P. (1986). *Petronius* The Satyricon *and Seneca* The Apocolocyntosis. Harmondsworth.

Tatum, J. (1972). 'Apuleius and metamorphosis', *American Journal of Philology* 93: 306–13.

(1979). *Apuleius and The Golden Ass*. Ithaca and London.

Walsh, P. G. (1970). *The Roman Novel*. Cambridge.

(1995). *Apuleius – The Golden Ass*. Oxford.

(1997). *Petronius – The Satyricon*. Oxford.

Wheelock, F. M., revised LaFleur, R. A. (2000). *Wheelock's Latin*, 6th edition. New York.

Winkler, J. J. (1985). *Auctor and Actor*. Berkeley.

Woodcock, E. C. (1959). *A New Latin Syntax*. London.